Critical Issues in Contemporary China

Critical Issues in Contemporary China offers up-to-date and in-depth coverage of the social, political and economic problems facing contemporary China. It provides students with a comprehensive analysis of a number of key issues including:

- critical developments in Chinese politics
- the privatisation of China's economy and social services
- regional economic inequalities
- environmental problems
- population growth and food security
- ethnic minorities
- social change
- social and economic inequalities
- cross-Strait relations with Taiwan.

By examining the three interrelated themes of stability, sustainable development and territorial integrity, the contributors raise important questions regarding the Chinese Communist Party's capacity to continue fast-paced economic development and maintain the territorial unity of China. *Critical Issues in Contemporary China* is both accessible and informative, with a number of useful pedagogical features that will equip undergraduates with the analytical skills needed to assess the political, economic and social challenges surrounding China as it enters the twenty-first century.

Czeslaw Tubilewicz is Assistant Professor and Co-Programme Leader of China Studies and International Studies at the Open University of Hong Kong.

Critical Issues in Contemporary China

Edited by
Czeslaw Tubilewicz

Routledge
Taylor & Francis Group

NEW YORK AND LONDON

香港公開大學出版社

OPEN UNIVERSITY
OF HONG KONG PRESS

First published 2006
by Routledge
2 Park Square, Milton Park, Abingdon,
Oxon OX14 4RN

Simultaneously published in the USA and
Canada
by Routledge
270 Madison Avenue, New York, NY 10016

*Routledge is an imprint of the Taylor & Francis
Group, an informa business*

© 2006 Open University of Hong Kong

Typeset in Century Old Style by
Bookcraft Ltd, Stroud, Gloucestershire
Printed and bound in Great Britain by
TJ International Ltd, Padstow, Cornwall

British Library Cataloguing in Publication Data
A catalogue record for this book is available from
the British Library

*Library of Congress Cataloging in Publication
Data*
Critical issues in contemporary China / edited by
Czeslaw Tubilewicz.
    p. cm
Includes bibliographical references and index.
1. China – Economic conditions – 2000– 2. China
– Social conditions – 2000– 3. China – Politics
and government – 2000– I. Tubilewicz, Czeslaw,
1968–
HC427.95.C753 2006
330.951–dc22   2006002906

ISBN10: 0-415-39584-4 (hbk)
ISBN10: 0-415-39585-2 (pbk)

ISBN13: 978-0-415-39584-7 (hbk)
ISBN13: 978-0-415-39585-4 (pbk)

Contents

CONTENTS

Illustrations

Figures

Tables

Contributors

Robert Fairbanks Ash is Professor of Economics at the School of Oriental and African Studies (SOAS), University of London. He has written or edited twelve books, and is the author of more than 30 articles and book chapters on a wide range of topics relating to the social and economic development of China, Hong Kong and Taiwan. His current research interests are China's regional economic development, food security, energy, population and employment, and social welfare issues.

Richard Louis Edmonds is Visiting Senior Lecturer in the Geography Department, King's College, University of London, and Associate Member, Center for East Asian Studies, University of Chicago. He has written extensively on China, Japan, Taiwan, Macau and Hong Kong. He is the author of *Patterns of China's Lost Harmony: A Survey of the Country's Environmental Degradation and Protection* (London: Routledge, 1994). Currently, he is working on environmental problems in China and land-use issues in Macau.

Colin Mackerras is Professor Emeritus in the School of International Business and Asian Studies, Griffith University, Australia. He has written twelve single-authored books, numerous articles and book chapters, as well as edited several books, on topics ranging from Chinese theatre, through China's ethnic minorities, to Western images of China. His most recent book is *China's Ethnic Minorities and Globalisation* (London: RoutledgeCurzon, 2003).

Ng Ka Po is Associate Professor of International Relations at Aichi Bunkyo University, Japan. His research interests include Chinese politics and security studies. He is the author of *Interpreting China's Military Power: Doctrine Makes Readiness* (New York: Frank Cass, 2005).

Bennis So Wai Yip is Assistant Professor of the Department of Public Policy and Management, I-Shou University, Taiwan. His publications focus on the private economy in China. He is now engaged in research projects on high-tech industrial policies in Taiwan and China, and public sector reforms.

Czeslaw Tubilewicz is Assistant Professor at the Open University of Hong Kong and Co-Leader of the China Studies Programme. He has published extensively on Taiwan's diplomatic and economic relations with the post-communist states. Currently, he is preparing a manuscript on Taiwan's economic diplomacy in the post-Cold War era.

Wang Shaoguang is Professor of Political Science at the Chinese University of Hong Kong and the chief editor of the *China Review*. He has authored, co-authored, and edited twenty books in Chinese and English, as well as contributed to numerous edited volumes and journals. His research interests include political economy, comparative politics, fiscal politics, democratisation, and economic and political development in former socialist countries and East Asian countries.

Acknowledgements

The editor wishes to thank Professor So Wai-chor of the OUHK, Mr Chris Baker of the OUHK and Professor Peter Cheung of the University of Hong Kong for their insightful comments on the original material developed for the OUHK course. The course was copy-edited by Mr Tim Maraun and produced by the OUHK's Educational Technology and Publishing Unit's Publishing Team.

The editor also wishes to thank Mr Chris Baker for his instructional design input and detailed review of the manuscript for this book.

Stability, development and unity in contemporary China

CZESLAW TUBILEWICZ

Introduction

The idea of publishing *Critical Issues in Contemporary China* came during the process of developing a course of the same name for undergraduate students enrolled in the China Studies Programme in the School of Arts and Social Sciences at the Open University of Hong Kong. Having offered students a number of courses that examined particular aspects of contemporary China's development, we realised the need for a course which would invite a critical analysis of key challenges facing China at the beginning of the twenty-first century. Some of these challenges, such as population growth, food security and the Taiwan issue, are obvious to those even remotely interested in Chinese affairs. Others, such as privatisation or rising inequalities, become evident only after a closer scrutiny of the wider consequences of the economic reforms initiated in the late 1970s. In this volume, we focus on the critical issues of political change; the privatisation of China's economy and social services; regional economic inequalities; environmental degradation; population growth and food security; ethnic minorities; social change and social inequality; and the question of Taiwan. The list could, of course, include other critical issues, such as human rights and law; the emergence of a civil society; labour unrest; corruption; reform of the financial system; energy security; and central government–provincial relations.

Although the chapters in this book are fairly distinct, focus on separate issues and can be read discretely, collectively they contribute to a discussion of the political and socioeconomic evolution of the Chinese state during the reform era. The contributors raise questions regarding the Chinese Communist Party's (CCP) capacity to continue fast-paced economic development without upsetting social stability or irreversibly damaging China's natural environment, and to restore and maintain China's territorial unity. In sum, although this book is by no means intended as an ultimate examination of all the challenges facing contemporary China, the analyses presented here critically reflect upon three broad, interrelated themes in China's contemporary development, namely:

- stability;
- sustainable development; and
- territorial integrity.

Stability in China prior to the reform era

In a country as populous as China, stability (*wending*) (whether political, social or economic) has often been a great concern. In the imperial period, population pressure (particularly when combined with a shortage of arable land and various ecological disasters) had destabilising effects upon Chinese society, and sometimes led to large-scale rebellions. Foreign demands made upon Chinese sovereignty in the mid-nineteenth and early twentieth centuries also exerted a destabilising influence, triggering uprisings and social turbulence. With the fall of the Qing dynasty in 1911, China experienced a protracted period of political instability, marked by hundreds of military conflicts between local military strongmen (warlords) and frequent changes of government. The accession of the Nationalist Party (Kuomintang, KMT) to power in 1928 failed to bring lasting political stability as the KMT government continued to struggle with warlords and the communist challenge until the Japanese invasion in 1937. The war with the Japanese was hardly a period of stability for the Chinese state, while the final chapter of Republican China, the civil war between the KMT and the CCP (1946–9), resulted in massive dislocations of population, economic destruction and violent political struggles.

The CCP's victory in 1949 brought an end to the incessant warfare that had engulfed China for a century, but, given the revolutionary ideology of the new ruling regime, it was not meant to bring social stability to China, at least not in the short term. The land reform (1950), which initiated social revolution in China's countryside, gave rise to intense class struggle, and claimed millions of lives. Subsequent mass movements, of which the Anti-rightist Campaign (1957–8), Great Leap Forward (1958–61) and the Cultural Revolution (1966–76) were the most significant, led to more social upheavals, resulting in more human tragedy. Although the CCP successfully restored economic growth to the pre-war levels by the early 1950s, the Chinese economy (both rural and urban) experienced protracted turbulence from the launch of the Great Leap Forward until the late 1970s.

In contrast to earlier periods in China's history, the social, economic and political instability of the People's Republic of China (PRC) – with the exception of ethnic conflicts in the border areas – was brought about by the party-state leadership, rather than by the enemies of the ruling regime. Communist China's leader, Mao Zedong, perceived society as characterised by numerous contradictions, in which ceaseless change and social upheaval were not only normal but necessary, so that the society could reach a higher level of proletarian consciousness. Furthermore, in Mao's view, revolution could be sustained only if all bourgeois influences were eliminated. However, since bourgeois tendencies could resurface within revolutionary institutions (such as the party apparatus and state bureaucracy), and these in turn could carry out counter-revolutionary restoration (Wang 1992: 54–5), continuous revolution (*jixi geming*) was necessary to guard against ideological revisionism. Hence Mao's dictum, 'to rebel is justified' (*zaofan youli*), coined as early as 1939 (Schram 1989: 172), encouraged the masses to rebel against the party hierarchy and state bureaucracy (and all forms of authority). Yet, continuous revolution notwithstanding, Mao's encouragement of rebellion at no point was meant to challenge his leadership within the party or the ruling position of the CCP. The Chinese Communist Party weathered leadership succession struggles and sociopolitical upheavals by ensuring the loyalty of the Chinese military, and extinguishing real or imagined opponents to its rule.

The death of Mao Zedong in 1976 ended the party's concern with the counter-revolutionary restoration, but did not bring immediate sociopolitical stability to China. In fact, the first post-Mao years were marked by continued power struggle within the CCP leadership and a debate about the direction of China's socioeconomic development. The eventual winner of the post-Mao succession process, Deng Xiaoping, feared the return of political and social instability (*luan*) à la Cultural Revolution, which had paralysed the party-state apparatus, inhibited economic development and polarised Chinese society. Therefore Deng gave priority to political and social stability, which became the basis for creating a favourable environment for dynamic economic development. Stability and development (*fazhan*) were the Deng leadership's main objectives.

Sources of instability in contemporary China

In the name of preventing social upheaval, Deng suppressed expressions of mass dissatisfaction with the CCP, of which the Democracy Wall movement (1978–9) and the Beijing Spring (1989) are the best-known examples. His resolve to maintain social and political stability in China – with tanks and bullets if necessary – carried the hidden cost of silencing dissenting voices and thus seriously restricted the political evolution of the communist party and state. Although Deng successfully imposed stability upon Chinese society, the speed with which the public's mourning for former party-state leader Hu Yaobang in April 1989 turned into large-scale demonstrations (engulfing major cities in China and uniting students and workers in their demands for democracy, and for Premier Li Peng's resignation) exposed the fragility of sociopolitical stability in China. This fragility was further underscored by the rapid collapse of communist regimes in the Soviet bloc from 1989 to 1991. Some China watchers therefore predicted the fall of the CCP, noting intense factional struggles and the absence of a charismatic leader to succeed Deng (Myers 1990: 462–4; Domes 1990: 469–70). Although this prediction proved wrong, others questioned the likelihood of social and political stability surviving Deng's death (Goldstone 1995; Waldron 1995). Still others did not rule out political instability in post-Deng China as a likely – although not necessarily exclusive or most likely – scenario (Dittmer and Wu 1995: 494; Baum 1996; Fewsmith 1997: 527–8). Yet Deng's departure in 1997 neither inspired any mass movements on the scale of the Beijing Spring, nor indeed gave rise to any factional struggles within the CCP or any organised challenge to the CCP's rule. Does this imply that neither Chinese politics nor society face contentious issues that might one day bring social unrest, large enough to contest the leadership of the CCP? Although none of the contributors to this volume suggest that contemporary China faces imminent collapse (Chang 2001), or that its economic development rests upon 'a volcanic stability' (He 2003), they agree that the economic reforms have released social and economic forces that are powerful enough to upset the political and socioeconomic status quo in contemporary China to the point of undermining the rule of the communist party, if not tearing the country apart.

Weaknesses of the political system

Ng Ka Po in Chapter 2 of this volume does not share the pessimism of some analysts regarding the decline of the CCP, its poor governance, or its increasing immobilism (Pei 1999 and 2002; Li and Bachman 1989: 90–3; Wang 2003: 38–41). In his view, Jiang Zemin, who emerged as the party-state leader after the Beijing Spring, successfully sustained China on the path of rapid economic growth without endangering the communist party's leadership position or dangerously eroding its legitimacy. Yet Ng acknowledges that potential sources of political instability did not disappear during the Jiang period. Although it managed to streamline state bureaucracy and leave greater room for the free market in the economy, the CCP under Jiang's stewardship failed to divest itself of the excessive control of state affairs, and thus prevented the state from developing its own institutional administrative capacity. This failure has also sustained the state's vulnerability to the ruling party's failings. The first peaceful and orderly transfer of power in post-imperial China, completed from 2002 to 2004, when Hu Jintao replaced Jiang as the CCP General Secretary, PRC President and the Chairman of the Central Military Commission, did not herald the institutionalisation of the leadership succession process. Potential power struggles within the CCP leadership still threaten political stability in China as they did during the Mao and immediate post-Mao years. Similarly, village-level elections, intended to give peasants a greater say in the local affairs, did not ease tensions in the most disaffected rural areas, as riots in Taishi village and Dongzhou village (both in Guangdong province) in 2005 amply demonstrated.

Jiang Zemin's Theory of the Three Represents, advanced in 2000, underscored the party's awareness of the disintegration of the social strata whose interests the CCP was established to represent and advance: peasants, workers and soldiers. While the share of workers and peasants in the CCP membership gradually declined (both in relative and absolute terms), the share of intellectuals, management, administrative and technical personnel increased. Enlightened with the Theory of the Three Represents (enshrined in the revised party constitution), the party also began welcoming private entrepreneurs, thus blurring – if not destroying – its proletarian image and undermining its legitimacy as a proletarian party. It remains to be seen how Hu Jintao will navigate through the CCP's ideological pitfalls and China's severe social inequalities to arrive at a 'socialist harmonious society'. It is certain, however, that he is as determined as his predecessors to fend off any challenges to the CCP's continued monopoly of power in China, be they ethnic or religious minorities, spiritual movements (such as *Falungong*), political opposition, or the information revolution that accompanies the development of China's mass media and personal communication technologies.

Economic inequalities

While the extent of political stability in post-Deng China is debatable, rising social instability has become so conspicuous in contemporary China that it is no longer a taboo subject even for the tightly censored Chinese media. Statistics of the number of collective protests, riots and other forms of resistance against authorities vary. Pei Minxin (2002: 106–7) wrote of the fourfold increase in the number of collective protests, from 8,700 in 1993 to 32,000 in 1999. George Gilboy and Eric

Heginbotham (2001: 34) counted 117 incidents of armed, violent protest in 2000, while in 2005 print media reported the number of riots to have surpassed 70,000 (*Standard* 2005, December 22; see also Chapter 8 in this volume).

While the causes of social unrest in contemporary China are numerous (and include a growing sense of political injustice and an absence of institutional mechanisms for resolving conflicts), the contributors to this volume consider the rising economic inequalities – intra-urban, intra-rural, intra-regional and inter-regional – as the main source of the increasing discontent among the Chinese citizenry. The widening gap – resulting from market reforms – between the haves and the have-nots has transformed China from one of the most egalitarian societies in the world during the Mao era into currently one of the most unequal. Colin Mackerras, in Chapter 8, notes that economic inequality in Chinese society (as measured by the Gini coefficient) has passed the 'alarm level' and continues to rise. Given corruption among party and state officials, both Wang Shaoguang (Chapter 4) and Mackerras (Chapter 8) tacitly agree with Pei's conclusion (2002: 108) that rising inequality is fuelling public anger against the state and party bureaucracy and stoking the Chinese public's perception that only those with privileged access to power benefit from economic reforms.

In the cities, the CCP's economic reforms have led to the closure, restructuring or privatisation of thousands of state-owned enterprises (SOE), resulting in rising urban unemployment (above 4 per cent according to official statistics in 2005 or above 11 per cent according to independent estimates, see Chapter 3 for more details). The state has offered little welfare protection for laid-off workers and as a result, unemployed workers have joined together in protests in cities and towns throughout the country. In the countryside, farmers have been exploited by local government officials who force the rural populace to pay onerous and arbitrary taxes and fees in order to finance local, extra-budgetary, non-agricultural development projects or personally enrich local cadres (see Ash in Chapter 6). Hundreds of millions of farmers have also been displaced by the rapid conversion of agricultural land for development, leaving millions with no land and no job, while the state rolls back social welfare provision. As crucial services (such as health care or education) are no longer affordable for the urban or rural poor (see Mackerras in Chapter 8), children are unlikely to escape their parents' poverty.

Bennis So in Chapter 3 suggests that one reason for the state's decreasing capacity to provide the citizens with sufficient welfare is the privatisation or restructuring of the state-owned enterprises. The SOEs often refuse to provide a social safety net for their employees, while private enterprises are even less concerned with welfare services for their employees. The government's reliance upon increasingly fewer and poorly performing SOEs for its revenue has contributed to the decreasing percentage of government revenue relative to GDP. In other words, the government does not have sufficient funding for essential welfare services and seeks to devolve responsibility for social welfare to various social groups, such as local communities, mass organisations, enterprises and families.

In focusing on the privatisation process in China, Bennis So does not engage with arguments related to the central government's strengthened revenue base (relative to the GDP and provincial budgets) that followed the fiscal and tax reforms in 1993–4 (Yang 2003: 44–5, and 2004: 122–6). Neither does Wang Shaoguang in Chapter 4, who agrees with So's thesis that the central government's capacity to generate revenue has fundamentally declined. However, Wang identifies increased decentralisation, in which provinces retain much of their revenue, as responsible for the government's shrinking share of national income, fiscal reforms notwithstanding. Wang argues that facing budgetary constraints, and being unwilling (and unable) to extract large surpluses from rich (coastal) provinces to subsidise the development of poorer regions, the Chinese government in the reform period (particularly after 1991) has presided over an era of widening inter- and intra-regional economic inequalities. Wang further argues that uneven economic development was neither a result of the invisible forces of the free market, nor, given China's vast size, an inevitable product of variations in geographical conditions, resource endowment, sectoral distribution of economic activities and socioeconomic development. Instead, uneven economic development became severe in post-Mao China because the reform leadership embraced a 'gradient theory' of development, in line with which the development of the coastal provinces was prioritised at the expense of declining support for the central and western (poorest) regions. Such a deliberate strategy allowed the rich provinces to mobilise local savings and retain most of these savings (rather than export their substantial proportion to poorer provinces as they used to do during the Mao era). In turn, the rich provinces (with a strong ability to mobilise local savings) attracted foreign investors, who were tempted to rich provinces by preferential policies extended by the central government. The state also located more than half of its capital investment in the coastal region. At the same time, the poor provinces did not enjoy preferential policies for foreign investors and benefited substantially less from inter-provincial capital flows.

In Wang's view, uneven economic development contributes directly to social instability as people living in regions where average incomes are remarkably lower than in other parts of the country or where incomes grow noticeably slower than elsewhere, are likely to vocally express their grievances and blame the local or central authorities for their plight. Wang suggests that Beijing should be concerned with the ominous trend of growing regional inequality and address the problem by reconsidering its skewed regional policies, rebuilding its extractive capacity, and overhauling the country's fiscal system to effect equalisation across regions.

Unrest among ethnic minorities

Unequal regional development also contributes to unrest in areas populated by ethnic minorities. By 2000, none of the five 'nationality autonomous regions' (or provinces populated by ethnic minorities: Tibet, Xinjiang, Inner Mongolia, Guangxi and Ningxia) or the three provinces where ethnic minorities comprised over one third of the population (Yunnan, Guizhou and Qinghai) enjoyed per capita GDP higher than the national average (Wang, Chapter 4). Colin Mackerras in Chapter 7 expresses concern over the social stability in economically underdeveloped minority regions and provides more data to suggest that minority areas are not only less developed but also suffer from far greater absolute poverty than other parts of China. The income gaps between minorities-populated areas and Han areas also overlap with religious, cultural and historical animosities between the Han and the minorities, and this reinforces the likelihood of inter-ethnic conflicts. Regardless of whether ethnic tensions lead to secessionist movements, terrorist attacks or isolated mass protests caused by particular grievances, their very existence renders China more unstable generally.

Both Wang and Mackerras applaud the central government's efforts to address the problem of growing regional inequality, of which the Western Development Programme is the main manifestation. Mackerras (Chapter 8) also acknowledges Beijing's achievements in reducing absolute poverty and gender inequality, as well as the government's determination to abolish agricultural taxes across the country in order to reduce urban–rural disparities and eliminate an important source of rural discontent. Hu Jintao has made stability and the fight against inequality his top priority. Although his predecessors succeeded in pushing through harsh market reforms while enjoying relative social and political stability, Hu understands that the continuity of the CCP's rule rests upon social stability as a prerequisite to political stability. He pins his hopes on sustained economic development, which has already appreciably improved the quality of life for many Chinese. It is hoped that the benefits of economic growth will eventually trickle down to all social classes, including those that initially lost out in the process of economic transformations. But can China sustain its precipitous economic growth long enough to ensure that the prosperity filters down to all social strata? To some, the spectre of large-scale social unrest remains a possibility, especially when China's economic growth slows down, leading to higher levels of popular frustration and accentuating sociopolitical problems currently concealed by the economic expansion (Pei 1999: 108; Perry and Selden 2000: 14).

Sustainable development

There is little doubt that Beijing is committed to sustaining economic growth, which has averaged 10 per cent per year since the early 1980s. Towards this goal, it has allowed the gradual and largely disguised privatisation of agriculture, industry and services (examined by Bennis So in Chapter 3). However, in the past decade, the CCP has also recognised that rapid economic growth that does not take into account the social and environmental costs of economic restructuring is not sustainable in the longer term. Thus, since 1994, when the Chinese government approved *China's Agenda 21: White Paper on China's Population, Environment and Development in the 21st Century*, Beijing has officially embarked upon sustainable development, defined as development that 'meets the needs of the present without compromising the ability of future generations to meet their own needs' (WCED 1987: 8).

Divided into twenty chapters, *China's Agenda 21* covered four issue areas: overall strategies for sustainable development; social development; economic development; and protection of resources and the environment. Unsurprisingly, economic development, measured by the GDP growth rate, was accorded the highest priority since '[o]nly when the economic growth rate reaches and is sustained at a certain level, can poverty be eradicated, people's livelihoods improved and the necessary forces and conditions for supporting sustainable development be provided'. Yet *Agenda 21* also emphasised the importance of social sustainability (paying particular attention to controlling population growth, eliminating poverty, promoting education, expanding job opportunities, and improving people's food, clothing, housing conditions, and health care) and environmental sustainability. *China's Agenda 21* did not neglect sustainability of agricultural development either. Its main objectives included an increase in agricultural productivity, enhancement of food production and food security, development of the rural economy and increase of rural people's incomes (*China's Agenda 21* 1994).

A decade after the publication of *China's Agenda 21*, Beijing released the *Programme of Action for Sustainable Development in China in the Early 21st Century* (*People's Daily* 2003, 26 July), in which it congratulated itself for making 'remarkable progress in sustainable development'. China maintained sustained and rapid economic growth; checked population growth; made progress in expanding education, developing social security, eradicating poverty and narrowing the regional gap in development; and strengthened ecological conservation and environmental protection. Yet, despite all these achievements, the Programme realistically noted persisting problems: an ageing population; inadequacy of social security; rising unemployment; widening regional inequalities; ongoing environmental degradation, and ecological deterioration. The contributors to this book agree that alongside some laudable achievements such as the reduction of absolute poverty, rising life expectancy, increasing literacy among men and women, and greater educational opportunities for youth and adults (see Chapter 8), China – in addition to coping with rising social dislocations and inequalities – also faces an environmental crisis. Moreover, the tension between its growing population and food security has not disappeared.

Environmental sustainability

As development that does not take nature's capacity into consideration is not considered sustainable in the long term, environmental sustainability – focused on maintaining the integrity, productivity and resilience of biological and physical systems – constitutes a key element of sustainable development (OECD 2001: 36). China's environmental predicaments are not new, and date back to ancient times when population growth and the scarcity of arable land necessitated intensive use of land. This led to a reduction in vegetation cover and facilitated soil erosion, flooding and increased silt loads in rivers. However, as Richard Edmonds argues in Chapter 5, the greatest damage to Chinese environment occurred in the post-1949 period when the communist regime set China on the path of accelerated industrialisation (with a focus on heavy industry) and encouraged the conquest of nature and economic growth at all cost. Thus, alongside resource degradation, China began facing a widespread and complex pollution problem created by the rapidly developing industrial sector. Edmonds devotes substantial attention to analysis of the seriousness of pollution in contemporary China by looking at water pollution, solid wastes, air pollution and noise pollution. Although Edmonds does not explicitly agree with Vaclav Smil's conclusion (1993, 191) that China's modernisation plans guarantee further extensive environmental degradation, destruction and pollution, he does agree that environmental problems in China are serious, and that their regulation and management requires urgent government action. More specifically, he suggests that the role of non-governmental organisations be expanded to monitor officials and enterprises that seek economic growth at any environmental cost. Furthermore, he argues that environmental education should be promoted to increase environmental awareness, and that environmental degradation be properly accounted for when calculating economic growth.

Population growth and food security

Natural resource degradation and population issues are closely interrelated. A growing population increases the demand on natural resources and other environmental services, possibly stretching resource use beyond its critical carrying capacity (OECD 2001: 44). China's population has fluctuated throughout centuries, expanding during the periods of peace and economic prosperity and contracting during wars and famines. In the Mao period, it more than doubled due to the absence of warfare, rare famines, generally improving diet, hygiene and health care, as well as the absence of population control measures, reflecting Mao's deliberate pro-natalist policy that favoured more births. What population can China support? Since the late 1970s, Chinese experts have suggested that the optimum desirable capacity of the land was a population of between 700 million and one billion (Edmonds). Thus, currently, China is overpopulated by at least 300 million. A major consequence of over-population is the maintenance of good quality cultivated land and of food security. In Chapter 5, Richard Edmonds notes a dramatic shrinkage of per capita availability of farmland, a progressing deterioration in the quality of farmland, and a decreasing availability of water per capita. These have an extreme impact on sustainable farming in China and excessive soil erosion, extensive deforestation and severe desertification contribute to already damaged ecosystems.

Despite rapid population growth during the Mao period, human development indicators (such as life expectancy, per capita income, food availability, access to education and health care) have improved rather than deteriorated in China. Yet the post-Mao leadership considered unchecked population growth not only as having potentially disastrous consequences on China's ecosystem and social welfare, but also as threatening Chinese economic development. Hence, in 1979, Beijing introduced the one-child policy. Although the policy met with resistance, especially in the countryside, and resulted in an increase in female infanticide and a skewed male–female ratio in favour of males, the Chinese government has succeeded in decreasing birth rates. Robert Ash's analysis of the one-child policy in Chapter 6 also suggests that this success, while temporarily solving the problem of unchecked population growth, created a problem that China had never faced in its long history: that of an ageing population. This problem is predicted to become acute by 2020 and negatively impact on China's economic growth and social security system.

The question of over-population raises a fear of food scarcity. According to Ash (Chapter 6), one of the most remarkable achievements of post-1949 Chinese governments has been the successful resolution of the tension between population growth and food supply. Despite the fact that China has only 7 per cent of the world's arable land and 21 per cent of the world's population, it has succeeded in feeding its rising population, resorting to food imports on a very limited scale. Food production during the Mao period, however, was not free of major problems, including a disastrous famine during the Great Leap Forward (1959–61) which claimed 30 million lives, and a stagnant per capita grain output throughout the first three decades of the communists' rule. Ash credits Deng's agricultural reforms (also briefly discussed in Chapter 3) with raising average per capita grain output (based on improvements in average yield rather than increases in grain-sown areas) and improving Chinese diet. As a result, the perennial threat of hunger, malnutrition and starvation has disappeared from China, while China became a net exporter of grain. Robert Ash, however, ends his examination on a cautionary note. Chinese agriculture faces severe water shortages, a contracting arable land base, stagnating rural incomes, and contracting output of cereals. As the consequences of Chinese agriculture's opening to international competition in the aftermath of China's entry to the World Trade Organization are yet to be known, the delicate balance between population growth and food security in China might evolve in unforeseeable ways.

China's territorial unity

The Chinese territory as we know it today resulted to a great extent from conquests made by China's last dynasty, the Qing, which more than doubled Ming China by incorporating non-Han (ethnic Chinese) areas, such as Tibet, Xinjiang, and the Qing's homeland, Manchuria. By the mid-nineteenth century, however, having lost the First Opium War with Great Britain (1839–42) and all subsequent military conflicts with the European powers and Japan, the Manchus were forced to cede parts of the Chinese empire to foreign powers and limit China's sovereignty in major trade centres by granting foreigners extraterritorial rights that exempted them from Chinese laws.

The fall of the Qing dynasty in 1911 and the establishment of the Republic of China in 1912 failed to end the process of China's territorial disintegration. Mongolia (supported by Russia) and Tibet (supported by Britain) declared independence, while Russian and later Soviet troops occupied Northern Mongolia, where with Soviet support, the Mongolian People's Republic was proclaimed in 1924. Chinese governments did not recognise Mongolia's sovereignty until 1945. The republican regime also did not recognise Tibetan sovereignty, but it exercised a minimal control over the province. In Xinjiang too, the republican government's effective control was weak in contrast to the influence enjoyed by the Soviet Union. The greatest blow to China's territorial integrity came in 1931, when Japan invaded Manchuria, and in 1937–8, when Tokyo occupied the territories east of the Guangzhou–Beijing line, where China's major ports and industrial centres were located.

A hundred years after the first unequal treaty was inked in 1842, the Chinese regained most of their lost territories. Germany lost its Chinese territories after the First World War, Soviet Russia gave up extraterritorial rights in China shortly after the Bolshevik revolution, and the United States and Britain gave up extraterritorial rights in 1943, with other powers quickly following suit. Having been defeated in 1945, Japan lost all of the occupied territories in China. The contribution of the Chinese Communist Party to consolidating China's territorial integrity took the form of expanding the central government's control over such areas as Xinjiang, Manchuria, Tibet, Yunnan and Inner Mongolia; areas that had remained under foreign influences for many decades. Only Outer Mongolia (whose sovereignty – out of deference to the Soviet Union – the People's Republic of China recognised in 1949), Taiwan (where the KMT took refuge after losing the Civil War in China in 1949), Hong Kong and Macau remained outside the CCP's control. With the return of Hong Kong and Macau to Chinese sovereignty in 1997 and 1999 respectively, the Taiwan issue became the most pressing item on the agenda of China's territorial unity.

Reunification with Taiwan

Czeslaw Tubilewicz in Chapter 9 discusses at length Chinese attempts to recover Taiwan, which throughout the 1950s relied primarily on military force and, since the late 1970s, have shifted to a peaceful offensive. Regardless of the tactics chosen, Beijing has failed to regain Taiwan and Tubilewicz doubts the CCP's capacity to accomplish national reunification in the foreseeable future. First, with its evolving democratisation, the Taiwanese public has had a greater say on the political future of Taiwan. And, given the rise of Taiwanese identity on the island, it is unlikely to support any immediate union with the mainland. Second, Beijing has yet to offer Taiwan an attractive reunification proposal. The current offer, a variation on the 'one country, two systems' formula which helped China reunify with Hong Kong and Macau, has lost much of its appeal among the islanders after China impeded the progression of political reforms in Hong Kong.

In light of Taipei's refusal to return to the mainland's embrace, the CCP has pinned its hopes on its military modernisation programme, which is intended to shift the military balance in the Taiwan Strait in China's favour and allow China a successful invasion of the island. Beijing has also supported the deepening of economic exchanges between the island and the mainland, hoping that these might eventually lead to Taiwan's loss of economic independence, and its reluctant or joyful return to China. Tubilewicz argues, however, that given the island's defences and the logistic difficulties of staging a surprise attack on the island, China's capacity to subdue the island militarily is debatable, even when other states (e.g. the United States) choose not to get involved in the Sino-Taiwanese conflict. Similarly, economic relations between the mainland and the island have evolved into a symbiotic, rather than a dependent partnership, and both sides have much to lose if either ceases cooperation.

Finally, Chapter 9 suggests that the importance of the Taiwan issue for China goes beyond a closure of the civil war chapter and a completion of the national reunification agenda. Because the CCP styled itself as an exclusive force for China's territorial integrity and sovereignty, the party's legitimacy to a great extent rests upon its ability to accomplish reunification with Taiwan in a nearer, rather than unspecified, future. Therefore, if Beijing manages to find a peaceful formula to the Taiwan issue, it would boost its legitimacy among the Chinese nationalists, thereby strengthening its mandate to rule China. If, however, it carries out the reunification by force, the resulting conflict with Taiwan could not only devastate the island's prosperity, but also undermine Chinese economic growth, upset social stability, and test the survival skills of the PRC regime. If war with Taiwan were to lead to social unrest, it could also trigger turbulence in border regions, with grave consequences for China's territorial unity.

Centrifugal forces in contemporary China

Throughout its long history, China has often been subjected to centrifugal forces. During the Qing period, the border regions, populated by ethnic minorities, enjoyed a large degree of autonomy, if not de facto sovereignty. After the fall of the Qing empire, the major check on provincial autonomy disappeared and China fragmented into smaller political and territorial units ruled by warlords, while major border regions declared independence. Warlordism continued beyond 1928, when the KMT nominally reunified the country, but the KMT's compromises with warlords allowed the warlords to rule most provinces with little regard to the central government. Although the KMT government gradually expanded its control of the lower Yangtze Valley to most provinces, Republican China was hardly a unified country when the Sino-Japanese war erupted in 1937, with the far west and southwest provinces enjoying the most complete autonomy (Sheridan 1975).

The CCP – through the unitary command structure of its armed forces – successfully eradicated warlordism from China's political scene. Yet, despite its success at extending the central government's control to all of China's regions, the centrifugal forces disappeared neither from Mao's China nor from China under the post-Mao leaderships. Prophecies of China disintegrating into independent or semi-independent strongholds (reminiscent of the warlords' era) or of transforming into a commonwealth of semi-independent regions intensified after the Beijing Spring (Cheng 1990: 196–7; Domes 1990: 471). These pessimistic predictions gained further credence when the Soviet Union disintegrated in 1991, quickly followed by Yugoslavia and Czechoslovakia. The vision of China's territorial disintegration (leading to the split into several new states, federalism or pseudo-federalism) was rooted in two interrelated phenomena: the rise of economic localism in post-Mao China, where – thanks to the economic reforms that demanded decentralisation if they were to succeed – provinces gained and then jealously guarded their autonomy in fiscal and other matters from the infringement of central authorities (Li and Bachman 1989; Chang 1992; Cheng 1999: 31–4), and the 'explosion' of regional communal identities (Friedman 1993). Other academics did not rule out a possible power struggle after Deng's death, resulting in radical devolutionary changes, including regional fragmentation (Waldron 1995: 151; Baum 1996: 167). At the same time, however, there were also voices urging against a premature proclamation of the death of the Chinese unitary state (Goodman and Segal 1994).

Academics have been notoriously unlucky at predicting the future. They failed to see the end of the Cold War or the fall of the Soviet Union (Gaddis 1992/1993) and, unsurprisingly, predictions of China's disintegration proved off the mark as well. The PRC survived the Beijing Spring, the disintegration of several former communist states, the post-Deng leadership transition, and the Asian Financial Crisis without experiencing territorial disintegration. In fact, the opposite happened as the Chinese territory expanded with Hong Kong and Macau's return to China's sovereignty. To account for the persistence of China's territorial unity, China-watchers focused on identifying factors explaining the strength of the Chinese unitary state, and cautioned against expecting the fragmentation of China in any foreseeable future (Naughton and Yang 2004). Two contributors to this volume, Wang Shaoguang (Chapter 4) and Colin Mackerras (Chapter 7) do not dispute arguments regarding the Chinese state's capacity to remake institutions and reshape its policies in ways that strengthen China's territorial unity. They remain, however, less optimistic about 'a dynamic tension between increasing diversity and national unity', implying that it is as likely to lead to territorial fragmentation, as to provide 'creative pressure that helps China's social and economic transformation moving forward' (Naughton and Yang 2004: 6–7).

Secessionist movements in ethnic areas

The capacity for territorial fragmentation is particularly of concern in the areas populated by non-Han people, which were incorporated into China by the Qing army. Colin Mackerras argues in Chapter 7 that two large border provinces populated by Tibetans and Uygurs, Tibet and Xinjiang, show the greatest desire for autonomy within, if not outright separation from, the PRC. In the 1920s, the Chinese communists argued in favour of transcending narrow patriotism and granting self-determination rights for Mongolia, Xinjiang, Tibet and Qinghai. By the late 1930s, however, they qualified their support for self-determination of the areas populated by ethnic minorities, requiring them to form some form of federal relationship with China (Hunt 1991: 194). Having established their rule in China, the communists did not change their views on the future of ethnic minority regions: the PRC constitutions never allowed for the secession of autonomous areas and Beijing used military means to suppress secessionist movements, especially the one in Tibet in 1959. The Deng Xiaoping regime's policies of according ethnic minorities wider scope of autonomy and improving minorities' livelihood did not extinguish secessionist sentiments in both provinces. A combination of factors ranging from ethnic identity and economic inequalities to religious freedoms and Han immigration contributed to the eruption of ethnic violence in Tibet and Xinjiang in the 1980s and 1990s, which had strong secessionist undertones. The establishment of independent Central Asian republics in the early 1990s further encouraged independence movements in China's border regions and a secessionist movement even emerged in Inner Mongolia, where pro-independence sentiments were relatively weaker than in other minority areas. Although Mackerras dismisses the likelihood of social and economic inequalities leading to fragmentation of China along ethnic lines, he does not dismiss the continuing challenge posed by the secessionist movements in Tibet and Xinjiang to China's territorial integrity. He suggests that Beijing should formulate 'sensitive and realistic' policies on the ethnic question to prevent any possibility that China could share the fate of Yugoslavia or the Soviet Union.

The peril of regional disintegration

In Chapter 4, Wang Shaoguang returns to his well-known thesis on the consequences of uneven regional development for China's territorial unity (Wang and Au 1999: 199–202). While Wang does not go as far as saying that uneven regional economic development might lead to warlordism (as the socioeconomic and political conditions of contemporary China differ greatly from those in the early twentieth century), he disagrees with those who either disparage the dangers posed to China's territorial integrity by unequal economic development or deny the very existence of regional inequalities (see, for example, Huang 1995: 66). In Wang's view, regional inequalities have the potential to undermine China's territorial unity as more developed regions might perceive the government's redistributive policies as unfair transfer of their resources and become attracted to the idea that their interests would be better served by seeking separation from Beijing. The experiences of the Soviet Union and Yugoslavia demonstrate the difficulty of maintaining territorial integrity under conditions of serious regional economic disparities. The difficulty of tackling uneven regional development in China, with its consequences for social stability and territorial integrity, is revealed in Wang's suggestion that Beijing should aim at more balanced regional development through redistributive policies that extract large surpluses from rich regions to benefit poor regions. Yet, these very policies, while possibly eradicating economic inequalities and contributing to social stability, could accelerate China's disintegration along the prosperity lines.

Development riddled with challenges

If the Chinese economy, in 2005 the world's fourth largest (when measured on the basis of the GDP) or second largest (if measured on the basis of purchasing price parity), encounters no significant obstacles in its rapid growth, it is predicted to match the United States' GDP between 2014 and 2050 (Casetti, 2003: 672). The analyses in this book, however, question Beijing's capacity to sustain economic growth. The primary concern is China's domestic stability. The economic transformation carries high opportunity costs, which Chinese society at the moment is willing to bear in an expectation of improved livelihood. However, increasing wealth has not been evenly distributed, with inequalities rising between regions, urban and rural areas, and within urban and rural societies. Confronted with frequent, albeit localised, rural and urban violent expressions of discontent, Hu Jintao has placed greater emphasis on social stability and a 'harmonious society' than his predecessor, Jiang Zemin. Yet, the effectiveness of his policies remains to be seen.

The spectre of social instability should be placed in the larger context of the increasingly questionable legitimacy of the Chinese Communist Party. Having pursued market reforms, the CCP is no longer seen as serving the interests of the underprivileged, but rather as a vehicle for the rich and powerful to further their influence and wealth. The Theory of Three Represents, while attempting to adapt the party to the new socioeconomic situation in China, reveals its evolving class character. How long can this nominally communist party sustain itself in power when it loses the support of the workers and peasants, because equal opportunities and equitable social welfare become no longer available in China?

The communist leadership is pinning its hopes on sustained economic growth, hoping this will deliver economic results to increasingly greater numbers of people. It is also basing its credibility on a self-styled image as the exclusive force for national unity, preventing China from disintegrating along ethnic or economic lines. Ironically, Beijing's use of Taiwan's protracted separation from the mainland in order to fan nationalist sentiments in China could backfire, as the mainland Chinese might become increasingly impatient when Taipei rejects Beijing's peaceful reunification offers, or unforgiving, when the CCP's coercive methods to recover the island fail. In either scenario, social instability, with dire consequences for the regime's survival and China's territorial integrity, is a distinct possibility.

Despite the serious challenges confronting contemporary China, this book suggests neither an imminent collapse of the CCP regime nor a collapse of China as a unitary state nor large-scale social unrest. Since its formation, the CCP has displayed a remarkable ability to adapt to evolving political and social environments. By 1950, it successfully reunified Chinese territory and thereafter initiated bold (although often socially divisive) policies which helped modernise the Chinese economy and establish social and economic equality. Realising the weaknesses of planned economy, the Chinese communists presided over an era of far-reaching and largely effective economic reforms and profound social change, without jeopardising its mandate to rule the country. Beijing's record of successful domestic strategies in the past two decades, its keen awareness of the critical issues discussed in this book, and its determination to pursue sustainable development, rather than merely sustained economic growth, augur well for its ability to resolve the critical political, economic and social issues faced by China in the early twenty-first century.

References

Baum, R. (1996) 'China After Deng: Ten Scenarios in Search of Reality', *China Quarterly* 145 (March): 153–75.

Casetti, E. (2003) 'Power Shifts and Economic Development: When Will China Overtake the USA?', *Journal of Peace Research* 40/6: 661–75.

Chang, G. G. (2001) *The Coming Collapse of China*, New York: Random House.

Chang, M. H. (1992) 'China's Future: Regionalism, Federation, or Disintegration', *Studies in Comparative Communism* 25/3 (September): 211–27.

Cheng, Chu-yuan (1990) *Behind the Tiananmen Massacre: Social, Political, and Economic Ferment in China*, Boulder, CO: Westview Press.

Cheng, J. Y. S. (1999) 'Local Government's Role in a Transitional Economy: The Case of Guangdong', in Zang Xiaowei (ed.), *China in the Reform Era*, Commack, NY: Nova Science Publishers, pp. 29–34.

China's Agenda 21: White Paper on China's Population, Environment and Development in the 21st Century (1994) retrieved from www.acca21.org.cn/indexe6.html, 2005, December 30.

Dittmer, L. and Wu, Yu-shan (1995) 'The Modernization of Factionalism in Chinese Politics', *World Politics* 47/4 (July): 467–94.

Domes, J. (1990) 'Four Ways Communism Could Die in China', in G. Hicks (ed.), *The Broken Mirror: China After Tiananmen*, Harlow, Essex: Longman, pp. 466–72.

Fewsmith, J. (1997) 'Reaction, Resurgence, and Succession: Chinese Politics Since Tiananmen', in R. MacFarquhar (ed.), *The Politics of China: The Eras of Mao and Deng*, Cambridge: Cambridge University Press, pp. 472–531.

Friedman, E. (1993) 'China's North-South Split and the Forces of Disintegration', *Current History* 92/575 (September): 270–4.

Gaddis, J. L. (1992/1993) 'International Relations Theory and the End of the Cold War', *International Security* 17/3 (Winter): 5–58.

Gilboy, G. and Heginbotham, E. (2001) 'China's Coming Transformation', *Foreign Affairs* 60/4 (July–August): 26–39.

Goldstone, J. A. (1995) 'The Coming Chinese Collapse', *Foreign Policy* 99 (Summer): 35–52.

Goodman, D. S. G. and Segal, G. (eds) (1994) *China Deconstructs: Politics, Trade and Regionalism*, London and New York: Routledge.

He Qinglian (2003) 'A Volcanic Stability', *Journal of Democracy* 14/1 (January): 66–72.

Huang Yasheng (1995) 'Why China Will Not Collapse', *Foreign Policy* 99 (Summer): 54–68.

Hunt, M. H. (1991) 'The May Fourth Era: China's Place in the World', in K. Lieberthal, J. Kallgren, R. MacFarquhar and F. Wakeman Jr (eds) *Perspectives on Modern China: Four Anniversaries*, Armonk and London: M. E. Sharpe, pp. 178–200.

Li Cheng and Bachman, D. (1989) 'Localism, Elitism, and Immobilism: Elite Formation and Social Change in Post-Mao China', *World Politics* 42/1 (October): 64–94.

Myers, R. H. (1990) 'The Next Power Struggle', in G. Hicks (ed.) *The Broken Mirror: China After Tiananmen*, Harlow, Essex: Longman, pp. 456–65.

Naughton, B. J. and Yang, D. L. (eds) (2004) *Holding China Together: Diversity and National Integration in the Post-Deng Era*, Cambridge: Cambridge University Press.

OECD (Organisation for Economic Cooperation and Development) (2001) *Sustainable Development: Critical Issues*, Paris: OECD.

Pei Minxin (1999) 'Will China Become Another Indonesia?', *Foreign Policy* 116 (Fall): 94–108.

—— (2002) 'China's Governance Crisis', *Foreign Affairs* 81/5 (September–October 2002): 97–109.

Perry, E. J. and Selden, M. (2000) 'Introduction: Reform and Resistance in Contemporary China', in E. J. Perry and M. Selden (eds), *Chinese Society: Change, Conflict and Resistance*, London and New York: Routledge, pp. 1–19.

Schram, S. (1989) *The Thought of Mao Tse-Tung*, Cambridge: Cambridge University Press.

Sheridan, J. E. (1975) *China in Disintegration: The Republican Era in Chinese History, 1912–1949*, New York: Free Press.

Smil, V. (1993) *China's Environmental Crisis: An Inquiry into the Limits of National Development*, Armonk and London: M. E. Sharpe.

Waldron, A. (1995) 'After Deng the Deluge: China's Next Leap Forward', *Foreign Affairs* 74/5 (September–October): 148–53.

Wang, J. C. F. (1992) *Contemporary Chinese Politics: An Introduction*, Englewood Cliffs, NJ: Prentice Hall.

Wang Shaoguang (2003) 'The Problems of State Weakness', *Journal of Democracy* 14 (1, January): 36–42.

Wang Shaoguang and Au Angang (1999) *The Political Economy of Uneven Development: The Case of China*. Armonk and London: M. E. Sharpe.

WCED (World Commission on Environment and Development) (1987) *Our Common Future*, Oxford: Oxford University Press.

Yang, D. L. (2003) 'State Capacity on the Rebound', *Journal of Democracy* 14/1 (January): 43–50.

—— (2004) 'Economic Transformation and State Rebuilding in China', in B. J. Naughton and D. L. Yang (eds), *Holding China Together: Diversity and National Integration in the Post-Deng Era*, Cambridge: Cambridge University Press, pp. 120–45.

2

Critical developments in Chinese politics

Ng Ka Po

Introduction

After more than fifty years in power, the Chinese Communist Party (CCP) is not exactly the same party it was in 1949, when it gained power in China, or for that matter in 1921, when it was established. It has had to adapt to changes in the domestic and international environments. This chapter will discuss the most critical challenges that face the CCP in the early twenty-first century that might potentially lead to its further transformation.

I begin this chapter by discussing the nature of the political regime and ideological leadership in China. I examine the role of ideology in the Chinese political system by analysing the evolution of the CCP's official ideology, particularly Jiang Zemin's 'Important Thought of the Three Represents' and Hu Jintao's idea of building a 'harmonious society'. While Chinese leaders have been keen to foster a political direction and justify their governance, ideology, in the reform era, has the additional function of responding to the possible political fallout of economic reform.

In the second section of the chapter, I address the question of government reform. For the sake of maintaining or enhancing political control, the CCP has consistently controlled China's political, economic and social sectors. But to maintain the momentum of economic reform, which now forms the basis of effective governance, a redefinition of government functions has been necessary, especially in the context of state–Party relations, political–economic relations and the civil service. Accordingly, I look at how the CCP has tried to reform government.

Things have not been static at the top of the Chinese government. Ever since the formation of the CCP in 1921, changes in its leadership have been characterised by power struggles. Deng Xiaoping was the first to attempt a peaceful transition of power. After initial failure to do so, he succeeded in 1989 when selecting Jiang Zemin as China's new leader. Jiang continued Deng's efforts to stabilise the leadership by overseeing the orderly leadership succession that resulted in Hu Jintao becoming the Party and state leader. Leadership succession is thus the third of China's critical contemporary political issues that is discussed.

The countryside has often been the source of political change and experimentation in China. While the current economic boom is clearly centred in China's major cities, the countryside has been leading the nation in an experiment with pluralistic institutions. The institution of grassroots-level elections in villages, and their departure from the tradition of mobilised political participation, raises a sensitive question: Does this signal the emergence of a Chinese liberal democratic system in the countryside? In the fourth section of this chapter, I will look at how this infant democratic practice operates within the existing political regime and assess its importance and its implications for future developments in state ideology and political and government reform.

I conclude the chapter by evaluating the threat to Party power that the information revolution poses and by looking at the CCP's response to this threat. The information revolution has replaced the industrial revolution as the major driving force of the contemporary age. This has rendered the traditional means of political control in China obsolete. Brute force and organisation are not as effective as they used to be because the information revolution has opened new fronts on the government's battle to maintain control. Controlling the flow of ideas and public discourse has become more difficult for the Party. The government has had to face this new challenge, and the final section of this chapter looks at how it maintains political control by controlling the dissemination of ideas and managing information.

Ideology

> They [the Chinese Communist leaders] have been 'hooked' on an ideology which for decades they have stubbornly insisted embraced the 'ultimate truth' and which, whether they still believe in it or not, they feel compelled to cling to as the justification for their monopolising of power. (Pye 1999: 569)

This is a comment by a veteran China scholar, Lucien Pye. Ideology may indeed look anachronistic in today's China, which is often depicted as one of the fastest growing economies in the world. However, ideology continues to influence the course of China's contemporary development.

Marxism-Leninism in China

Before the establishment of the PRC, CCP leaders, from Chen Duxiu to Wang Ming, are said to have adopted various 'policy lines or platforms' (*luxian*). These are different from 'political thought' (*sixiang*), which refers to the systematic interpretation of political ideas. Political 'thought' has delineated important epochs in the CCP's development. In Chinese Communist lexicon, there is Maoism or Mao Zedong Thought, Deng Xiaoping Theory (*lilun*) and Jiang Zemin's Important Thought of the Three Represents (*sange daibiao*). At the beginning of 2005, the Hu Jintao leadership introduced the new concept of a Socialist Harmonious Society. All of these are supposed to be developments of Marxism-Leninism, the basic foundation of all Communist ideologies.

Mao Zedong Thought

Despite its criticism of the Mao-instigated Cultural Revolution, the CCP still regards Maoism highly. The Party considers Mao Zedong Thought as an important Chinese contribution to the development of Marxism-Leninism and one of the pillars of its ideological worldview. Years after his death in 1976, Mao's ideology continues to provide a legitimising utility for any Chinese leader who wishes to claim ideological orthodoxy. As such, it forms the foundation of Chinese political ideology from which incumbent leaders have to derive their new policies and 'visions'. The major features of Maoism include:

1   voluntarism, which, built upon the concept of the mass line and egalitarianism, is executed through mass mobilisation and campaigning;
2   anti-intellectualism;
3   contradictions and the united front by which the CCP unites with elements of secondary contradictions to confront the principal;
4   classes and class struggles; and
5   self-reliance (Lieberthal 2004: 60–77).

Maoism is sometimes labelled 'sinicised Marxism'. His emphasis on class struggle produced a radical form of putting the concept of contradiction and dialectical materialism into practice, which proved to cost China a much needed political stability. In the face of a war-torn and economically devastated China, Mao's voluntarism was able to mobilise public enthusiasm for the purpose of reconstruction; however, it was also used for the purpose of destroying enemies. His emphasis on self-reliance had a negative impact on China's international relations, economic development and technological advancement, and his distrust of intellectuals also brought the pursuit of knowledge to a virtual standstill in the country.

Deng Xiaoping Theory

Deng Xiaoping wanted to moderate Mao's emphasis on politics and redirect the country towards economic growth. His vision for China was to 'build socialism with Chinese characteristics'. Building on a Marxist-Leninist ideological foundation, he managed to give his programme some flexibility, and the Chinese characteristics that he emphasised were adaptability and pragmatism. Two of the most famous elements of his Theory are 'seeking truth from facts' and 'practice is the sole criterion for examining truth'. Deng is often considered as a pragmatist, known for his advocacy of economic reforms. However, there is also a political, orthodox dimension of his theory, namely, the Four Basic Principles. These are:

1   adherence to the socialist road;
2   upholding the dictatorship of the proletariat;
3   upholding the Communist Party leadership; and
4   upholding Marxism-Leninism and Mao Zedong Thought.

When Deng Xiaoping was in power, political campaigns, albeit on a much smaller scale than those during Mao's years, were still an important means of political purges and mobilisation. Campaigns under Deng included the Criticise the Gang of Four campaign of 1977, the Anti-Spiritual Pollution campaign of 1983, and the Anti-Bourgeois Liberalisation campaign of 1987. Deng also oversaw the military suppression of the student movement in June 1989. His reform must be seen within the context of these ideological perimeters, for it is within this ideological straitjacket that China's economic modernisation proceeded.

Jiang Zemin's Important Thought of the Three Represents

If Marx and Engels were right in asserting that changes to socioeconomic substructures facilitate changes in the superstructure (including politics and ideology), then more than two decades of economic reform and the increasing weight of the market economy should have created considerable changes in China's political superstructure that solicit responses. Unlike his political predecessors, Jiang was somewhat slow to articulate his political beliefs into theories. He expressed his Three Represents theory only in February 2000 while making an inspection trip to Guangdong. However Jiang's theory did not gain momentum until he pushed it again during his speech commemorating the eightieth anniversary of the CCP in 2001. The Three Represents mean:

1   the CCP must represent 'the requirements of the development of China's advanced productive forces';
2   the CCP must represent 'the orientation of the development of China's advanced culture';
3   the CCP must represent 'the fundamental interests of the overwhelming majority of the people in China'.

The Three Represents theory essentially reiterates the importance of economic construction but points out the additional cultural dimensions of people's living standard. The CCP had to rally support by showing people ideational leadership. Since recent decades had led to a tainted image of the Party as bureaucratic, sluggish, and out of touch with international ideational development, the Party needed to reinvigorate itself.

As Jiang reinterpreted the social representation of the CCP as the workers' vanguard party, he argued that economic reform had caused social changes, with the emergence of new social strata (*jieceng*). Note the use of 'social strata', rather than the more common 'social class' (*jieji*). Jiang credits the members of these new strata, including small businesses (*getihu*) and owners of private enterprises, with contributing to socialist construction through honest labour and law-abiding practices. Consequently, he ideologically reconciles the efforts of entrepreneurs with the virtues of social construction, and the entrepreneurs are thus united with the workers. While Deng Xiaoping tried to develop socialism in China by embracing some capitalist forms of economy, Jiang Zemin was ready to welcome 'capitalist' members to the CCP. To put words into deeds, four business owners (including two CCP members) were awarded the May 1 Labour Medal in 2002 (*South China Morning Post*, 20 April 2002). Contrary to high expectations, however, only five representatives of the private sector attended the Sixteenth Party Congress (November 2002), even though there were more than 2,100 delegates. None of the 350 members of the Central Committee elected during the Congress was from the private entrepreneurship and there was only one among the 158 alternative members (Fewsmith 2003: 14).

In addition to implicitly embracing entrepreneurs, Jiang has strongly urged the Party to renew itself by serving the interests of the people (*wei renmin fuwu*) and steering clear of corruption. Increasing unemployment and the government's limited ability to provide a safety net are challenging the CCP's claim to be a proletarian party, and unless the government can balance the need for continued economic development with the need to protect the interests of the common people, the third point of Jiang's Three Represents will become an empty phrase.

Building a 'socialist harmonious society'

It was at the fourth plenum of the Sixteenth Party Congress in September 2004 that the concept of 'socialist harmonious society' was first advocated. This concept began to gain momentum after study sessions were organised for Politburo members as well as for local government and Party leaders in the spring of 2005 (Xinhua News Agency 2005a; Yang 2005). It was officially introduced in the 'Government Work Report' at the third plenum of the Tenth National People's Congress in March 2005.

Building a 'socialist harmonious society' can be regarded as an addition to Deng's vision of a 'better-off' (*xiaokang*) society and the social relationship dimension of Jiang's Three Represents. The concept of a 'socialist harmonious society' claims to embrace the ideals of democracy and rule by law (*fazhi*); sincerity and fraternity; energy, stability and order; and a harmony between humans and nature (Liu 2005: 428). While promotion of this programme allows Jiang's successor, Hu Jintao, to assert his ideological leadership, it also serves practical purposes. It is expected to strengthen the Party's governing capability by revitalising social creativity, improving social construction and management, and maintaining social stability (Yang 2005). More importantly, it is also a tacit acknowledgement that society is rife with various fault lines and that China is facing the threat of social instability. Forces that threaten to tear China's social fabric include the expanding gap between the rich and the poor (as well as between city and rural developments); land disputes; employment pressure in cities; rampant corruption; bureaucratism; the unsettled psychology of a people adapting to fast socioeconomic changes; the irresponsible use of natural resources; and ethnic problems (Li 2004: 5–10; BBC, 28 September 2005).

According to views expressed in official media, the concept of building a 'socialist harmonious society' has an extensive scope of concern and the Hu leadership is ready to involve virtually all sociopolitical sectors, including law, labour, and the army. It is noteworthy that, unlike the Three Represents which is essentially inward-looking, this concept also has an international application. The speech Hu Jintao made at a meeting to commemorate the sixtieth anniversary of the United Nations was about building a 'harmonious world' on the principles of inclusion, multilateralism, fairness, peace, and co-prosperity, as well as on the cooperation between major powers (Ruan 2005; Ouyang 2005).

Every leader in China has marked his reign with an ideological imprint. Since Mao's revolution, it has been necessary for a Communist Party leader to show that he is pioneering an ideational front and is leading his fellow members. This was particularly important for those without revolution credentials. Jiang who, in policy terms, did not greatly deviate from the path set by Deng, needed to justify and summarise his governance. His ideological leadership was crowned by the introduction of his Important Thought to the revised Party Charter at the Sixteenth Party Congress. Like his predecessors, Hu Jintao also offers China an ideological re-imagining of Marxism-Leninism. Time will be needed to see whether his vision of building a 'socialist harmonious society' is an ideological breakthrough or a façade for high-handed social control and whether this can mandate the CCP's continuing governance.

Ideology loses its political function when it fails to translate words into actions. Its successful implementation relies on sound institutions, particularly political institutions. Government reform, therefore, is a key element in ideological and political evolution.

Government reform

In order to retain full control of the state's overall development, the CCP has, since 1949, largely controlled government agencies and directly managed their everyday functions. However, as a result of the challenges posed to Marxism-Leninism in China by decades of economic reform, the relationship between the CCP and the Chinese government (which translates Communist Party's ideas into national policies) has changed significantly. This change is analysed below.

The Party's control of government

The Marxist-Leninist dictatorship of the proletariat is more commonly known in China as the people's democratic dictatorship (*renmin minzhu zhuanzheng*). The government or the administrative arm is placed under the leadership of the ruling CCP and executes its decisions and policies. Since the establishment of the PRC, the CCP has systematically penetrated the government to assure complete political control at all levels. Kenneth Lieberthal (2004: 233–40) has identified several measures that the CCP has used to control government:

1   *nomenklatura*: a patronage system borrowed from the former Soviet Union for senior cadres that allows the Party to control their career moves;
2   interlocking directorates: this involves key Party officials holding concurrent government appointments. This practice allows Party control through personnel appointments;
3   leadership groups that coordinate between the CCP and government and policy recommendations;
4   Party core groups made up of Party members in the state apparatus to translate Party decisions into government policies; and
5   the promotion of Party platforms through regular meetings and study sessions.

In recent years it has been widely recognised in the CCP that these measures for controlling government have caused rigidity in governance and have contributed to excessive Party control over state affairs. It could be argued that, prior to its economic reforms, the chief purpose of the government was to ensure the success of the proletariat dictatorship in the class struggle that followed the CCP's victory in 1949. By 1981, the CCP no longer believed that class struggle was the principal contradiction in Chinese society and thought instead that the government should focus on developing productivity. This re-evaluation prompted corresponding adjustments in the government's relations with the Communist Party.

Restructuring the relationship between government and the Party

State bureaucracies all over the world face the temptation of expansion. But once their budgets become overblown, they are compelled to streamline their staffing. China is no different in this respect. However, there is one additional factor that featured in China's government reform: the idea of separating the state from the Party. Given the fact that China practises a mono-party system, any separation of the government from the Party is unlikely. The reforms, therefore, can only tackle the issue of the degree of micro-management by the Party apparatus.

As early as 1980, Deng Xiaoping pointed out the urgency of solving the problems of 'the combination of Party and government functions' and that of 'substituting the Party for the government' (*dangzheng bufen, yidang daizheng*). Deng argued that rather than weakening Party leadership, separating the operations of the government and the Party would actually strengthen the Party leadership. Since then, there have been five respective rounds of government structural reform (in 1982, 1988, 1993, 1998 and 2003).

The 1998 reforms saw probably the most dramatic streamlining, but still made no attempt to divorce the Party from the management of the day-to-day state affairs. Fifteen State Council ministries and commissions were removed, four were newly formed, and three were renamed. More than 200 tasks were transferred to business units, social agencies and local administrations. Such massive size reduction was unsurprising because it was built upon the failure of previous reforms – the state apparatus remained locked in the vicious cycle of streamlining–expansion–streamlining (Zhang, Bo and Li 2003: 171).

The latest round of government reforms took place in 2003, and was aimed at reforming government functions. They made little mention of streamlining, but their emphasis on rule by law and functional reform deserves attention. Without compromising Party leadership, Jiang Zemin highlighted that the CCP could actually translate its policy platforms into national will and send its selected personnel to state leadership, through legal procedures. Some intellectuals readily hailed this as a new theory of 'three powers' vis-à-vis the triune of 'legislature, executive, and judiciary' (Fu, Yuan and Rui 2004: 265). However, this elation may be premature because if the tradition of Party penetration of the government is to stay intact and all political and legal institutions continue to serve one ultimate purpose – to facilitate CCP rule – the check on the use of political power would at best be frail and ephemeral. But functional reform looks more optimistic, and the state has been under great pressure to respond to socioeconomic changes.

The state and the economy

A major theme of the 1998 restructuring was 'the separation of government from enterprise' (*zhengqi fenkai*), largely because the reform of the early 1980s to turn industrial ministries into general corporations (*zong gongsi*) had proved to be inadequate. In the 1998 reforms, these general corporations were reorganised into business corporations (*qiye jituan*), which shunned their previous state administrative roles. While consolidating functions into fewer organs, the State Council, in response to the expanding non-public economy, shifted the focus of traditional economic planning agencies to macroeconomic regulation (Zhang, Yang and Feng 1998: 82–4). (These changes are discussed in more detail in Chapter 3, which deals with the issue of privatisation.) The Ministry of State Resources and the Ministry of Information Industry were created to cope with the demands for new economic management and reflect emerging economic developments.

The additional pressure for reform brought by China's accession to the WTO in 2001 cannot be overstated. The functional reforms in 2003 had to go deeper than those of 1998. Zhu Rongji made this clear at the NPC when he claimed that 'under the socialist market economy, government functions are mainly for regulating the economy, monitoring the market, and delivering social management and public services'. China's planned economy was weakened with the reorganisation of the State Planning and Development Commission into the National Development and Reform Commission. Important new organs such as the China Banking Regulatory Commission, the State-Owned Assets Supervision and Administration Commission and the Ministry of Commerce were created to consolidate functions previously scattered among several agencies. These new organs sought to respond to new economic challenges such as the gradual opening of financial markets, the further separation of ownership from management, and an increasing volume of commercial activities (Fu, Yuan and Rui 2004: 264; Fan 2003: 14–15). Previous state interventions, auditing and approval systems, and measures to support economic development were to be changed; and China had to prepare for possible risks as its economic system was to further open up (Ruan 2001: 206; *Liaowang News Weekly*, 3 March 2003: 52). While the state had to withdraw from direct intervention in the economy, it was expected to take a more active role in the creation of an amiable economic environment and provide the delivery of public goods (Zhang, Bo and Li 2003: 107–21).

The state and society

A notable instance of government adaptation to changing socioeconomic demands was the establishment of the Ministry of Labour and Social Security in 1998 to take charge of social insurance responsibilities. At the same time, the State Drug Supervision and Administration Bureau was established to oversee the drug market, drug policies and administration (Zhang, Yang and Feng 1998: 83). The 2003 reforms contributed towards increasing public safety by expanding the latter bureau to include also food safety and by upgrading the Production Safety Bureau. These 1998 and 2003 reforms show that the government has become more conscious of its responsibilities for social management and welfare. However, a series of food safety scandals and coal mine explosions in 2005 betrayed the fact that diligent implementation is far more important than the mere existence of institutions.

Reflecting on the fifty years of PRC experience, John Burns commented that China had virtually no autonomous trade unions or other civil society organisations (Burns 1999: 580). Even though it was formed by workers, the CCP has been wary of any independent trade union organisations. The All-China Federation of Trade Unions (ACFTU) is practically the only legitimate workers' organisation in China. Based on the Leninist organisation principle, it has a dual role: on the one hand, it conveys the objectives and directives of the Party and state to the workers and, on the other, it mobilises the workers to meet state economic objectives (Feng 2001: 70–1). But this artificial balance puts the ACFTU in a dilemma: it cannot actually represent and promote the interest of its constituents (i.e. the workers) because ultimately it owes its allegiance to the Party. This is also the problem facing other supposedly civic organisations and interest groups.

However, economic reforms and the information revolution, as will be discussed below, may eventually provide new opportunities for independent civic groups to function in new ways. The continuous streamlining of the government and the PLA and the reforms to SOEs have created a sizeable redundant labour force while the poor income derived from agricultural production continues to produce an increasing population of peasant labour. In the face of increasing unemployment and concomitant social stability problems, the government itself is in great financial difficulty, preventing it from taking up the responsibility for job placement and social security on its own. A way out is to encourage social initiatives and to tap the financial resources of society. Thus recent years have already seen a growing number of social welfare agencies and organisations. It remains to be seen how these social groups may evolve.

With Jiang Zemin's 'Three Represents' codified in the Party and state documents, the Hu Jintao leadership is now seeking to create a vision of building a harmonious socialist society and preserve the CCP's ruling mandate or legitimacy. There are real problems that urgently need solutions. Although government reforms have gradually shifted focus from the size and number of institutions to their functions, the ruling Party is still reluctant to reform the power relationship that underpins all these institutions. In summary, the CCP has permitted changes to the extent of Party control, rather than allowing genuine alternatives to this control to develop.

Leadership succession

The government reforms mentioned in the previous section will help little in improving CCP governance if the Party fails to deliver a stable leadership. Ever since the formation of the CCP in 1921, changes of leadership have been characterised by power struggles, condemnations and purges of losing factions. Mao's rule was characterised by violent succession intrigues, and Deng Xiaoping's accession to power in the late 1970s and the fall of Zhao Ziyang in 1989 had the PLA in the background. It was not until Deng Xiaoping's reign that the CCP began serious efforts to implement a smooth leadership succession. Since 1989, this process has so far operated successfully and both Jiang and Hu have succeeded to the leadership without major social or political upheavals. In this section of the chapter, I discuss and evaluate this critical issue of leadership succession.

The transfer of power

The fact that the same party has been in power for more than 50 years may create a false sense of political stability and continuity in China. The official CCP history's segmentation of the Party leadership into three generations also presents an over-simplified picture. As the CCP grew from an underground political organisation in the 1920s to the ruling party of China, it went through incessant power struggles, which sometimes took the form of political purges and involved the use of violence. This is not surprising. In a regime that lacks institutionalised arrangements for alternate government and a clear definition of legitimacy, politicians have to engage in constant power struggles not only for political dominance but also for their own self-preservation. Furthermore, the army, being the most coherent organisation in a state where no institutionalised succession arrangements exist, usually serves a coercive function and exercises uncontested political influence.

Leadership succession in CCP history

Table 2.1 summarises the history of CCP leadership succession and shows that most of the CCP leaders have been disgraced in the process of succession. Some were thrown out of the CCP, including its founder, Chen Duxiu. Lin Biao lost his life in an allegedly failed military coup to usurp power. Those who fared better were relegated to minor or ceremonial positions after the purge, such as Li Lisan and Wang Ming. Even Mao Zedong, the leader longest in power, experienced severe political setbacks before he won a decisive victory over his opponents at the Zunyi Conference of 1935. Zhou Enlai is a notable exception but he had never been a serious contender for the topmost position nor had he been designated as 'heir apparent'. Hua Guofeng was, with the benefit of hindsight, doomed to be a transitional leader. Without a solid power base and claiming legitimacy simply on a directive by the late Mao Zedong, Hua could not pose any serious challenges. Deng Xiaoping is certainly the most dramatic figure. He had been on the top right

Table 2.1 Major CCP leaders in succession

Party member	Roles and fates
Chen Duxiu	GS 1921–7 Expelled from CCP, 1929
Qu Qiubai	1927–8 Discredited for 'leftist putschism'
Xiang Zhongfa	Chair, PB and CC 1928 Executed by the KMT 1931
Li Lisan	PB 1928 Discredited for 'left adventurism'; dismissed from all posts, 1930
Wang Ming	PB, 1931 Discredited for 'rightist capitulationism', 1938 and 1945
Mao Zedong	Chair, PB, CC and Sec, 1945 Died in 1976
Zhang Guotao	VC, provisional central govt, Chinese Soviet Republic, 1931 Split with Mao in 1935; defected to the KMT in 1938
Zhou Enlai	Premier, 1949; PBSC and VC, CCP CC, 1956 Died in 1976
Liu Shaoqi	Chair, NPCSC, 1954; PBSC and VC, CCP CC, 1956; state chair and chair, national defence committee, 1959 Discredited as the greatest 'capitalist roader' in the Party. Died 1969
Lin Biao	Marshall, 1955; PB, 1956; VC, CCP CC, 1958; Minister of Defence, 1959; PBSC and VC, CCP CC, 1969; Mao's 'close comrade-in-arms' Killed in failed military coup, 1971
Hua Guofeng	1st state VC and premier, April 1976; chair, CCP CC, and CCP CMC, Oct 1976 Discredited for his 'Two whatevers' (liangge fanshi); resigned from premiership, 1980; resigned from CCP CC and CMC chair, 1981
Deng Xiaoping	GS, CCP CC 1954; GS, CCP CC, and PBSC 1956; dismissed of all posts, 1966; Vice Premier and PB 1973; VC, CCP CC, and PBSC, 1975; dismissed of all posts, 1976; reinstated, 1977; Chair, CCP CMC, 1981; chair, Central Advisory Committee, 1982; resigned from CMC, 1989 Died in 1997
Hu Yaobang	PB, 1978; PBSC and GS, CCP CC, 1980 Discredited for 'contravening the principle of collective leadership and committing mistakes over important political principles'; relieved of GS duty, 1987. Died 1989

Party member	Roles and fates
Zhao Ziyang	PB, 1979; Premier and PBSC, 1980; GS, CCP CC, and 1st VC, CCP CMC, 1987 Discredited for mishandling the mass movement in 1989; dismissed from all posts, 1989. Died 2005
Jiang Zemin	PB, 1987; GS, CCP CC, and PBSC, and Chair, CMC, 1989; state president, 1993 Retired from his positions of GS, CCP CC in 2002, state president in 2003, Chair, CMC in 2004
Hu Jintao	1st secretary, CYL secretariat, 1984; PBSC, 1992; CCP Secretariat, and Pres, Central Party School, 1993; state VP, 1998; VC, CMC, 1999; GS, CCP CC, 2002; state president, 2003; Chair, CMC, 2004

Abbreviations:

CC	CCP Central Committee	PB	Politburo
CMC	Central Military Commission	SC	Standing Committee
CYL	Communist Youth League	VC	Vice-Chairman
GS	General Secretary	VP	Vice-President
KMT	Kuomintang		

Note: The post of CCP CC chairman was abolished at the Twelfth Party Congress, 1982

after the establishment of the PRC. Still, he was twice stripped of power, in 1966 and again 1975. Deng was reinstated in 1977 and eventually rose to the zenith of power. Jiang Zemin's accession to the post of General Secretary is anomalous in the sense that he himself had not 'defeated' fellow contenders. He was simply chosen to take that position. Hu Jintao had consistently been moving up since the 1990s and at the Sixteenth CCP Congress emerged as the new leader.

The role of the army in CCP leadership succession

CCP leadership succession in the pre-PRC period was abrupt and violent but political violence peaked during Mao Zedong's rule. Liu Shaoqi, together with his policy supporters, especially Deng Xiaoping, became political targets in the Cultural Revolution. Eventually, Liu fell ill and died. Then, amid the fervour of that mass movement, Mao named Marshall Lin Biao as his 'heir apparent' and called him his 'close comrade-in-arms' (*qinmi zhanyou*). This relationship was not accidental because the PLA was then the only state instrument that could provide order and remained cohesive. Soon after, Lin Biao allegedly attempted a coup, failed, and paid the price of his own life. Shortly after Mao passed away in 1976, the moderates led by Marshall Ye Jianying and with the support of the army were able to force the Gang of Four out of power. This seemed to vindicate Mao's dictum, 'political power grows out of the gun barrel'. The reign of the succeeding Hua

Guofeng, without any power base, was short-lived. After brief political recuperation, Deng Xiaoping returned triumphantly in 1977 and soon became the Chairman of the Central Military Commission (CMC). The CMC is China's highest military command authority. Although there are a state CMC and a Party CMC under the CCP Central Committee, their membership overlap and both are essentially the same body. Since the founding of the PRC, the CMC chairmen have been Mao Zedong, Hua Guofeng, Deng Xiaoping, and Jiang Zemin. Currently, the Chairman is Hu Jintao.

Deng Xiaoping did not follow Mao's high-profile practice of naming successors. Instead, he carefully groomed the 'third echelon' (*disan tidui*) leadership. This third generation of Chinese leaders was meant to succeed the two previous generations (Mao Zedong being the first generation, and Deng Xiaoping the second). As Deng receded from direct leaderhip roles, he played the role of the patriarch and provided behind-the-stage support for his groomed leaders. Deng also applied Mao's dictum on the political use of the military: 'Our principle is the Party commands the gun but the gun should never be allowed to command the Party' (Mao 1993 [1938]: 421).

By revising the Military Ranking Regulations in 1988, Deng made it possible for a civilian to lead the Central Military Commission and secured a way for his successors, who had virtually no military credentials at all, to take command of this important post. Zhao Ziyang, who had won Deng's patronage for his staunch support for economic reform, was given first vice-chairmanship of the CMC but was discredited in 1989 because of his refusal to take a tough stance against the mass protest movement that summer. Again, the army moved to the centre of the political stage as it marched into Tiananmen Square. Jiang Zemin, who had been known little in Beijing, was called from Shanghai to take up the post of Party General Secretary in 1989 and not coincidentally was later to take up the leadership of the CMC.

Many China watchers speculated on whether the Jiang leadership would survive the post-Deng political struggles. Knowing the weakness of Jiang's political credentials, Deng continued to play the patriarch. Jiang was made the 'core of the third generation of leaders' with an emphasis on collective leadership. He was flanked in the Party, state and military by Deng's supporters. Most importantly, Deng persuaded other veterans to retire with him from active politics.

Under Deng's patronage, Jiang Zemin gradually consolidated his power base. He began to install his men in important positions in the Party, state and army. To ensure 'control of the gun', Jiang promoted more generals than any other Chinese leader. Taking advantage of revised military legislations, Jiang also strictly enforced the retirement age requirements for military officers and made frequent personnel reshuffles of Military Regional commanders.

Jiang's succession strategies

Even before he was elected General Secretary of the CCP Central Committee in November 2002, Hu Jintao had been widely expected to become the next leader.

Jiang Zemin followed Deng Xiaoping's practice of grooming protégés and first promoted Hu to prominence by securing him a position at the Politburo Standing Committee and the CCP Secretariat in 1992 and 1993 respectively. The next move was expanding Hu's power base to the state (as state Vice-President in 1998) and then to the army (as Vice-Chairman of the Central Military Commission in 2003). In addition to Jiang's patronage, other supporters were likely responsible for Hu's rise to power, as Hu was appointed to important positions when Deng Xiaoping was still alive. It has also been argued that Hu owed his ascension to power to a faction led by Chen Yun, a party veteran of Deng's stature (You 2002: 127).

Jiang Zemin did not have the stature of Deng Xiaoping when he assumed the leadership, so while he was leader he diligently built up an image of himself as a leader of epic reforms during epic times and this image has managed to put him on a par with Deng in CCP history. (This is particularly evident on the ideological front, an area already discussed.) However, Jiang had little policy legacy to pass on to his successor as Deng Xiaoping had done and he has retained his influence in politics by installing his stewards in senior positions.

Hu's leadership

Hu Jintao seems to have weathered the leadership succession well. Indeed, his succession was the first that witnessed no political disgrace of a predecessor. In 2004, he got his licence for real leadership by attaining CMC chairmanship. Although various study sessions, organised by the CCP, government, and the army continue to deliberate Jiang's Three Represents, Hu Jintao is making his ideological mark through his 'comments on historical missions' and giving 'important directives' to the army, no doubt to emphasise the change of leadership (*Jiefangjun Bao*, 28 September 2005). However, in reality, the PLA has lately become more focused on its own professional interests than on king-making.

Hu Jintao has so far had a good start to his leadership. In an article published in the June 2003 issue of *Banyuetan* (Fortnightly talk), a Xinhua News Agency semi-monthly, Hu's leadership was praised for its resolute, wise and efficient decision-making and its ability to meet a series of 'tests', most notably the SARS epidemic. Obviously, Hu Jintao has scored points and effectively proven the efficacy of his leadership. Some had anticipated a more liberal regime before Hu got the top job. However, in the few years he has been in power, he has shown no signs of being a Chinese Gorbachev, or of relaxing political control.

Looking back, perhaps Jiang Zemin's most important contributions to Chinese political succession were his institutionalisation of the retirement system and the continuous professionalisation of the PLA. While these measures were a move in a positive direction, they did not completely institutionalise succession and fall short of solving the legitimacy problem. At best, they are good precedents that will take time to evolve into norms and institutions. Since the succession issue continues to be at the mercy of strong and contentious leaders, the question of leadership succession still has the potential to affect China's political stability.

Grassroots-level elections: an experiment with pluralism

Marxist-Leninist regimes are distinguished from Western liberal democracies by their mistrust of pluralism. In the place of pluralism, Marxist-Leninist regimes have created democratic centralism. The democracy element allows public policy deliberations and elections while centralism requires absolute obedience to resolutions and decisions made by the highest authority. Referring to this principle of democratic centralism, Chinese political leaders claim that their country has never lacked democracy and that there are channels for political participation.

However, while there is no viable alternative political organisation to the CCP in China, diverse and pluralist interests have emerged as a result of socioeconomic changes. The villages, where the economic reform programme first began, are not surprisingly also the place to see the beginning of the political experiment of pluralism, which is the subject of this section.

Political participation in China

Political participation in China has for a long time focused on political mobilisation, mainly in the form of mass campaigns organised along Mao Zedong's mass line (*qunzhong luxian*). The policy of political campaigning came to a climax during the Cultural Revolution but gradually lost its favour among leaders during the 1980s because it proved to be damaging to economic development. Other major forms of political participation include membership in quasi-official organisations, such as the ACFTU, and 'democratic parties' which, however, neither compete with the CCP for political power nor field any truly independent candidates in elections (Liu and Zhang 1995: 345).

The CCP obviously provides an important channel of political participation. CCP membership remains a credential for successful careers in most of China's institutions although the expanding market economy is diluting its value. To maintain its ruling efficacy, the CCP needs to recruit the best people. Thus, Jiang's Three Represents theory serves to legitimise the admission of business owners and entrepreneurs to reflect changes in China's socioeconomic composition. A study by Mōri Kazuko (2003: 12) shows that the proportion of labourers and peasants in the CCP membership has been consistently dwindling (from 80.4 per cent in 1956 to 56.6 per cent in 1987 and 49.1 per cent in 2001) while that of intellectuals, and management, administrative and technical personnel, has been growing steadily (from 14.8 per cent in 1956 to 27.7 per cent in 1987 and 30.8 per cent in 2001).

As for the National People's Congress (NPC), China's legislative body, direct elections are restricted to the township and county levels and candidacy depends on 'consultation with' the CCP. In addition, the CCP can easily reduce the number of candidates when numbers far exceed that of deputy seats. It is these electoral arrangements that make the direct elections of the villager committees so significant in Chinese politics.

Villager committees: the origin of grassroots democracy

In 1980, a village in Yizhou city of Guangxi province took the initiative to elect China's first villager committee to help organise production and social welfare. Other villages in the same province followed suit. This practice was endorsed and given legal status by the state when the national constitution was revised in 1982. All this came about because the Party was desperate to find an alternative to the people's commune for administrative purposes after the introduction of rural economic reforms. As the dismantling of the people's commune accelerated in 1983 and was completed in 1984, rural township government was put in its place to represent the state and execute its policies. At the same time, villager committees replaced production brigades (*shengchan dadui*). By 1985, nearly 950,000 such committees were established (Fan 2001).

In 1987, when the NPC promulgated the Organic Law on the Villager Committee (Provisional), it brought the villager committee experiment to a new stage by specifying the organisation and functions of the committee. In 1990 it was decided that each county should select several villages to promote and demonstrate village self-administration. By the time the provisional legislation on villager committees was revised and finalised in 1998, about a quarter of Chinese counties participated in this political experiment. Most villages conducted two or three rounds of elections and 60 per cent of them formed their own villagers' representative assemblies (Zhan 2001).

As the 1998 law clarified and improved the processes of elections, decision-making and administrative arrangements, the villager committee decisively left the experimental stage and was institutionalised. According to Ministry of Civil Affairs statistics, there were more than 730,000 villager committees nationwide with over 3.1 million committee members by the end of 2000 (Ministry of Civil Affairs 2001).

The villager committee and its election process

The villager committee is not part of the government structure. It has no political power and is officially under the purview of the civil affairs department. It is responsible mainly for social welfare, arbitration, public security, birth control, public hygiene, and collecting taxes and levies on behalf of the government (Jin 2000: 61). A villager committee is usually composed of a director, deputy director(s) and committee members, totalling three to seven people, and is accountable to a villager assembly. Below it are several subordinate working committees (Ministry of Civil Affairs 2002).

The application of democratic principles to village elections, as they are practised, is specified in the Organic Law on the Villager Committee of 1998. A villager committee election is valid if over half of the electorate cast their votes. The outcome is decided by simple majority. The villager committee has a term of three years. Villager committee members can be re-elected and may serve another term once their first three-year term has expired. (For more information about the election mechanisms, the following websites are particularly useful:

www.chinarural.org and www.chinaelections.org.) The specific forms of villager committee elections can vary across localities.

The election process begins with the nomination of candidates. According to the law, this nomination process should be free of Party or government interference. This stage produces an initial list of candidates that is finalised at primaries or by other means, such as consultation. The final number of candidates must exceed that of the offices available. While multi-candidacy assures competitiveness, many villages go further to organise vote canvassing activities. These campaigning exercises have raised villagers' interest in and knowledge of the election and their candidates. Moreover, these exercises help individual candidates overcome the incumbents' advantages of recognition.

Well over two decades have elapsed since the beginning of the experiment in villager committee elections. The committees have generally held several elections and successfully returned with 'alternate committees', but there remain a lot of problems, both internal and external, with the villager self-rule system. This is not surprising when we consider the discrepancy between the villager committee system and China's overall governance. The relationship between the Party branch and the villager committee constitutes one of the most complicated issues in villager self-administration (Fo 2001: 21; Lang and Lang 2005: 29). Furthermore, the CCP can undermine committees when there is a clash between Party policy and decisions made by villager committees. Problems associated with the proper functioning of villager committees have been partly due to interference from local CCP branches.

Challenges to grassroots democracy in China

According to the CCP charter, a Party branch should be established in every village where there are three or more Party members, and the Party branch is expected to 'lead' the villager committee. Such 'leadership' can easily become naked interference. Indeed, the implementation of villager committee decisions, especially about taxation, can be greatly frustrated by Party directives. Another serious impediment to villager self-administration is the 'management' of village finances by the township government. 'Supervision' over village financial arrangements by government bodies has often degenerated into direct control. Without financial autonomy, the functioning of the villager committee is obviously greatly impaired (Jin 2000: 62).

CCP and government interference is not the only challenge to the grassroots democracy of villager elections. The weak legal institution and poor legal knowledge among the villagers have hindered the development of grassroots democracy. Kinship politics, bribery and corruption also muddy the legitimacy of village elections. China's democratic political culture has yet to mature and indifference to election procedures suggests villagers' insufficient understanding of and poor sensitivity to their own political rights and the importance of proper procedures (Wei 2004: 91; Yuan 2004: 20; Pan 2005: 35; Yang 2005: 65–6).

However, the inadequacies of the system do not negate the value of the institution of grassroots committees. Moreover, there are signs that villager self-administration is gradually improving. The rigging of elections by local clans, for example, has diminished significantly and is now regarded as an 'isolated' problem (Liu 2001: 73). Clearly, democracy involves learning, and learning takes time.

Significance of grassroots democracy

The pluralist elections in rural China are politically significant because they represent an alternative model for the transfer and exercise of political power. They operate on the principles of political equality, accountability, recall, and competitive and pluralist elections. They also follow procedures of secret balloting and open vote counting. The successful execution of grassroots village elections may also create pressure for wider political reforms that quietly change Chinese political culture. In the summer of 2005, the villagers of Taishi in Guangdong province staged a tenacious struggle to recall an unpopular village committee director. What made this incident remarkable was the villagers' insistence on exercising their constitutional rights. This event also represents increasing political consciousness among the peasants (BBC, 1 September 2005). The government's response to protests in Taishi – centred on silencing the protesters through intimidation and the arrest of 'troublemakers', rather than investigating their demands – underscores the limitations of rural democracy in China.

The information revolution and political control

Although economic reform prompted villagers to create their own committees and prompted the government to adapt itself to the increasing marketisation of the economy, the government has been wary of developments on the ideological front. While Jiang Zemin responded to ideological challenges by proposing his Three Represents theory, neither he nor Hu has directly addressed the challenges posed by the information revolution. As more Chinese consumers gain access to electronic media, the dissemination of information by electronic media is set to challenge the state's monopoly over information and threaten state power by influencing public opinion. In this final section of the chapter, I consider the possible political threats that are raised by the information revolution, and the CCP's actual and likely future responses to these threats. Before considering how threats from the information revolution may emerge, it is useful to look at how the CCP uses surveillance and information networks to exert and maintain political power.

Social surveillance and ideological control

To achieve political stability, the state attempts to prevent overt conflicts and, if conflicts do occur, it tries to solve or suppress them as soon as possible. Thus, China has built up an elaborate law enforcement establishment along with its surveillance system which consists of several organisational components: the *danwei* (occupational unit) system, the *hukou* (household registration) system and the personal file or dossiers (*dang'an*) system. Together they control personal careers and movements (Burns 1994: 5, 32–4).

The control of information is another means that the state uses to mould a person's behaviour, facilitate compliance or create political consensus (albeit superficial). It has the advantage of avoiding the need for open social coercion or it precludes or at least reduces the visibility of conflicts. In China, the political campaigns of the Mao era have been gradually replaced by propaganda campaigns in which the Party controls information input and dissemination with the purpose of galvanising popular support for its policies.

An important player in this process is the CCP Central Committee's Propaganda Department which is responsible for unifying the interpretation of Party and government policies as well as handling reports of major affairs. This department also supervises the mass print and electronic media. Since the Party believes in *no* politically neutral reporting, it holds that the press should serve the interests and ideas of the ruling Party and adhere to its responsibility to provide 'correct directions for public opinion'. The General Administration of Press and Publication implements Party directives on press activity and maintains control of the press through its licensing system. As for the electronic media, the government, through its State Administration of Radio, Film and Television, has constantly monitored the content of the media and does not hesitate to interfere in programme reception if something is judged threatening. Perhaps the most difficult of all electronic media to control is the radio, which is cheap and popular among Chinese people, and the BBC and Voice of America are able to broadcast to Chinese audiences using short-wave frequencies. Although the Chinese government has so far generally managed to maintain control over the opinions expressed in the print and electronic media, the increasing growth and popularity of computers and internet access in recent years has created a new front for China's campaign against dissenting opinions.

The growth of information flow

Despite numerous measures aimed at controlling computer mediated information, the need for timely information, the global trend of developing a knowledge-based economy, and the increasing affordability of computers and internet access have inadvertently opened the floodgates to a flow of information into China. Importantly, an increasing amount of computer hardware and software is now being manufactured in China.

In recent years, there has been a significant increase in the number of magazine and newspaper titles published in China. Between 1990 and 2003, the numbers jumped from 5,751 to 9,074 and from 1,444 to 2,119 respectively (NBS 2000 and 2004). However, these increases in print information pale in comparison with the breathtaking growth of the telecommunications sector. According to figures released by the Ministry of Information Industry, China had laid 3.38 million kilometres of fibre-optic cable telecommunications lines by 2004. The growth of telephone density and the dramatic increase in the number of mobile phone users and internet service subscribers are represented the tables below.

Table 2.2 clearly shows the trends in the telecommunications boom. Most importantly, the internet has emerged as the fastest growing means of communication since the government began to allow commercial internet accounts in 1995. Table 2.3 gives the details of growth in internet usage.

The rapid growth in internet use in China is obvious. However, as we look at Tables 2.2 and 2.3, we should not just focus our attention on the growth in user numbers. We should also be mindful of the expanding functions of these forms of

Table 2.2 The growth of selected communications services

Year	Number of fixed-line telephones per 100 people	Mobile phone subscribers
1990	1.11	18 300
1995	4.00	3 629 400
2000	20.10	84 533 000
2001	25.90	144 800 000
2002	17.50	207 000 000
2003	21.20	268 693 000
2004	24.90	334 824 000
2005 (June)	26.00	372 776 000

Source: Except for data before 2001, which is from NBS 2001: 539, other figures are based on statistical reports of various years on communication industry operations supplied online in the Ministry of Information Industry homepage: www.mii.gov.cn/mii/hyzw/tjxx.html.

Notes
1 According to the source, the number of internet service subscribers includes dial-up subscribers and ISDN subscribers.
2 The 2002 figure is based on statistics released in 2003 but the Ministry of Information Industry has changed its statistical calibre since 2003 from 'completion target' (zhibiao) to 'actual cases of completion' (wancheng yewu).

Table 2.3 The growth of internet usage in China

Year	Number of computers connected to the internet	Number of internet service subscribers
1997	299 000	620 000
1998	747 000	2 100 000
1999	3 500 000	8 900 000
2000	8 920 000	22 500 000
2001	12 540 000	33 700 000
2002	20 830 000	59 100 000
2003	30 890 000	79 500 000
2004	41 600 000	94 000 000

Source: Compiled from CINIC reports (October 1997, January 1999, January 2000, January 2001, January 2002, January 2003, January 2004, January 2005, July 2005); www.cnnic.net.cn.

Notes:
1 This survey was first conducted in 1997.
2 All cut-off dates of the statistical data are 31 December, except for 1997, where the cut-off date is 31 October.

communications. For example, a mobile phone can now transmit text messages and images as well as voice messages and what was once a means of communicating spoken information can now also document and broadcast news, events and opinions. Moreover, the introduction and increasing popularity of broadband technology has facilitated faster download times and allows for the online transmission of information via text, sound and images.

The state's responses to the information revolution

In 1989, shortly after the Tiananmen incident on 4 June, people overseas tried to break through China's information blockades by faxing foreign press reports to China. Some activists in the US had even reportedly distributed lists of fax numbers of organisations in China to Chinese students abroad. In response, the Chinese government began to tighten the control over the use of fax machines. Today, the internet is a much more powerful information tool than the fax machine, and internet users can interactively search for and obtain information on just about any subject.

Publications and information that are banned by the government may find their way on to the internet. The outlawed Falungong group once managed to use the internet to tell its story to the Chinese people. Moreover, online chat rooms are popular forums for expressing critical opinions (not necessarily against the government). While information deviating from the official view may cause confusion and dissension among the people, the internet may also serve as a platform for organising people. The latter is certainly no less threatening than the former to the government. Consequently, the government is taking significant measures to control and manage the flow of cyber-information.

Administrative and legal measures

Beijing is well aware that information is an instrument of power. In order to minimise its damaging effects, it has adopted a series of administrative and legal measures. A search of the legislation database in October 2005 on the *Legal Daily* (*Fazhi ribao*) online showed that the central government had issued over 280 rules and regulations on communications and almost 150 on internet control. The Chinese government has untiringly expanded and updated its legal regulatory regime of internet access, services, and content control. Major measures include elaborate registration and approval systems applied to entities from Internet Service Providers (ISPs) to internet cafés and practically charging ISPs with responsibilities for monitoring their users. A series of fires involving internet cafés in 2002 gave the government licence to close down a large number of internet cafés and to reinforce greater information control (Bezlova 2005). A set of rules on internet news information promulgated in 2005 further tightened government control on internet content provision by raising the financial capital threshold for running such information services, denying foreign ownership and expanding the scope of the provider's responsibility for monitoring electronic bulletin boards and chat rooms (Xinhua News Agency 2005b).

Concomitant with the promulgation of stricter regulations is a strengthening of law enforcement. China's first internet police unit was organised in the late 1990s. As of early 2001, over 20 provinces or equivalent level administrations had formed their own internet police units, with a total force of almost 1,000. Shortly after their establishment, they reportedly cracked cases of computer crimes (Xinhua News Agency 2001a). This was reinforced by the addition of 'undercover agents' in 2005 who now monitor internet bulletin boards and chat rooms and defend the government against attacks (*Nanfang Weekend Newspaper*, 19 May 2005).

However, the challenge that the information revolution poses to governance lies not only in its exposure of people to alternative ideas and perspectives. The government faces the prospect of either considering information technology a threat, or of viewing it as a modern method of political control. The Chinese government seems to be opting for the latter and has been taking active measures to make use of the internet. The Government Online project, with its portal at www.gov.cn, was launched in 1999 and was operational on the Chinese National Day of 2005. This site indicates Beijing's determination to harness information technology, instead of attempting to defeat it.

Although Chinese government agencies are only just beginning to utilise the electronic platform for administrative purposes, they recognise that utilising the internet has distinct policy advantages. It helps to promote China's international image by promoting official policy transparency; and it provides a convenient channel to propagate official views and ideology.

Many of China's official newspapers and periodicals have also gone online, ranging from such heavyweights as the *People's Daily* (*Renmin ribao*) (www.people.com.cn) to local and specialised titles such as *Shaanxi Daily* (*Shaanxi ribao*) (www.sxdaily.com.cn) and *Zhongguo Minbing* (*China Militia*) (www.chinamil.com.cn/site1/zgmb/zgmb.htm). Important political speeches and commentaries, statistical data, and policy White Papers are accessible online as well.

The Chinese government has in recent years shown a greater awareness of the importance of public discourse, especially at the international level. It is managing to participate in discourse battles (though still largely in a polemical manner), and it is trying to use the internet (as one of many means) to defend its political stance amid criticism, and even mount publicity counter-offensives. Thus, appearing on official government homepages are White Papers on human rights, military policy, Taiwan policy, and poverty relief projects. (These can be found on the *People's Daily* homepage, and on the Xinhua News Agency homepage: www.xinhua.org.) Indeed, China is going beyond passive defence of its policies to launch counter-attacks on its major trade and ideological adversaries.

Technological control

In addition to these administrative and legal measures, China operates extensive and sophisticated internet filtering through technological means. Utilising western technologies, it is able to block access to certain politically sensitive internet sites, especially those preaching anti-communist ideologies as well as those maintained by human rights groups, outlawed organisations (most notably, the Falungong), and foreign news networks, including the Voice of America and BBC (OpenNet Initiative 2005). Another method is traffic analysis, which allows the authorities to screen email traffic and track down the senders of sensitive messages. Although the effectiveness of traffic analysis technology is doubtful, it at least serves as some deterrence. Since information security is regarded not simply as a matter of censorship and ideological work but as an integral part of national security, China is likely to increase its investments in related projects and step up its efforts for dominating cyberspace (Shen 2004). The Chinese government has also successfully co-opted multinational internet service providers to exercise self-censorship (so that, for example, certain 'offensive' terms cannot be searched through popular search engines). Furthermore, some of these providers have now actively joined the state's surveillance programme. In late 2005, a Chinese journalist was sentenced to ten years in jail for leaking 'state secrets' after Yahoo revealed his identity to the Chinese authorities (Marquand 2005).

To what extent does the information revolution challenge the state?

While the impact of the information revolution on Chinese governance is evident, it should not be overestimated. We should keep in mind several factors when we try to understand and analyse the phenomenon of the information revolution.

First, the influence of foreign information is limited by the average education and foreign language proficiency of most Chinese people. According to a 2002 survey by the China Internet Network Information Centre (CINIC), Chinese internet surfers get almost 80 per cent of their information in *Chinese* and, in fact, more than 70 per cent of their information comes from mainland Chinese internet sites. While we cannot discount that the content of individual sites is a factor, language ability may also contribute to their limited exposure to foreign media, particularly English sites.

Another aspect that deserves our attention is the possible correlation between information accessibility and wealth. The coastal east leads the west by a wide margin in its number of internet users, its growth rate of mobile phone users, and in its fixed-asset investments in communication infrastructures (CINIC 2003).

The third factor limiting the impact of the internet relates to broad psychological and sociological values in China. It is doubtful how much internet surfing can change value systems that have been built over a lifelong socialisation process. Users may just visit those sites that reinforce rather than challenge their views. Moreover, according to a July 2005 CINIC survey, a significant 45.6 per cent of internet users said they went online to download music, suggesting that leisure and entertainment are a major motivation for internet usage in China. However, the same survey showed that more than half of the internet users were aged below 24 and that students accounted for the biggest occupational group (33.2 percent). This finding is notable. Although these young people do not yet have the high earning and spending power of most other internet users, they are perhaps the most likely to be open to new ideological and psychological views of the world.

Given the Chinese state's intent to monopolise power by creating an ideologically homogeneous society, the information revolution is set to create political problems. The first 'casualty' is the official propaganda machine, which may become less effective in shaping public opinion. But, more importantly, once varying opinions are formed, people can get organised. Alternative organisations beyond official control are certainly a nightmare for a one-party system. In addition, information security has become an important component of national security, and the military may take a more active role in information control. Information technology developments will show a trend towards civil–military integration.

Ultimately however, the government has to accept the political risks associated with the internet because it has to take advantage of the information revolution to sustain its economic growth and support its credentials for rule. The development of information services has also become a key factor in attracting foreign investment. Thus, the Chinese government itself directly benefits from the information revolution. Moreover, so far at least, the state has been successful controlling the flow of information in China. Despite the proliferation of information, the state controls national network infrastructures and produces a substantial percentage of the content online. The internet is also being used to promote state ideas and raise public awareness of social and political experiments.

Conclusion

Over the past fifty years, the CCP has weathered various challenges. However, if it is to retain its monopoly on power, it has to adapt to the new political demands unleashed by decades of economic reforms. The information revolution and the need for new ways to organise economic activities in villages have precipitated changes in the power relationship between the state and the people. More transparency, accountability and 'democracy' (even in the sense of democratic centralism) are necessary. The government bureaucracy must find ways to get out of the vicious cycle of expansion, streamlining, and expansion by restraining state power through institutional means, not simply on a policy basis. This need for institutionalisation applies also to leadership succession. Personality politics has cost China much political stability in the past. The 'refined' Marxist-Leninist ideology of China's leaders is no longer sufficient to legitimise the Communist regime. It is now up to Hu Jintao to show the Chinese people a new vision.

Despite all these changes, we must also remember the continuity of Chinese politics. Deng Xiaoping's pragmatism and Jiang Zemin's continuous emphasis on economic reform do not diminish the prominence of politics in Chinese governance. It must be remembered that mindful of the international consequences and possible setbacks to economic reform and opening, Chinese leaders did not hesitate to forcefully suppress popular opposition in Beijing. Deng himself said (at his reception of the martial law enforcement army units) that the armed suppression was the right decision because the people aimed at 'overthrowing Communist leadership'. Improving public relations may simply go along with the development of enhanced surveillance and coercive means. Holding on to state power has been and continues to be the main objective of the CCP.

References

Banyuetan (2003) 'China's New Government Rushing to the "Tests"', (in Chinese), 26 June, news.xinhuanet.com.

Bezlova, A. (2005) 'Fire Tragedy the Price of Beijing's Net Crackdown', *Asia Times*, 20 June.

Burns, J. P. (1994) '*Renshi dang'an*: China's cadre dossier system', *Chinese Law and Government* 27/2: 5–104.

—— (1999) 'The People's Republic of China at 50: National Political Reform', *China Quarterly* 159: 580–94.

CINIC (China Internet Network Information Center) (various years) *Zhongguo hulian wangluo fazhan zhuangkuang tongji baogao* (China's Internet Network Development Statistical Report) www.cnnic.net.cn.

Fan, X. C. (2003) 'Comparing Several Major Government Reforms Since the Founding of the Country', *Beijing xinzheng xueyuan xuebao* (Journal of Beijing College of Public Administration) 6: 11–16.

Fan, Y. (2001) 'The Evolution and Characteristics of the Villager Committee Election System' (in Chinese), *Zhongguo nongcun guance* (China Villages Observation) 1: 54–63.

Feng, T. Q. (2001) 'The Changing Labour Relations and Basic Characteristics of the Chinese Trade Union' (in Chinese), *Hong Kong Journal of Social Sciences* 21 (Winter): 70–1.

Fewsmith, J. (2003) 'The Sixteenth National Party Congress: The Succession that Didn't Happen', *China Quarterly* 173: 1–16.

Fo, J. G. (2001) 'Properly Dealing with the Relations Between the Village Party Branch of the Chinese Communist Party and Villager Committees' (in Chinese), *Shaoguan xueyuan xuebao, shehui kexue* (Journal of Shaoguan University, Social Sciences) 22/7: 21–5.

Fu, D. Y., Yuan, Y. Z. and Rui, G. Q. (2004) *Xingzheng gaige yu zhidu chuangxin* (Public Administration Reform and Institutional Innovation), Shanghai: Sanlian.

Jin, T. J. (2000) 'Villager Self-rule Under the Arrangement of "Rural Government, Village Self-rule"', (in Chinese) *Shehui zhuyi yanjiu* (Socialism Studies) 4: 61–4.

Lang, Y. X. and Lang, Y. G. (2005) 'Village Party Branches and Village Elections', *Ningbo dangxiao xuebao* (Journal of Ningbao Party School) 1: 29–33.

Li, P. (2004) 'Construct a Harmonious Society: China Under the Guidance of Scientific Development Perspectives' in X. Ru, X. Lu and P. Li (chief eds) *2005 nian: zhongguo shehui xingshi fenxi yu yuce* (Analysis and Forecast of China's Social Development [2005]), Beijing: Shehui kexue wenxian chubanshe, pp. 1–17.

Lieberthal, K. (2004) *Governing China: From Revolution Through Reform*, New York: Norton.

Liu, H. and Zhang, M. S. (1995) 'The Characteristics and Development of Our Country's Direct Election System', in Research Office, the NPC Standing Committee Office (ed.) *Renmin daibiao dahui chengli sishi zhounian jinian wenji* (Selection of Essays Commemorating the Fortieth Anniversary of the People's Congress), Beijing: Zhongguo minzhu fazhi chubanshe, pp. 340–6.

Liu, L. (2005) 'Promote the building of socialist harmonious society,' in *Shijie quanguo renda sanci huiyi 'zhengfu gongzuo baogao'* (Supplementary Readings to the 'Government Work Report' at the Third Plenum of the Tenth National People's Congress), Beijing: Renmin chubanshe and Zhongguo yanshi chubanshe, pp. 427–47.

Liu, Y. (2001) 'Villager Self-administration Development after Democratic Elections' (in Chinese), *Zhongguo nongcun guance* (China Villages Observation) 3: 70–6.

Mao, Z. (1993) [1938] 'The Problem of War and Strategy' (in Chinese), *Mao Zedong junshi wenji* (Selected Military Works by Mao Zedong), vol. 2, Beijing: Junshi kexue chubanshe and zhongyang wenxian chubanshe, pp. 416–33.

Marquand, R. (2005) 'Yahoo, Chinese Police, and a Jailed Journalist,' *Christian Science Monitor*, 9 September.

Ministry of Civil Affairs (2002) 'Grassroots Level Political Authorities and Community Development', www.mca.gov.cn/manual/index.html.

Mōri, K. (2003) 'The Sixteenth Party Congress and Future Chinese Political Development', *Kokusai Mondai* (International Affairs) 514 (January): 2–16.

NBS (National Bureau of Statistics) (2000, 2001, 2004) *Zhongguo tongji nianjian* (China Statistical Yearbook), www.stats.gov.cn.

OpenNet Initiative (2005) *Internet Filtering in China, 2004–2005: A Country Study*, www.opennetinitiative.net/studies/china/. (The OpenNet Initiative is a collaborative partnership between three leading academic institutions: the Citizen Lab at the Munk Centre for International Studies, University of Toronto; Berkman Center for Internet and Society at Harvard Law School; and the Advanced Network Research Group at the Cambridge Security Programme, University of Cambridge.)

Organic Law on the Villager Committee of the People's Republic of China (1998) www.mca.gov.cn/laws/law7.html.

Ouyang, X. (2005) 'Study Hu Jinto's UN Speech: Cooperation Between Major Powers Guarantees the Building of a Harmonious World', *Jiefangjun Bao* (Liberation Army Daily), 24 September, www.chinamil.com.cn.

Pan, H. L. (2005) 'New Problems of Villager Committee Elections and Their Solutions', *Zhongguo minzheng* (China Civil Affairs) 4: 35.

Pye, L. (1999) 'An Overview of 50 Years of the People's Republic of China: Some Progress, but Big Problems Remain', *China Quarterly* 159 :569–79.

Ruan, C. F. (2001) *WTO yu zhengfu gaige* (WTO and Government Reform), Beijing: Jingji chubanshe.

Ruan, Z. Z. (2005) 'Study Hu Jintao's UN Speech: China Advocates and Promotes the Building of a Harmonious World', *Jiefangjun Bao*, 21 September, www.chinamil.com.cn.

Shen, W. G. (2004) 'Sound the Alarm of National Information Frontier Security', *Zhongguo guofang bao* (China National Defence News), 9 November.

Village Department, the Bureau of Grassroots Level Governance and Community Development, the Ministry of Civil Affairs (2001) 'Democratic Centralism Does Not Apply to the Direct Election at Villages, the Township Party Committee and Government Should Protect the Rights and Interests of Party Members and Villagers According to Law' (in Chinese), *Xiangzhen luntan* (Township Forum) 9, www.chinarural.org/xzlt.htm.

Wei, X. H. (2004) 'The Effect of Villager Committee Election on Village Relations: Field Investigation of Villager Committee Elections in Economically Backward Regions', *Shehui zhuyi yanjiu* (Socialism Studies) 2: 91–3.

Xinhua News Agency (2001a) 'The Market Daily: China Forms International Internet Security Control Police Units', 23 March, www.xinhua.org.

—— (2001b) '20,000 Internet Cafés Across The Country Were Outlawed', 11 December, www.xinhua.org.

—— (2005a) 'Hu Jintao Chairs Politburo Collective Study Sessions and Makes Important Speech', 22 February, www.xinhuanet.com.

Yang, H. L. (2005) 'Legal Reflections on the Widespread Briberies in Villagers Committee Elections', *Xuexi luntan* (Tribune of Study[sic]) 2: 66–9.

You, J. (2002) 'Profile: the Heir Apparent', *China Journal* 48: 125–34.

Yuan, M. S. (2004) 'Analysis of the First Case of Prosecuting the Villagers Committee', *Hunan gong'an gaodeng zhuanke xuexiao xuebao* (Journal of Hunan Public Security College), 6: 20–3.

Zhan, C. C. (2001) 'The Current Situation and the Future Development Direction of Villager Self-rule' (in Chinese), www.chinarural.org/llyt/xrzs/zhang/01.htm.

Zhang, D. X., Bo, G. L. and Li, J. P. (2003) *Zhongguo zhengfu gaige de fangxiang* (The Direction of China's Government Reforms), Beijing: Renmin chubanshe.

Zhang, M. M. (2005) 'Study Hu Jinto's UN Speech: Insist on the Spirit of Inclusion', *Jiefangjun Bao*, 28 September, www.chinamil.com.cn.

Zhang, W. M., Yang, X. Q. and Feng, Y. S. (1998) *Zhongguo zhengfu jigou yu xingzheng guanli tizhi gaige* (Reform of Chinese Government Agencies and Public Administrative Institutions), Guangxi: Guangxi shifan daxue chubanshe.

ther reading

Bai, G. and Zhao, S. X. (2001) *Xuanju yu zhili* (Election and governance), Beijing: Zhongguo Shehui Kexue Chubanshe.

'China Leadership Monitor', an online magazine run by the Hoover Institution, Stanford University, www.chinaleadershipmonitor.org.

Dittmer, L. (2003) 'Leadership Change and Chinese Political Development', *China Quarterly* 176: 903-925.

Guo, Z. and Bertstein, T. P. (2004) 'The Impact of Elections on the Village Structure of Power: the Relations between the Village Committees and Party Branches', *Journal of Contemporary China* 13/39: 257–75.

Hughes, C. R. and Wacker, G. (eds) (2003) *China and the Internet: Politics of the Digital Leap Forward*, London: RoutledgeCurzon.

Li, C. (2003) 'The "New Deal": Politics and Policies of the Hu Administration', *Journal of Asian and African Studies* 38/4–5: 329–46.

Lukes, S. (1974) *Power: A Radical View*, London: Macmillan.

O'Brien, K. J. and Li L. J. (2000) 'Accommodating "Democracy" in a One-Party State: Introducing Village Elections in China', *China Quarterly* 162: 465–89.

Xinhua News Agency (2005b) 'Full Text of 'Rules on the Administration of Internet Information News Services', 26 September, www.xinhuanet.com.

Yang, T. Y. and Yan, L. (2003) 'The Strategic Intentions of Building a Harmonious Society', *Liaowang xinwen zhoukan* (Outlook News Weekly), 21 February, www.xinhuanet.com.

3

Privatisation

Bennis So Wai Yip

Introduction

With the rise of New Right ideology in Western Europe from the late 1970s to early 1980s, privatisation became a global trend. It reached its peak when the collapse of the Soviet bloc in the late 1980s and early 1990s triggered a series of large-scale privatisation reforms in the former communist countries. There is little doubt that the Chinese leadership noticed the privatisation drive in Western Europe and privatisation initiatives in the former communist economies. Yet their own policies, which – as this chapter will argue – would eventually lead to a gradual privatisation of the state-owned economy and the emergence of a private sector, owed little (if anything) to the European experience.

The impact of privatisation is much more profound in a socialist country than in a capitalist country. In a socialist country, privatisation changes the fundamental economic structure of a planned economy, transforms the state–society relationship, and has far-reaching implications for the ruling communist party's control of the state's economic and social resources. For that reason, the Chinese communist leadership never adopted an outright and explicit privatisation programme. Instead, the opening-up policy adopted in the post-Mao period fostered an indirect and gradual process of privatisation. Since the southern tour of Deng Xiaoping in early 1992, this process has become an important and irreversible part of China's economic transformation.

What is privatisation?

The narrow definition: privatisation from above

Definitions of privatisation can generally be classified as either narrow or broad. In the narrow definition, privatisation refers to the sale or transfer of state assets, usually state- or publicly-owned enterprises, to individuals or private firms. Mass privatisation, the direct transfer of state assets (through the distribution of vouchers or coupons) to the population for free or for a nominal charge, was practised by some former communist countries in the early 1990s. Another form of privatisation is the management-employee buyout (MEBO), which is the sale of an enterprise to its management and employees. This form is usually adopted to privatise small state enterprises. With reference to the post-communist transitional economies, the direct privatisation of the state sector is sometimes referred to as 'privatisation from above' (Ners 1995).

The broad definition: privatisation from below

In the broad definition, privatisation refers to any attempt to reduce the size and scope of the state, and to strengthen market forces in the provision of public services. This kind of privatisation does not necessarily result in a transfer of state assets. It can refer to

- abolishing state monopoly;
- relaxing the restrictions on private-sector activities; or
- allowing entry of more private firms.

These methods of reducing state control are also referred to as deregulation. An example would be a government's issuing of licences to private firms to operate telecommunications services in an effort to break up the monopoly of a state telecom. Another method for reducing state monopolies is to withdraw the government/public sector from certain industries or service provisions so that the state is gradually displaced by the private sector. This process is known as displacement. A broad definition of privatisation also includes the policies of delegation and contracting-out. These policies involve a government delegating the provision of public services to private firms, or leasing a public enterprise to private management.

The rise of new private enterprises outside the state sector in post-communist transitional economies is sometimes considered a form of privatisation, and is referred to as 'privatisation from below' (Ners 1995). This kind of privatisation resembles the method of displacement in the sense that it aims at gradually replacing the old state sector with a newly established private sector and the new sector's acquisition of the state sector.

While academic discussions usually only refer to the narrow definition of privatisation, in this chapter, the term 'privatisation' includes both the broad and narrow definitions. It is questionable whether the transfer of state ownership in China would have occurred if a broad form of privatisation had not occurred first. Although we focus on the privatisation of the Chinese economy in this chapter, we will also note the emerging privatisation of the social sector.

An 'unintended' privatisation in China

To this day, the Chinese government has officially denied that privatisation has been taking place in China. Unlike other post-communist countries, China has never articulated an explicit privatisation programme. The official term for 'privatisation' (*siyouhua*) refers to the sale or transfer of state-owned enterprises (SOEs) to private firms that do not have private 'legal person' status (*siren gongsi*; see the Glossary at the end of this chapter). Despite this, the government did admit to the limited sale and 'stockification' of SOEs after Deng's historic southern tour in 1992. The official discourse now tolerates the euphemistic term 'denationalisation' (*feiguoyouhua* or *minyinghua*; see Glossary). If adopting the broad definition of privatisation, it can be said that the privatisation process started long before the 1990s, and that the post-Mao reform policies indirectly resulted in the fait accompli of privatisation, though privatisation was not the initial goal of these reforms. This section reviews how the Chinese Communist Party's (CCP) policies in the post-Mao period hastened the emergence of rural and urban privatisation.

'Crossing the river by groping for stones'

Post-Mao reform policy-making has been compared to 'crossing the river by groping for stones' (*mozhe shitou guohe*). The metaphor refers to the situation that pro-reform Party leaders found themselves in at the beginning of the reform period. Although they did not know which point of the opposite river bank they would eventually reach (i.e. the ultimate goal of reforms), they knew that they had to 'cross the river' (i.e. needed to carry out reforms). While an ultimate goal was not clear to the Party leaders at the beginning of the reform process, they believed that the 'stones' positioned before them would in fact point in a definite direction, and that the closer they came to the opposite bank, the clearer their goal would become. As a result of this strategy, policy-making was relatively passive at the beginning but became more active once goals became clearer. In other words, the consequences of reforms were to a large extent not a result of the state's definite plan or intent.

'Crossing the river' does not mean that choices associated with reforms had no basis. The break with radical Maoism paved the way for the adoption of an alternative moderate approach to economic development: the line of Deng Xiaoping and Chen Yun. The Deng-Chen approach had already emerged in the Mao period, and in line with Mao, they did not subscribe to the Soviet-style planned economy. Their approach advocated a limited use of the market as a supplement to the state-planned economy. Chen, who had been in charge of economic policies since the outset of the People's Republic, supported sideline production by rural households and the production of other small-scale commodities. The progressive decentralisation in the Mao era and the move away from the Soviet model resulted in a further devolution of control over SOEs. Pilot schemes increasing the autonomy of SOEs and profit retention were carried out in over 6,000 enterprises in the early 1980s. This new approach allowed more autonomy and changed the incentive mechanism. It is important to note, however, that the Party did not articulate a clear blueprint for reforms until 1984.

Rural privatisation

Although the central government had not formulated systematic reform policies, a spontaneous reform was taking place in rural areas. This reform took place on three fronts:

1   land division and agricultural decommunisation;
2   township village enterprises; and
3   a private economy.

These reforms were accompanied with an overall relaxation of the state's control.

Land division and agricultural decommunisation

After the completion of agricultural collectivisation in the mid-1950s, collective farming became the main form of production in rural areas, although limited side-line private production was also allowed (except during the late 1950s). Since collective farming had failed to raise productivity and rural incomes in the late 1970s and early 1980s, some peasants began dividing land up for individual household cultivation. This practice was officially prohibited at the time. The best-known case of spontaneous division of collectivised land took place in a production brigade in Fengyang County, Anhui province, in 1978. Opinions over this division were divided among local and central leaders. However, in light of the substantial increases of agricultural output that occurred in the areas where farming land had been decollectivised, the Deng Xiaoping leadership endorsed household farming in 1980. The rural household responsibility system was rapidly adopted across the country, and by 1984, 99 per cent of rural households participated in household farming (Naughton 1995: 141).

It is important to note that land division did not mean that land ownership was directly transferred to individual peasants; land division only related to managerial decentralisation. Land was still owned by villages but contracted to peasant households for farming. The contract for management was first set at three years. In order to avoid short-term behaviour, it was soon lengthened to 15 years. By the end of the contract, it was extended to 30 years on top of the original contract period in 1993. Under the household responsibility system, each household had to grow a contracted amount of particular crops (essentially grains, cotton and oil crops) and sell them to the state at planned prices. Having fulfilled their contracted obligations, peasants could then farm any crops and sell them to the market. Although agricultural reform was not carried out in the form of the privatisation of land ownership, peasants claimed most property rights of the land, including the rights to use the land and the residual incomes for sold produce after fulfilling state quotas. Only in 2001, did the state purchase quota system start to be abolished in certain provinces. However, its demise was fast and it was abolished nationwide in 2004.

Township village enterprises (TVEs)

Alongside agricultural restructuring, restrictions on rural industrialisation were relaxed. Rural industry originated from the pre-reform 'commune and brigade enterprises' that had been underdeveloped because 90 per cent of the rural population was engaged in farming. Rural industries were intended to provide agricultural producers with goods, but they received little local raw material input because of the state monopoly on procurement (Naughton 1994: 144–5). After 1984, commune and brigade enterprises, renamed 'township village enterprises' (TVEs), were allowed to process rural raw materials (after state monopoly on the purchase of agricultural materials was relaxed) and supply consumer goods to cities. The legitimisation of rural industries was based upon the ostensible collective ownership of most TVEs. TVEs were supposed to be a further development of existing commune-brigade enterprises and were intended to strengthen public ownership in the countryside. However, since most TVEs were set up or managed by rural local governments and were operated outside of the state plan and bureaucracy, they differed from the public enterprises of a traditional planned economy. Sometimes, the collective ownership of TVEs was in name only because only collective ownership could legitimise their operation. In addition, various new forms of ownership were tested by TVEs, including joint-stock forms (Kraus 1991: 103).

Rural individual private economy

In addition to the sideline production in rural households, the self-employed individual economy, i.e. the *getihu*, was allowed. The *getihu* had existed in the Maoist era, though of course, this sector was infinitesimal then. Despite the existence of forms of private economy in the rural economy, the employment of labour was problematic because it implied 'exploitation of others', something that was clearly taboo in a socialist society. In 1981, the government promulgated Policy Regulations on Urban Non-Agricultural Individual Business, allowing the *getihu* to employ one to two helpers and not more than five apprentices. Derived from the Regulations, the employment of less than eight workers was thus considered as involving no exploitation. (A few years later, a 'private enterprise' (*siying qiye*) was defined as a private economic entity that employed more than seven wage workers.) In practice, many rural private firms went beyond this limitation. Though faced with spontaneous growth in the private sector, the Party did not suppress its development in the early 1980s because it considered the private economy too weak to challenge its leadership. The state clearly thought that it would not be difficult to address any 'negative' consequences that might emerge from the growth of a private sector.

The policy-making associated with rural reform emphasised the Party's traditional line of 'seeking truth from fact' (*shishi qiushi*). Deng maintained this line and his subsequent decisions led to further liberalisation and privatisation of the Chinese economy. It should be noted that the privatisation of the rural farming was completed rapidly, without significant resistance. A non-agricultural private economy burgeoned in rural areas. The number of rural *getihu* increased from about 160,000 in 1978 to over 7 million in 1984 (Kraus 1991: 64).

Urban privatisation

The unexpected success of rural reforms emboldened the Party leaders to step up reform and take it into urban areas in 1984. At the Third Plenum of the CCP Twelfth Central Committee in October 1984, the Party decided to establish an institution of 'socialism with Chinese characteristics', in which, instead of fully depending upon planning, the Chinese socialist economy was to become a 'planned commodity economy' in which the market, as a supplementary but indispensable force, was to remedy the shortcomings of mandatory planning. By the same token, instead of pure public ownership, diversified types of ownership were allowed, including not just *getihu* but also Sino-foreign joint ventures under the dominance of public ownership. And for the first time, the Party allowed the leasing or contracting-out of small SOEs to collectives or individuals. This should be considered as the first incidence of privatisation by delegation in post-Mao China, revealing a new economic system that combined planning with the market, although the latter was subservient to the former.

SOE reform

As part of its SOE reform policy, the Party further expanded the managerial auton-omy of enterprises and enabled them to respond to market forces. Accordingly, a policy of separating the Party from SOEs was adopted. The authority of the Party secretary in an SOE was largely curtailed, and restricted to ideological matters and to the supervision of overall policy. By contrast, the authority of the business manager was greatly enlarged through the manager responsibility system. Under this system, the manager of the SOE became the legal-person representative of the enterprise and enjoyed a high degree of autonomy in business, financial and personnel management. But the manager also had to shoulder the ultimate responsibility of the enterprise's performance. Instead of simply accomplishing an assigned state plan, the enterprise produced goods in accordance with a contract that was negotiated with its supervisory agency. The enterprise was allowed to keep a large portion of above-target revenues. Under this contract system, some managers were expected to be risk-bearers. Some long-term contracts required a personal security deposit from the manager, and in all cases enterprises were sup-posed to fulfil their profit delivery obligations regardless of total profit earned.

Urban individual economy

The individual economy in cities was still a marginal sector in the 1980s, because most city dwellers had secure jobs under the state system. The social status of *getihu* was very low at that time. The state also monopolised most available mate-rials in cities so that urban *getihu* concentrated upon service industries such as repairs, carpentry, photography, eateries, catering and transport – the economic gap left by the state sector. Most *getihu* businesspeople were retirees and rusti-cated urban youths who had been sent to the countryside during the Cultural Rev-olution. Allowing these workers to run *getihu* was an expedient way of resolving the problem of surplus labour.

Legitimisation of the private economy

However, the overall private economy became increasingly significant in contrib-uting to the national economy. According to the official statistics, the private sector only constituted 2 to 5 per cent of gross industrial output (GIO) in 1985–9 (NBS 1990: 412). However, in some regions like Wenzhou prefecture in Zhejiang province, the figure was higher. It is worth noting that the official figures did not include the output of many de facto private firms that falsely registered them-selves as collectives, so-called 'red-hat' firms or 'disguised' collectives (*jiajiti*). False registration could legitimise their operation and help them receive preferential treatment offered by the government only to public firms. More importantly, private firms with more than seven employees became too rampant to be ignored. The Party could not but openly settle the question of the legitimacy of private enterprises.

At the CCP Thirteenth National Congress in October 1987, the Party formally endorsed the existence of private enterprises. The Party justified that China remained in the 'primary stage of socialism'. At that stage, the principal contradiction was between the growing material and cultural needs of the people, and backward production. Based on this premise, the private sector should be allowed, as 'practice proved that a certain degree of development of the private sector promoted production'. The reformist Party leaders still believed that the existence of the private sector would not threaten socialism in China because the private sector was bound up with the public sector, which remained predominant.

The private economy was legalised by constitutional amendment in 1988, though the private sector was described in the constitution as 'a supplement to the socialist public economy', thus clearly occupying an inferior position to the state sector. In the same year, the State Council promulgated Provisional Regulations on Private Enterprises to regulate the operation of private enterprises. Private enterprises were divided into three types (see Glossary for definitions):

1   wholly individually-owned enterprises;
2   partnership enterprises; and
3   limited liability companies.

Private enterprises did not proliferate in the first years after legitimisation because of a nationwide campaign against Bourgeois Liberalisation. The subsequent line of anti-bourgeois ideology after the Tiananmen protests of 1989 further caused a setback for the private sector. In addition, the conservative faction of the Party queried the political nature of various market reform measures, questioning whether they served the ends of 'socialism' or 'capitalism'. As a result, the pace of reforms came to a standstill in 1989–91.

Post-1992 acceleration

The southern tour of Deng Xiaoping in spring 1992 broke through this impasse. During the tour, Deng put forward his seminal idea of 'three advances' (sange youliyu). He declared three criteria by which to judge whether reforms were 'socialist'. Reforms had to advance

1   the development of productive forces;
2   the enhancement of the overall capacity of the country; and
3   the improvement of people's living standards.

In short, any measures that helped to develop the economy were not antithetical to socialism. Deng indicated that a planned economy was not synonymous with a socialist economy. Planning and market regulation could not be used to draw distinctions between socialism and capitalism. Both were only means of controlling economic activities that could be employed by both capitalist and socialist countries. Deng's definition of socialism paved the way for a complete transition to a market economy. At the Fourteenth National Party Congress in October 1992, the Party resolved to establish a 'socialist market economy' in place of the 'planned commodity economy'.

The reform of SOEs shifted from management reform into property rights reform from 1993 onwards. The property rights of an enterprise were to be clearly defined by means of establishing a 'modern enterprise system' in which the ownership and the rights of the enterprise were separated by turning the enterprise into an independent legal entity, i.e. corporatisation. And ownership of the enterprise would become scattered. This was a new attempt to separate government from enterprises. The incorporated SOEs no longer depended upon the administrative resource appropriation from the state, and needed to operate independently in the market.

The property rights reform also marked an explicit attempt at privatisation in the narrow sense of the definition. First, it encouraged inter-sectoral business cooperation including the participation of the private sector. In other words, private capital could enter the state sector. Second, the sale of small-sized SOEs was allowed. Third, large SOEs were allowed to go public and were listed on the domestic (in Shanghai and Shenzhen) and foreign stock markets, albeit the number of stockified SOEs was strictly controlled and the state had to hold a majority stake.

This new corporate regime was governed by the Company Law, enacted in 1993. The new law did not classify enterprises in terms of ownership. It only governed two sorts of legal entities – a limited company and a shareholding company (*gufen youxian gongsi*) that could be invested in or owned by various sorts of economic entities, i.e. legal persons and Chinese citizens (see Glossary). The law also established a legal base for the transfer/sale of shares among companies.

Despite a decade of reform, changes within SOEs have remained the least successful among the post-Mao reforms. In light of the state's inability to carry out reform of hundreds of thousands of state enterprises, the Party resolved to concentrate on restructuring only the largest SOEs. In 1995, it adopted the policy of 'grasp the large, let the small go' (*zhuada fangxiao*), which meant the State only put resources into the 1,000 or so largest SOEs by reorganising them into conglomerates. Debt-ridden and inefficient small SOEs would be sold off, leased out or allowed to go bankrupt. The new policy accelerated the privatisation of SOEs much more quickly than the central government expected. By early 1997, over 70 per cent of SOEs in Liaoning, Shandong, Guangdong and Fujian provinces had been privatised, and over 50 per cent in Sichuan. In some sub-provincial places, especially in prosperous regions, SOEs no longer existed. Some local governments even announced that no small SOEs would be set up in the future (Lau 1998: 10).

Table 3.1 Industrial output shared by different sorts of ownership (100 million yuan)

Year	National gross industrial output	State-owned and state-holding enterprises (share in %)		Collective enterprises (share in %)		Others (share in %)	
1978	4 237	3 289	(77.63)	948	(22.37)		
1980	5 034	3 782	(75.13)	1 227	(24.37)	25	(0.50)
1985	8 768	5 586	(63.71)	3 029	(34.55)	153	(1.74)
1989	14 731	7 721	(52.41)	6 236	(42.33)	774	(5.26)
1990	15 796	7 949	(50.32)	6 799	(43.04)	1 048	(6.64)
1991	18 208	8 634	(47.42)	8 050	(44.21)	1 524	(8.37)
1992	22 901	9 705	(42.38)	10 730	(46.85)	2 466	(10.77)
1993	29 394	10 258	(34.90)	14 486	(49.28)	4 650	(15.82)
1994	37 012	10 925	(29.52)	18 093	(48.88)	7 994	(21.60)
1995	43 769	11 821	(27.01)	20 843	(47.62)	11 105	(25.37)
1996	51 312	12 427	(24.22)	25 195	(49.10)	13 690	(26.68)
1997	57 885	12 555	(21.69)	27 767	(47.97)	17 563	(30.34)
1998	64 653	12 568	(19.44)	30249	(46.79)	21836	(33.77)

Source: NBS 2000, 409.

Note: Data in this table calculated at comparable prices.

After almost two decades of reform, the state-owned economy's share in the total economy had plummeted by the end of the 1990s. In 1980, the state sector accounted for 75 per cent of the gross industrial output, and this had been reduced to just 22 per cent in 1997. Conversely, the non-public industrial sector, composed of indigenous and foreign private industries, rose from 0.5 per cent in 1980 to 30 per cent in 1997 (see Table 3.1).

China's experiments in the shareholding system engendered debates over whether the system should be considered 'public' or 'private'. The Party responded to this issue at the Fifteenth National Party Congress.

From the Fifteenth National Party Congress to the present

At the Fifteenth National Party Congress in 1997, the then Party Secretary, Jiang Zemin, pointed out that the public sector consisted of state-owned and collective enterprises, and state-owned and collective stakes in enterprises of mixed owner-ship. Jiang stressed that public ownership could be realised in diverse forms. The shareholding system could be one means of realising public ownership as long as the state or collective bodies held a controlling stake in the enterprises. Sticking to the previous Party line, Jiang repeated that the state-owned economy should play a 'leading' role in the national economy. However, this leading role was not realised in terms of the share of the state sector in the national economy but in terms of the degree of state control. In this sense, only key sectors of the national economic backbone should be dominated by the state sector, whereas the overall economic share of the state sector might decrease. The state's leading role should be strengthened in terms of quality, not quantity. The Party Congress also endorsed the non-public economy (*feigong jingji*) as an 'important component' of the socialist market economy. The new phrase 'important component' was written into the constitution amended at the 1999 National People's Congress and the Party yielded to the reality that the state/public economic sector was shrinking significantly.

From the Fifteenth National Party Congress up to the present time, the Chinese government has downplayed the issue of ownership. No longer focusing on the public–private divide, the government's industrial policy has been formu-lated to support selected branches of industry, regardless of their form of owner-ship. In many respects, in terms of government policies, the private sector now enjoys equal treatment with the public sector, though discrimination against the private sector has been reported at the implementation level. Emboldened by the 1997 Party Congress, many 'disguised' collectives re-registered themselves as officially licensed private enterprises. The incidence of privatised TVEs also soared in rural areas. The number of TVEs registered as a collective contracted from about 670,000 among a total of 21,100,000 TVEs in 2001 to about 290,000 among 21,700,000 in 2003 (www.agri.gov.cn/sjzl/). Many previously restricted areas of business have been gradually opened to private capital. In February 2005, the State Council promulgated a policy to further open some previously state-monopolised sectors to private investment, including infrastructure construction, public utilities and even the national defence industry. Private capital has now entered some previously sensitive industries, like banking, aviation and oil.

In addition, the ideological barrier to 'stockification' has been removed and the flotation of SOEs has steadily increased. Over 1,300 public companies are now listed on the Shanghai or Shenzhen Stock Exchange, among which about 93 per cent have sprung from SOEs. However, the floating of SOEs has not resulted in full-scale privatisation. The initial aim of founding a securities market was to revi-talise the ailing SOEs by introducing public monitoring, but without losing state control. Hence, state and corporate shares in listed SOEs were banned from being traded on the market and these two types of shares usually constituted over 50 per cent of the companies' equity. Obviously, the lower transferability of the companies' equity did not impose sufficient external pressure upon managers to improve management. In recent years, the state has therefore further enhanced the transferability of state equity. The total number of SOEs has gradually decreased, and was down to about 150,000 in 2003. The reduction rate has averaged 7.2 per cent since 1998. However, the government claims that the value of SOEs' assets keeps growing with an annual average rate of 26.4 per cent (Tong 2004).

To be sure, state investment remains very active and state-owned assets are still growing in absolute value. However, state agencies now seldom establish purely state-owned companies. Mixed ownership with private capital and shareholders has become the major pattern of newly established state-funded companies, and the management of these companies is usually delegated to private management.

Privatisation in China does not follow a premeditated and comprehensive plan. Essentially, the CCP has taken small steps in response to the consequences of each preceding step. Each step or response has in turn prodded the Party on to adopt an increasingly bold policy of privatisation. In this regard, it is important to note that local initiative, especially in rural areas, has played a significant part in pushing privatisation forward. Localities initiated and tested different reforms, and the household farming and stockification processes were spontaneous trials by peasants and local enterprises respectively. After their success, the central government endorsed, promoted, legalised and regulated them. It is also important to note that the privatisation in the urban industrial sector was spearheaded by the achievements of the privatisation process in rural areas.

Political economy of privatisation in China

The previous section reviewed the course of privatisation in terms of state policies. To a large extent, privatisation in China was spontaneous, and state policies cannot account very well for the course of privatisation. This section makes sense of the course of privatisation by providing an account of political economy and by looking at privatisation from below and from above.

Privatisation from below

In contrast to the 'shock therapy' approach taken by Eastern Europe and the Russian Federation, China's approach to economic reform has been gradual or incremental. Chinese economist Fan Gang describes the Chinese reform process as an institutional transition in which substantial economic development relies upon the growth of a non-state sector (the new system outside the old economic sectors) while the existing old sectors are left intact without a major structural change. The aim of this strategy is to gradually replace the state sector with the non-state sector, and at the same time attenuate the pain for state employees and their resistance to SOE reforms, especially in the case of bankruptcy (Fan 1998). In other words, Fan's comment suggests that privatisation in China primarily comes from below. Another mechanism for privatisation is the regional competition fostered by post-Mao decentralisation that has led to better economic performance among producers (Qian and Xu 1993; Montinola *et al.* 1995; Zhang and Li 1998).

The non-state sector

It should be clear that the 'non-state' sector in China is not equivalent to a private sector. Non-state enterprises (or *minying qiye*) refer to collective, cooperative, shareholding, individual and private, and state-owned people-managed (*guoyou minying*) enterprises. (*Minying qiye* do not include foreign-funded enterprises.) Among these enterprises, collective, cooperative and state-owned people-managed enterprises lay claim to public ownership in an official sense. The key distinction between the state and the non-state sector is that the state sector is allocated funds from the government budget and operates under state administrative control, whereas the non-state sector is financially self-reliant and does not receive any budgetary funds. As a result, the management in a non-state enterprise enjoys a higher degree of managerial autonomy and is also responsible for its own profits and losses. (Some urban collectives established in the early 1970s for rusticated urban youth are exceptional cases. These enterprises were subject to planned control, although they were all inferior to state enterprises in status and were allocated fewer resources.)

State-owned people-managed enterprises

Likewise, the so-called 'state-owned people-managed enterprise' usually refers to an urban spin-off from a state agency. The founding of this kind of enterprise is usually based upon seed capital provided by a state agency, and such an enterprise is operated by a private management that enjoys a high degree of autonomy. Some of the high-tech enterprises that have proliferated since the mid-1980s (such as the information technology conglomerate Lenovo), are examples of state-owned people-managed enterprises. Such high-tech enterprises numbered over 5,500 in 2002 (Huang 2004: 535). Since these enterprises receive seed capital derived from a state agency, they could be registered as state-owned enterprises.

This kind of enterprise is different from a traditional SOE in that the source of funding is not directly from a government budget, but extra-budgetary sources or the retained capital of a state agency. In addition, this enterprise never experiences traditional planned control, so it seldom inherits the burdens and practices of socialism. As I noted earlier, the state is still active in investing, and to a certain extent, new state investment is derived from extra-budgetary sources. This new type of state-holding/state-funded enterprise has a hybrid ownership with both state and private capital/shares.

Collective enterprises and TVEs

Rapid growth in industrial output from the non-state sector in China has been remarkable. Among all non-state enterprises, the collective sector was the first to claim a niche in the state-dominated system. In the 1980s, about a third of gross industrial output (GIO) was registered by the output of collective enterprises. In the 1990s, it overtook the state sector, accounting for a majority of the GIO (see Table 3.1).

A majority of the industrial output of collective enterprises is derived from township village enterprises (TVEs). The proliferation of TVEs was based upon four factors:

1   their legitimacy was guaranteed by their public ownership status from the outset;
2   their public ownership status and their link to rural governments allowed them to make use of collective assets in townships and villages and secure access to bank loans;
3   the huge population reserve in rural areas provided ample cheap labour to the TVEs; and
4   they are a market-oriented sector that has a competitive edge over SOEs.

The growth of TVEs provided a pre-condition for subsequent accelerated privatisation. It helped accumulate capital for would-be peasant entrepreneurs who later launched their own businesses or even bought out SOEs. The rural business ventures nourished ranks of entrepreneurs that China had been devoid of in the pre-reform period. The TVEs were also the first to create a competitive environment that asserted pressure on SOEs to restructure. The growth of the TVEs was privatisation in the sense that collective assets were utilised to further the accumulation of private capital. The shortage of capital among poor peasants made the activation/privatisation of collective assets indispensable for the growth of a private economy. In addition, it should be noted that many TVEs were private enterprises from their inception, including many 'disguised' collective enterprises.

The urban private economy

Privatisation in urban areas had a similar evolution. Although urban reforms lagged behind rural reforms, urban privatisation also began in the mid-1980s. Starting from 1984, the state allowed the leasing and contracting-out of small SOEs to collectives and individuals, who were usually state employees. By 1987, some 60 per cent of all small state-owned firms had been leased out (Kraus 1991: 110). These firms were concentrated in the service sector, e.g. retail outlets and food shops. Although state ownership was kept intact, leasing produced urban private entrepreneurs who made use of state resources to earn seed capital to later launch their own businesses. From the mid-1980s, scientific technicians were also encouraged by the state to join the ranks of entrepreneurs and launch high-tech firms, like Lenovo. Although they usually founded firms under the sponsorship of state universities or research institutes and registered as state-owned or collective enterprises, these firms were quasi-private like their rural counterparts. Some technicians accumulated seed capital in these non-state enterprises and later started their own private firms. These state employees and technicians, along with other cadres-turned-entrepreneurs, made up the majority of urban private entrepreneurs.

After a decade of capital accumulation and budding entrepreneurship, private enterprises proliferated in the 1990s, especially after Deng's southern tour and the promulgation of the Company Law. Emboldened by the Party redefinition of the non-public economy in 1997 as an 'important component' of the socialist market economy, many 'disguised' collective enterprises re-registered themselves as private limited companies. In addition, some outstanding private enterprises have expanded into public companies by establishing shareholding companies (see Table 3.2) or even going public on the stock market. By the end of 2003, about 18 per cent of public companies listed on the stock exchange markets in Shanghai and Shenzhen were controlled by indigenous private enterprises (CSRC 2004: 162). And there were over 3,000,000 private enterprises in 2003 (see Table 3.2).

Foreign direct investment

The entry of foreign investment into China has played an indispensable role in the process of privatisation from below. Since the beginning of the reform era in 1980, foreign direct investment (FDI) has increasingly flowed into China. The growth in FDI was fuelled initially by China's proximity to capitalist Hong Kong and Taiwan and by other overseas Chinese investors. The growth rate of FDI accelerated and reached a peak right after 1992 with expanding capital inflow from major industrialised countries such as the United States and Japan. In 1992–3, the growth rates of foreign-funded enterprises and real foreign investment exceeded 100 per cent (Zhang and Ming 2000: 71). During the period from 1979 to 2003, China absorbed a total of US$943.1 billion worth of FDI (DTEERS 2004). The share of foreign-funded industries in GIO grew from 9.47 per cent in 1994 to 15.92 per cent in 1999 (NBS 1999–2000).

FDI has greatly hastened China's foreign trade. In 2004, China overtook Japan to become the third largest trading country. Exports as a portion of GDP jumped from 16.1 per cent in 1990 to 30.9 per cent in 2003 and foreign-funded firms' contributions to exports have also drastically surged, accounting for over 50 per cent since 2001 (DTEERS 2004). FDI was important for privatisation from below, especially in the early years of reforms, because it provided needed capital to the budding indigenous private sector. At the same time, it helped establish a market environment outside of the deeply entrenched state planning system. Foreign enterprises offered high remuneration to a local elite of would-be entrepreneurs who obtained advanced management experience and seed capital from these enterprises. This in turn greatly facilitated later transition to a market economy and the privatisation of the state sector. In contrast, Russia's transition was plagued by a shortage of FDI, and the opening up of its domestic economy in fact facilitated capital flight from Russia (Murray 2000).

Table 3.2 Official statistics for the growth of private enterprises (1989–2003)

Year	Total number of private enterprises	Growth rate (%)	Number of wholly-individually owned enterprises and share	Growth rate (%)	Number of partnership enterprises and share	Growth rate (%)	Number of limited companies and share	Growth rate (%)	Number of shareholding companies and share	Growth rate (%)
1989	90 581		48 172 (53%)		38 573 (43%)		3 836 (4%)			
1990	98 141	8.4	53 491 (55%)	11.0	40 303 (41%)	4.5	4 347 (4%)	13.3		
1991	107 843	9.9	60 613 (56%)	13.3	40 552 (38%)	0.6	6 678 (6%)	53.6		
1992	139 633	29.5	77 268 (55%)	27.5	44 692 (32%)	10.2	17 673 (13%)	164.7		
1993	237 919	70.4	114 944 (48%)	48.8	56 722 (24%)	26.9	66 253 (28%)	274.9		
1994	432 240	81.7	209 852 (49%)	82.6	86 594 (20%)	52.7	135 794 (31%)	105.0		
1995	664 330*	53.7	301 153 (45%)	43.5	118 354 (18%)	36.7	245 272* (37%)	80.6		
1996	840 612*	25.5	358 453 (43%)	19.0	127 763 (15%)	8.0	353 242* (42%)	44.0		

Year										
1997	994 647*	18.3	387 534 (39%)	8.1	130 668 (13%)	2.3	478 396* (48%)	35.4		
1998	1 252 659*	25.9	441 734 (35%)	14.0	137 661 (11%)	5.4	673 682* (54%)	40.8		
1999	1 508 857	20.5	494 673 (33%)	12.0	133 492 (9%)	−3.0	880 577 (58%)	30.7	115 (0.008%)	
2000	1 761 769	16.8	499 787 (28%)	1.0	174 694 (10%)	30.9	1 086 973 (62%)	23.4	315 (0.01%)	173.9
2001	2 028 548	15.1	517 251 (25%)	3.5	131 142 (7%)	−24.9	1 379 866 (68%)	26.9	289 (0.01%)	−8.3
2002	2 435 282	20.1	570 010 (23%)	10.2	124 774 (5%)	−4.9	1 739 969 (71%)	26.1	529 (0.02%)	83
2003	3 005 524	23.4	661 704 (22%)	16.1	120 553 (4%)	−3.4	2 222 664 (74%)	27.7	603 (0.02%)	14
		29.9		22.2		10.1		67.7		65.7

* The original aggregate data do not include private limited companies that were registered in accordance with the Company Law in Beijing. The data from 1995–8 shown in this table have been revised by adding these private limited companies in Beijing.

Source: NBICM 1989–2003

Privatisation from above

Local governments have been indirectly supporting privatisation by tolerating 'disguised' collectives, the growth of private firms and the sale of SOEs. Why do local states adopt a strategy that curtails the state's control over economy? One reason is that local governments are obliged to boost economic development under their jurisdiction, and because of the post-Mao drive to decentralisation, they face tighter budget constraints (Montinola *et al*. 1995). Privatisation is seen as a superior strategy for managing some of these constraints. It should be noted that in the most prosperous provinces, such as Guangdong, Jiangsu and Zhejiang, the share of the private/non-state sector in the economy tends to be much higher. Shanghai, a major industrial and economic hub in pre-reform China, experienced slow economic growth before the mid-1990s when the private/non-state economy still only accounted for a minor share of the municipal economy (Qian and Xu 1993: 141; Zhang and Ming 2000: 47). In addition, local governments can cut subsidies to loss-making SOEs and at the same time draw revenue by selling off SOEs (Wang *et al*. 2001).

Competition among jurisdictions pushed local governments to experiment with reforms. Negatively, some local governments adopted local protectionism, erecting trade barriers against marketisation so as to prevent competition with outside goods. Indeed, local protectionism prevailed in the 1980s. However, local governments could not exercise monopoly over the entire national economy. The lowest level governments had less strength to assert a monopoly. For this reason, some other local governments opted instead to provide a hospitable environment for capital and factory owners, for example by establishing a basis for secure property rights and market-facilitating institutions. Those jurisdictions that failed to provide a favourable environment found that capital and factory owners moved to other jurisdictions (Montinola *et al*. 1995: 58).

Successful reforms were then imitated. Regions that adopted privatisation regularly provided successful models. These initiatives usually came from the lowest-level governments, which felt the greatest pressure to change because they were allocated the fewest resources by higher-level governments. Two well-known cases are Shunde in Guangdong Province and Chucheng in Shandong Province, which as early as the mid-1990s launched large-scale privatisation programmes by selling off their SOEs to the private sector or by stockification, including restructuring enterprises into employee-owned firms.

In the early 1990s a number of factors contributed to increased levels of gradual privatisation. Firstly, regional competition obviously curtailed the ability of local governments to erect trade barriers. At the same time, the absorption of foreign investment in certain coastal regions and the entry of foreign goods made the first breach in the local state monopoly. The new entrepreneurial class accordingly sought places that offered favourable conditions, so there was a gradual shift from regional protectionism toward marketisation in the 1990s. Since the growing size of TVEs increased monitoring costs for local governments, and rural local officials lacked the sophistication and professional knowledge to operate a larger scale of production in a more marketised environment, it became imperative for rural local states to yield the ownership of enterprises to professional managers in order to align them with the development goals of the state (Yep 2000). Furthermore, an increase in the privatisation of TVEs, usually by means of MEBO, occurred from the early 1990s (Oi 1999; Chen 2000; Yep 2000). Likewise, urban spin-offs also clarified their property rights structure, yielding part of their ownership to senior staff in order to align the staff with the long-term development goals of the spin-offs.

Such a gradual privatisation is also found in the SOEs' reform. Although corporatisation and stockification were aimed at creating modern corporate governance structures and introducing public monitoring without full-scale privatisation, these changes indirectly paved the way for privatisation. Although incorporated or stockified state enterprises have become the majority of SOEs since 2000, their performance has not improved so far (Zhang 2004). This can be attributed to the generally poor corporate governance structure of the SOEs; their failure to get rid of administrative intervention; and the failure of private shareholders to exercise their rights to monitor enterprises (Chen 2005). However, at the same time, local governments and enterprises make use of SOE reform policy to accelerate de facto privatisation by spinning off subsidiary private companies or selling off subsidiary companies, welfare services, and company housing (Hassard *et al.* 2002). Since 1998, the privatisation of small and medium-sized SOEs by means of MEBO has proliferated with acquiescence from local governments. However, since many MEBO practices have been condemned as illicitly stripping off state assets, central authorities have recently issued regulations to try to limit and control these practices.

The private sector has also got involved in the privatisation of SOEs. First, mature indigenous private enterprises began to privatise SOEs from the early 1990s, under the euphemistic term 'participation in SOE reforms'. According to an estimate based on a nationwide survey of indigenous private enterprises, about 550,000 out of some 3,000,000 private enterprises in 2003 were restructured enterprises from SOEs or other publicly-owned enterprises (*China Business Times*, 3 February 2005).

Before China's accession to the World Trade Organization (WTO) in 2002, foreign investors were generally not allowed to hold a majority stake of joint ventures. In fact, very few foreign investors were interested in taking over SOEs because of the high transaction costs of such operations and the low quality of the assets which included high debt levels, obsolete technology, inefficient management, and shrinking market share (Huchet 2000: 40). However, since a large-scale equity restructuring and divestment of underperforming SOEs and attempts by foreign investors to further expand their market share in China, acquisitions of SOEs by foreign companies have surged in recent years: the value of annual transactions has grown from about US$5 billion before 2003 to US$10–12 billion in 2004. Although the amount just accounted for 10 to 20 percent of total annual FDI, it reveals a new trend of privatisation development (Woodard and Wang 2004).

In sum, an irreversible trend toward further privatisation of SOEs is likely. However, this does not mean that rapid, all-around privatisation of SOEs will ensue. This is because:

1   large-scale privatisation would result in social instability, particularly among laid-off workers;
2   the Communist Party would face a crisis of legitimacy if it overtly pushed privatisation;
3   privatisation is not a cure-all for large SOEs (as the failure of mass privatisation in the former Soviet bloc illustrates); and
4   the Party does not believe that the state should withdraw completely from the economy, especially from those industries for which there is a natural monopoly or which are key to national security, such as the telecommunications industry.

Consequences of privatisation in China

China's privatisation has proceeded in a slow and incremental manner, evolving from an implicit process in the 1980s into an explicit one in the 1990s. The consequences of privatisation have gradually surfaced over the past decade. Needless to say, as noted earlier, privatisation has resulted in a gradual contraction of the state economy's share of the national economy. The state economy no longer accounts for the majority of economic output. The state has also gradually lost its monopoly of resources control and allocation – a hallmark of the classical socialist economy. It was estimated in 2003 that private property in China was worth 2800 billion yuan, as against 1100 billion yuan held by the state (Lian 2004: 67). With private wealth now dominating this socialist country, the state's major economic function has shifted to the exercise of macroeconomic management. National economic gain has been achieved by rationalising property rights, solving the principal–agent problem caused by public ownership. Privatisation has also led to national fiscal restructuring, a decline of the state's control over society, political liberalisation, the rise of unemployment and the privatisation of social welfare and service provisions.

Fiscal consequences

One consequence of privatisation is the structural change of the state's fiscal extraction. The percentage of government revenue relative to GDP has been shrinking since the reform, from 31.2 per cent in 1978 to the nadir at around 10 per cent in 1995–6, gradually recovering in the ensuing years and back to 18.6 per cent in 2003 (MoF 2004: 331). Despite outstanding economic performance and soaring national income in the past two decades, increases in government revenue did not match national economic growth. The government has maintained mounting fiscal deficits since 1979, except for 1985.

There are a number of reasons for these deficits. First of all, the government relied upon SOEs for more than 70 per cent of its revenue in the 1990s (Lee *et al.* 1999: 12), but SOEs were performing poorly. In fact, the government needed to subsidise the growing number of loss-making SOEs. Subsidies amounted to 728.7 billion Renminbi between 1985 and 2003 (MoF 2004: 332–3). At the same time, the non-state sector's contribution to government revenue did not keep up with the sector's rapid growth. TVEs and foreign-funded firms enjoyed a lower tax rate, and tax evasion, which was most pronounced among indigenous private enterprises, was rampant because the taxation system was underdeveloped. The personal income tax, which was neglected in the planning era and usually contributes 30–50 per cent of tax revenue in developed countries, only accounted for less than 2 per cent before the mid-1990s.

However, the government has recently strengthened the mechanisms for tax collection from the private sector. The share of personal income tax rose from 3.9 per cent in 1999 to 7.1 per cent in 2003 (MoF 2000–4). The share of taxes paid by indigenous private enterprises, foreign companies and *getihu* rapidly increased and overtook the contribution by SOEs in 2002. In 2004, taxes paid by the former accounted for 33.3 per cent while those paid by by the latter declined to 26.6 per cent (Huang 2005: 8).

Decline of the state's control over society

The most pronounced consequence of privatisation in a socialist country is the decline of the state's control over society. People become less dependent upon the state as the state no longer monopolises most economic resources. A private sphere outside the state domain is gradually formulated and expands. This has a profound impact upon the state–society relationship.

In China, the decline of state control is seen in the disintegration of the *danwei* (work unit) system which is a grass-root unit founded in the Mao era. This system is applied to all urban state agencies, including factories, hospitals and schools, and operates as a multifunctional 'miniature society' that monopolises resource provision, including welfare and social services for all affiliated members. It was also the key interface between the urban population and the political system. Instead of using functional bureaucracies, as in other societies, the CCP only made use of the *danwei* as an extension of the state to deal with people. The *danwei* was the work unit from which the Party was able to organise and carry out political education and mass campaigns, and to control the mobility of people.

With marketisation, the *danwei* ceased to be the sole source of resources, and it also suffered from a fiscal crisis that made it unable to continue to support welfare and social service provision. More importantly, people were able to develop careers working in non-state units or setting up their own businesses. A job market has been emerging in China, albeit it is far from mature. In 2003, 73.2 per cent of the urban employed working population was not in state units (NBS 2004: 119). People can now obtain various goods and services from markets, not necessarily through a *danwei*. People no longer live in such an isolated 'miniature society'. They can have more interfaces with society and they can survive without the patronage of a *danwei*.

Accelerated industrialisation has also activated the rural surplus labour force. Rural workers not only enter TVEs in the countryside but are now hired as a cheaper source of labour for urban enterprises. It was estimated in 1998 that there were about 80 million floating rural labourers in China (Wang 2001: 33). The new rich from the countryside and small towns are also entering urban areas to seek business opportunities. They can even purchase an urban residency from a municipal government. The state is no longer able to effectively exercise control over population mobility.

The rise of an entrepreneurial class and democratisation

The decline of a Communist regime and the growth of a private sphere are often associated with democratisation in Western political theory. Private forces, including private entrepreneurs, were implicated in the democratic movement in 1989. The failure of the movement to a large extent reflected the state's strong control in the 1980s. However, the 1990s witnessed a remarkable proliferation of private enterprises. It is high time to re-examine the prospects of democratisation in terms of privatisation and the subsequent emergence of a middle class or bourgeoisie.

Up to now, no scholarly study has come to an affirmative conclusion on the contribution of the new rich to China's democratisation. First of all, despite rapid growth, the middle class remains underdeveloped, and is still only a minority of the total population (He 2000: 78). Second, the new rich to a large extent emerged after the 1989 democratic movement, and many of them went into business feeling disenchanted with politics. They tend to be politically apathetic or sceptical of participation in politics through official channels. Third, the Chinese entrepreneurial class tends to support an authoritarian regime, with authoritarianism shifting from 'politics takes command' to 'economics takes command'. In this view, the regime offers favourable and stable conditions for business, while democratic transition may bring about uncertainty (He 1997: 157; Parris 1999). Fourth, a considerable number of the new rich are former government officials or their relatives, and they have retained close ties with the government. They have a vested interest in Communist rule. Many entrepreneurs form a loose coalition with government officials, engaging in power/money exchange (*quanqian jiaoyi*). In this arrangement, officials use their political power to get involved in market activities, while entrepreneurs use their economic power to gain entry into the political arena. Both officials and entrepreneurs can make money in this way (Choi and Zhou 2001: 126).

Despite these factors limiting democratisation, there are some noteworthy trends to the contrary. First, intense regional and global competition is forcing local governments to establish fair institutions for sustainable development so as to absorb more outside investment. To help establish such a favourable environment, more political participation from all walks of life, especially from the well-educated middle class, is encouraged. Competition may bring about not only marketisation but also political liberalisation, even though the latter may not necessarily take a form that is in line with the Western model. Second, after two decades of opening up, foreign ideas have gradually penetrated people's consciousness. In recent years, hundreds of thousands of Western-trained Chinese have returned to China to further their careers. Their eventual input into China's social and political development should not be overlooked. China's entry into the WTO has also accelerated the inflow of foreign values and will force the government to conform to various international norms, including more institutionalisation and transparency of public governance. Third, the political apathy of entrepreneurs may be a transient phenomenon. In fact, more and more entrepreneurs have been co-opted into the Chinese parliamentary system – i.e. the People's Congress and People's Political Consultative Conference – where they can influence the state's policy-making. They are not seeking to exercise their influence through an opposition party but from within the CCP (Hong 2004).

The rise of unemployment

While the decline of the socialist state grants people freedom, the cost is a loss of the security previously granted by an all-encompassing state. It is apparent that privatisation, as well as marketisation, entails a physical shrinking of the state, which results in job losses for millions of people. Such large-scale unemployment has the potential to cause enormous social unrest. Downsizing of the state accelerated in the second half of the 1990s and the overwhelming majority of victims have been workers at SOEs. Under the policy of 'grasp the large, let the small go', numerous SOEs have laid off workers since 1994–5 in an attempt to reduce deficits and avoid debts. The number of laid-off SOE workers climbed from 3.68 million in 1995 to a peak at 6.19 million in 1999 (Giles *et al.* 2005: 150). The unemployment rate soared accordingly. The official urban unemployment rate climbed from 2.3 per cent in 1991–2 up to 3.1 per cent in the second half of the 1990s, and further up to above 4 per cent in the first years of the twenty-first century (NBS and MLSS 2001: 67; DRC 2004: 934).

It is generally believed that the official figures downplay the real unemployment situation because of unreliable data. Moreover, the narrow official definition of unemployment only includes registered unemployed people. According to one estimate, the urban unemployment rate should have been 5.5 per cent in 1992, and 12.5 per cent in 1999 (Xue and Zhong 2003: 394). Another source has estimated that the real urban unemployment rate actually reached 11.1 per cent in 2002 (Gile *et al.* 2005).

The primary consequence of unemployment and privatisation is social unrest. A variety of actions against bankruptcy, salary arrears, and the restructuring or sale of SOEs have been reported, especially in regions where SOEs are concentrated, such as in the northeast and some inland provinces. Actions include visits to government offices; demonstrations, marches in and blocking of streets or railways; letters of complaint to officials; sit-ins in front of government buildings; petitions; and protest rallies. Such actions are occasionally more violent, including sabotaging factory equipment, attacking offices, committing arson against state property, and detaining, attacking and even killing managers and bosses.

Urban unemployment is one of the major factors leading to social instability, albeit the fallout from unemployment has yet to induce a political crisis. The government is trying hard to placate the urban workforce whose loyalty is the foundation of Communist rule. In 1994, a re-employment programme was introduced. The government is also establishing a social safety net in cities to maintain a minimum subsistence for the urban poor.

To a large extent, further legitimisation of the non-public economy in the 1990s was an attempt to use the private sector to absorb the labour released from SOEs. However, the private sector had a limited ability to absorb these layoffs. In 2000, indigenous private enterprises only accounted for one-third of job resettlement of which about one-fifth set up their own firms to fend for themselves (*People's Daily*, 28 February 2001: 6).

Privatisation of welfare and social service systems

With its retreat from direct economic production and management, the state also has to establish a new mechanism to take over some non-production functions that were the responsibility of the *danwei* such as welfare and social service provision. Although, in light of the budget crisis, the government cannot realistically take as much responsibility for provision of these services as the *danwei* had. Instead, privatisation of the welfare and social service system has accompanied economic privatisation.

The reform of the welfare and social services system began as early as the 1980s, when economic privatisation was about to begin. While this reform was slow at the beginning, it became more pressing in the 1990s. The major impetus was the heavy welfare burden borne by SOEs, which curtailed their competitiveness and eroded state revenue. Consequently, the state has had to separate welfare provision from economic entities.

The guiding concept of reforms has been 'socialisation of social welfare'. Socialisation (*shehuihua*) refers to devolving responsibility into different levels of society, including local communities, mass organisations, enterprises, families and individuals. Socialisation to a large extent is tantamount to the Western notion of privatisation (Wong 2001: 57). However, socialisation stresses a diversification of service providers. Load-shedding has mainly occurred in three areas of reform:

1   housing;
2   pensions; and
3   medical care.

The goal of housing reform is to commodify housing supply, establish a real estate market to supply commodity housing (*shangpin fang*) to urban residents, and abolish the *danwei*'s free or subsidised housing supply system. Pension reform seeks to establish a variety of so-called 'social pooling' schemes for pension funding, administration and delivery. Instead of an individual enterprise, a group of enterprises joins together to form a pool of funding, so as to distribute risk and burden. Under the new scheme, both employees and employers have to contribute to the pool. The contribution rates vary in different places. In addition, pension insurance schemes established by enterprises and individual pension schemes run by commercial insurance companies are allowed to supplement the social pooling. Similar to this is the medical care reform which seeks to reduce state subsidies by establishing a contribution-based health insurance programme that is funded by both employees and employers (Gu 2001a, 2001b).

Most privatisation programmes of welfare and social services began only at the close of the 1990s. Their effect will not be clear for some time. However, it is clear that the state is adopting a 'welfare pluralism' approach, diversifying the sources and responsibility for welfare and social service provision. To be sure, the transition to a market-oriented system will take some time, since policy implementation usually meets resistance from many social groups in urban areas who have vested interests in the existing institutional arrangement. Also, the state is reluctant to implement a 'big bang' transition that might trigger a political and social crisis. As a result, urbanities in China are still highly dependent upon the state for welfare provision (Lee and Wong 2001) and this high degree of dependency may be maintained in the coming decade. Gradualism remains the dominant approach to this aspect of privatisation.

Conclusion

Privatisation in China was a consequence of Deng's strategy of 'crossing the river by groping for stones'. There was no premeditated plan for privatising the socialist economy. In fact, Party policy has restricted the practice of privatisation in a nominal sense. Ironically, there has been no consensus in China on the definition of privatisation. When conservative Party leaders adopt the broad definition, liberal Party leaders and those local officials who benefit from privatisation adopt the narrow definition. This ambiguity has allowed room for privatisation's evolution.

However, it has also meant that privatisation's evolution has not been straightforward. In the early years of reform, only partial private property rights were granted to 'quasi-private entrepreneurs' in reforming SOEs and other post-Mao non-state non-private enterprises. When the development of these enterprises met a bottleneck after vested interests in partial privatisation had been formed, the government could only yield more property rights to these vested interests. This helped avert direct confrontation with socialist ideology and allowed people more time to accept and adapt themselves to the new system. However, it also made it difficult to deal with the legacy of ambiguous property rights of numerous enterprises, especially collective properties. Property rights disputes are becoming more evident as entrepreneurs' consciousness of these rights increases. Now the central government is enacting a law to protect private property rights.

Since privatisation is still under way in China, and many variables and uncertainties are involved, any assessment of its possible long-term effects can be only tentative. As noted towards the end of this chapter, privatisation of the welfare and social service system is continuing. The Chinese government still needs to face severe fiscal stress. The unavoidable result has been the privatisation of various parts of the socialist state. Furthermore, since China's accession to the WTO, privatisation or deregulation measures have been applied to the financial, insurance and telecommunications sectors, and various service sectors that were once restricted.

Nonetheless, this ongoing process of privatisation does not suggest that China and Western capitalism are converging. It is true that China is merging with the international economic order because of the continuing tide of global privatisation and because of mounting pressure to come into line with international (Anglo-American) standards. The marketisation that has accompanied these changes has also led to sharp economic inequality within the population, which is a common phenomenon in many market economies.

However, while Western New Right ideas and Chinese reforms have occurred simultaneously, they have different backgrounds. Chinese reforms have been driven mainly by social and economic transition, whereas Western reforms have come from social discontent with the pathology of the bureaucracy as well as from the rise of new management paradigms. China's economic reforms (which have arrived without substantial political change) are producing a new version of capitalism. When economic logic takes command in China, capital (rather than democracy) takes command. China is becoming more capitalist but not necessarily more democratic.

Some observers expect that economic development will hasten democracy in China. Economic development doubtless will result in political change, but this might not mean Western democracy. The variables and conditions in contemporary China are different from those that produced Western democracy hundreds of years ago. Furthermore, Western democracy is changing, and in some ways is being challenged by the depoliticising logic of economics. Privatisation in China is also possibly one instance of this depoliticisation, since allowing the pursuit of wealth can be a means of distracting people from the pursuit of radical political reform.

One thing that we can say with certainty is that China is no longer a classical socialist state. Two of three hallmarks of the classical socialist state – public ownership and the command economy – have faded away. The only remaining hallmark is Party rule.

Glossary: key terms related to privatisation in China

Collective enterprise (*jiti qiye*)	An enterprise equally owned by all members within the enterprise. It is not a joint-stock enterprise so the ownership cannot be divided by members, and individual owners cannot sell the ownership to other people.

Denationalisation (*feiguoyouhua/minyinghua*)	A process consisting of non-state enterprises replacing, taking over, or merging with SOEs. SOEs are converted into privately-managed joint ventures with either domestic or foreign enterprises, or are reorganised into privately-managed joint-stock companies.
Self-employed individual (*getihu*)	A tiny firm owned usually by one person, a family or a couple of persons. According to state regulations, it should not employ more than seven persons.
Limited liability company (*youxian gongsi*)	According to the Provisional Regulations on Private Enterprises, it is an enterprise formed by share capital and invested in by at least two but generally not more than 30 persons who bear liability according to the amount of their investment. These enterprises need to carry the word 'limited liability company' (*youxian zeren gongsi*) or 'limited company' (*youxian gongsi*) in the concern's name. In addition, the 'company' possesses a separate 'legal person' status. The wholly individual-owned enterprise and the partnership enterprise cannot carry the name 'company' (*gongsi*). According to the 1993 Company Law, the upper limit of shareholders is 50 persons. The shareholders can be either natural or legal persons.
Non-public economy (*feigong jingji*)	This encompasses indigenous private and foreign-funded firms.
Non-state enterprise (*fei guoyou qiye/minying qiye*)	This consists of collective, cooperative, shareholding, individual and private, and state-owned people-managed enterprises. Please note that *minying qiye* usually does not include foreign-funded enterprises.
'Legal person' status	A 'legal person' is an entity on which the legal system confers rights and imposes duties. A legal person can refer to an artificial or statutory body such as a company. A company, as a legal person, has a separate and independent personality from a natural person (human being) who manages or represents the company. The properties of the company and the natural person are clearly separated
Partnership enterprise (*hehuo qiye*)	An enterprise jointly invested in and operated by two or more persons in accordance with an agreement concluded by them. The enterprise also bears unlimited liability. According to the Provisional Regulations on Private Enterprises, it should have over seven employees. But according to the 1997 Partnership Enterprises Law, no minimum number of employees is stipu-

	lated. In practice, the distinction between the enterprise and *getihu* is not clear now.
Privatisation (*siyouhua*)	Transfer or sale of state assets to private firms without legal person status or natural persons.
Shareholding company (*gufen youxian gongsi*)	A shareholding company is similar to a limited liability company in the sense that the shareholders bear liability according to the amount of their investment. However, the shareholding company is established by means of promotion or by means of share offer. Only the shareholding company can issue shares to the public and list on the stock market. The minimum registered capital is ten million yuan.
Socialisation (*shehuihua*)	Devolution of a state responsibility into diverse parts of a society.
State-owned enterprise (*guoyou qiye*)	A state-funded enterprise, not necessarily managed by the state bureaucracy.
State-run enterprise (*guoying qiye*)	A state-funded enterprise managed by the state bureaucracy .
Wholly individually-owned enterprise (*duzi qiye*)	An enterprise invested in and operated by one person who enterprise bears unlimited liability for the enterprise's debts. According to the Provisional Regulations on Private Enterprises, it should have over seven employees. But according to the 1999 Wholly Individually-owned Enterprises Law, no minimum number of employees is stipulated. In practice, the distinction between the enterprise and *getihu* is not clear now.

References

Chen, H. Y. (2000) *The Institutional Transition of China's Township and Village Enterprises: Market Liberalization, Contractual Form Innovation, and Privatisation*, Aldershot: Ashgate.

Chen, J. J. (2005) 'Corporatisation of China's State-owned Enterprises and Corporate Governance', in David Brown and Alasdair MacBean (eds), *Challenges for China's Development: An Enterprise Perspective*, London: Routledge.

Choi, E. K. and Zhou, K. X. (2001) 'Entrepreneurs and Politics in the Chinese Transitional Economy: Political Connections and Rent-seeking', *China Review* 1/1: 111–35.

CSRC (China Securities Regulatory Commission) (2004) *China Securities and Future Statistical Yearbook* (in Chinese), Shanghai: Baijia Publishing House.

DRC (Development Research Centre of the State Council) (2004) *Almanac of China's Economy* (in Chinese), Beijing: Publishing House of Almanac of China's Economy.

DTEERS (Department of Trade and External Economic Relations Statistics, National Bureau of Statistics) (2004) *China External Economic Statistical Yearbook 2004* (in Chinese), Beijing: China Statistical Bureau Press.

Fan, G. (1998) 'Development of the Nonstate Sector and Reform of State Enterprises in China', in J. A. Dorn (ed.), *China in the New Millennium: Market Reforms and Social Development*, Washington, DC: Cato Institute.

Giles, J., Park, A. and Zhang, J. (2005) 'What is China's True Unemployment Rate?', *China Economic Review* 16/2: 149–70.

Gu, E. X. (2001a) 'Beyond the Property Rights Approach: Welfare Policy and the Reform of State-owned Enterprises in China', *Development and Change* 32/1: 129–50.

—— (2001b) 'Dismantling the Chinese Mini-welfare State? Marketization and the Politics of Institutional Transformation, 1979–1999', *Communist and Post-Communist Studies* 341: 91–111.

Hassard, J., Morris, J. and Sheehan, J. (2002) 'The Elusive Market: Privatisation, Politics and State-Enterprise Reform in China', *British Journal of Management* 13/3: 221–31.

He, B. G. (1997) *The Democratic Implications of Civil Society in China*, London: Macmillan Press.

He, Q. L. (2000) 'China's Listing Social Structure', *New Left Review* 5 (September/October): 69–99.

Hong, Z. (2004) 'Mapping the Evolution and Transformation of the New Private Entrepreneurs in China', *Journal of Chinese Political Science* 9/1: 23–42.

Huang, M. (ed.) (2004) *The Development Report of Non-state-owned Economy in China no.1 (2003)* (in Chinese), Beijing: Social Sciences Academic Press.

—— (ed.) (2005) *The Development Report of Non-state-owned Economy in China no.2 (2004)* (in Chinese), Beijing: Social

Kraus, W. (1991) *Private Business in China: Revival between Ideology and Pragmatism*, Honolulu: University of Hawaii Press.

Lau, R. W. K. (1998) 'The 15th Congress of the Chinese Communist Party: Milestone in China's Privatisation', Hong Kong: Division of Social Studies, City University of Hong Kong.

Lee, G. O. M., Wong, L. and Mok, K. H. (1999) 'The Decline of State-Owned Enterprises in China: Extent and Causes', Occasional Paper Series No. 2, Hong Kong: Department of Public and Social Administration, City University of Hong Kong.

Lee, P. N.-S. and Wong, C. K. (2001) 'The Tale of Two Chinese Cities: Rolling Back the Boundary of the Welfare State During the Reform Era', in P. N.-S. Lee and C. W.-H. Lo (eds), *Remaking China's Public Management*, Westport: Quorum Books.

Lian, Y. M. (ed.) (2004) *Quantitative Report on China* (in Chinese), Beijing: China Modern Economic Publishing House.

MoF (Ministry of Finance) (various years) *Finance Yearbook of China* (in Chinese), Beijing: China Finance Magazine Publishing House.

Montinola, G. Y. Y., and Weingast, B. R. (1995) 'Federalism, Chinese Style: The Political Basis for Economic Success in China', *World Politics* 48/1: 50–81.

Murray, B. (2000) 'Dollars and Sense: Foreign Investment in Russia and China', *Problem of Post-Communism* 47 (July/August): 24–33.

Naughton, B. (1994) 'Chinese Institutional Innovation and Privatisation from Below', *American Economic Review* 84/2: 266–70.

—— (1995) *Growing Out of the Plan: Chinese Economic Reform, 1978–1993*, New York: Cambridge University Press.

NBICM (National Bureau of Industrial and Commercial Management) (various years) *Statistical Materials of China Industry and Commerce* (in Chinese), Beijing: Industrial and Commercial Press.

NBS (National Bureau of Statistics) (various years) *China Statistical Yearbook* (in Chinese), Beijing: China Statistical Bureau Press.

NBS and MLSS (Department of Population, Social, Science and Technology Statistics, National Bureau of Statistics and Department of Planning and Finance, Ministry of Labour and Social Security) (2001) *China Labour Statistical Yearbook* (in Chinese), Beijing: China Statistics Press.

Ners, K. J. (1995) 'Privatisation (from Above, Below, Or Mass Privatisation) Versus Generic Private Enterprise Building', *Communist Economies and Economic Transformation* 7/1: 105–16.

Oi, J. C. (1999) *Rural China Takes Off: Institutional Foundation of Economic Reform*, Berkeley: University of California Press.

Parris, K. (1999) 'Entrepreneurs and Citizenship in China', *Problems of Post-Communism* 46/1: 43–61.

Qian, Y. Y. and Xu, C. G. (1993) 'Why China's Economic Reforms Differ: the M-form Hierarchy and Entry/expansion of the Non-state Sector', *Economics of Transition* 1/2: 135–70.

Tong, P. (2004) 'Emerging Performance of State Economic Structural Adjustment, The Performance of SOEs Has Greatly Improved' (in Chinese). Retrieved 15 November 2005, from www.sasac.gov.cn/gzjg/tjpj/xjpj/200503090145.htm.

Wang, C. (2001) 'Unemployment in Current Economic Growth and Solution' (in Chinese), *Labor Economics* 2: 30–40.

Wang, H. L., Li, D. K., and Lui, T. M. (2001) 'Why Has the Government Abandoned the Property Rights of SOEs' (in Chinese), *Economic Research Journal* 399 (August): 61–70, 85.

Wong, L. (2001) 'Welfare Policy Reform', in L. Wong and N. Flynn (eds), *The Market in Chinese Social Policy*, Basingstoke: Palgrave.

Woodard, K. and Wang, A. Q. (2004) 'Acquisitions in China: A View of the Field', *China Business Review* 13/6: 34–8.

Xue, J. and Zhong, W. (2003) 'Unemployment, Poverty and Income Disparity', *Asian Economic Journal* 17/4: 383–405.

Yep, R. (2000) 'Bringing the Managers In: A Case of Rising Influence of Enterprise Managers in Rural China,' *Issues and Studies* 36/4: 132–65.

Zhang, H. Y. and Ming, Z. L. (eds) (2000) *Report on the Development of China's Private Economies (1999)* (in Chinese), Beijing: Social Science Document Press.

Zhang, L. Y. (2004) 'The Roles of Corporatization and Stock Market Listing in Reforming China's State Industry', *World Development* 32/12: 2031–47.

Zhang, W. Y. and Li, S. H. (1998) 'Regional Competition and Privatisation of SOEs in China', (in Chinese), *Economic Research Journal* 12 (December): 13–22.

4

Uneven economic development

Wang Shaoguang

Introduction

Uneven development is a universal phenomenon. It exists in almost all large countries, developing and developed alike. Examples include India, Indonesia, Mexico, Brazil, Canada, Great Britain, France, Italy and the United States. China is no exception.

The regional inequality that results from uneven development is of interest for a variety of reasons. First, the problem of regional disparity is a problem of economic growth. If all regions had grown at the same pace, there would be no income differences between regions in the first place. Even if regional gaps exist, as long as poor regions are able to grow faster than rich ones, the former would converge with the latter and the initial differences would thereby disappear in due course. Some economic theories predict convergence, but the empirical evidence has been a subject of debate. In any event, it is an undeniable fact that regional disparities persist in most countries. To find the root causes of regional disparities, we have to trace the long-term growth paths of different regions in the national economy and to understand the dynamics of regional growth.

Second, regional disparity is an ethical issue. Unless the process of economic development is intrinsically even, society is always confronted with the fundamental contradiction between ethically motivated efforts to establish socioeconomic parity in space and the economically more advantageous strategy of letting inequality increase, as long as it makes the whole economy grow faster. No one denies the importance of attaining a high overall growth rate, but the question to investigate here is: who benefits from the rapid economic growth? Both economic growth and fairness in the distribution of income are desirable. Unfortunately, the two goals are often in conflict with each other. The maximisation of growth could worsen the problem of inequality, whereas the pursuit of equality may slow down national growth. A development strategy should not concern itself simply with the maximisation of one objective at the expense of the other: it has to consider the trade-off between them. However, it is impossible to find out where the optimal point lies, for the problem involves ethical judgements. The study of regional disparity makes it explicit that any development strategy is founded on the basis of a certain ethical principle.

Third, regional disparity is an issue of political significance, because regional economic disparities may have adverse effects on the political stability and unity of the nation. The relation between inequality and political instability is a close one. In countless instances, real and perceived inequities give rise to political conflicts. Inter-regional inequality could be a source of political conflict, just as inequalities between social groups are. Regions are not just geographic and economic entities but also social and political ones. Residents of one region tend to care more about the welfare of other residents than about the welfare of inhabitants of other regions. As a result, there tends to be a widespread sense of grievance among the people living in regions where average incomes are noticeably lower than in other regions of the country, or the incomes are growing noticeably slower. They may regard an insufficiently sympathetic central government as partly responsible for their plight.

Meanwhile, those living in more developed regions are likely to perceive that their economies are the backbone of the nation. If the central government intervenes to correct regional disparities in such a way that the high-income regions have to subsidise the poor ones, then these regions are likely to believe that such fiscal transfers to low-growth regions are just a waste of money because, in their view, trying to sustain inefficient economic activity is irrational. Thus, any attempt to redistribute resources across regions is likely to provoke resistance from rich regions.

In other words, persistent regional disparities may not only frustrate people living in relatively impoverished regions but also alienate those living in affluent regions. History suggests that when regional disparities become excessive, catastrophic political consequences could occur. Especially when ethnic, religious, and linguistic differences are combined with economic disparities, the result could be an explosive situation. Examples include secessionist movements in the Punjab of India; Bougainville of Papua New Guinea; Quebec in Canada; the Lombardy region of Italy; Katanga in Zaire; Biafra in Nigeria; and Scotland, Wales and Northern Ireland in Great Britain. One factor contributing to the disintegration of both the former Yugoslavia and the former Soviet Union was growing income gaps among their ethnically populated republics. In 1993, Mahbub Ul Haq, the principal author of the UNDP's *Human Development Report*, warned that the widening of regional disparities was threatening the unity and stability of seventeen countries. In particular, his team predicted that Rwanda was in danger of disintegration, and Chiapas in Mexico might soon become a trouble spot. Barely before their report came out, troubles occurred in both places. Ul Haq later pointed out:

> Regional disparity is an especially powerful index because poverty itself cannot interpret the disintegration of a county. But if the poor people are concentrated in one region, they can easily be organized, just as in the peasant uprising in the Chiapas region of Mexico. When we were studying Mexico, the data of the Chiapas region was already catching our attention. Although the Mexican government was not happy, we still predicted that the region might become a trouble spot. And it has proved that we are right.

Covering 9.6 million square kilometres, China is the third largest country in the world. Given its gigantic size, it is perhaps inevitable to find significant spatial variations in geographical condition, resource endowment, the sectoral distribution of economic activity, and the level of socioeconomic development. Indeed, the UNDP's *Human Development Report* (1994) listed China as one of the countries in which regional gaps had become excessively large. The UNDP's advice to China in 1994 was that 'it will need to take care that existing regional disparities do not widen further. Thoughtful state intervention will be required to ensure a more equitable distribution of social services.' Given the UNDP's good record in predicting national disintegration elsewhere, its advice should not be taken lightly.

In fact, since the mid-1990s, geographers, economists, sociologists, and political scientists both inside and outside the country have been fiercely debating three issues concerning regional inequality in China:

1   What are the key factors that have contributed to changes in regional disparities?
2   Have China's reforms ameliorated or aggravated existing regional inequalities?
3   Should the Chinese government do anything to narrow regional disparities?

The purpose of this chapter is to explore various key issues in the current debate over the spatial effects of reforms. I begin the analysis by looking at the historical roots of uneven development and initial attempts to address regional imbalance. I then look at how and why regional disparities have widened since 1978. In addition to examining the broad patterns of regional disparities, the chapter investigates both the economic and political factors that have caused these patterns. Until comparatively recently, economics, politics and ethics were seen as parts of an indivisible whole. However, as modern economics evolves, the importance of ethical and political perspectives has substantially weakened. This chapter argues that regional disparity can only be fully understood by applying the perspectives and insights of economics, politics and ethics. That is why, rather than dealing with regional disparity solely from an economic perspective, I take a political economy approach. As well as describing the economic basis of regional disparities, I investigate the political and social factors that have shaped these developments. After doing so, I end the chapter with a brief discussion of institutional prerequisites that are necessary if the government is to ease tensions caused by real and perceived regional gaps.

A historical overview of regional economic development

When the Chinese Communists came to power in 1949, they inherited an extremely lopsided economy. Industrial activities were to a large extent concentrated in what was then called Manchuria (the modern-day northeast provinces of Heilongjiang, Jilin, and Liaoning) and a few major coastal cities such as Shanghai, Xiamen and Guangzhou. Although the coastal provinces accounted for only 11.34 per cent of the land, they were the source of 77.6 per cent of total industrial output. The rest of the country produced only 22.4 per cent of the total industrial output. In particular, western China lagged far behind. Only 8 per cent of the total industrial output originated in this region, despite the fact it took up over half of the country's territory (Sheng and Feng 1991: 666).

Regional development during the Mao years

The new Communist government made a strong commitment to achieving balanced distribution of productive capacity and income. The First Five-Year Plan (1953–7) of the People's Republic gave high priority to the development of new industrial bases in north, northwest and central China. Among the 694 industrial projects built during this period, most were located in the inland areas (Bo 1991:

475). But Mao hoped to see more changes. In his famous 1956 speech, 'On Ten Major Relationships', he again dwelt on the relations between the coast and the interior. In his view, it was both economically irrational and politically unacceptable to keep 70 per cent of industry in the coastal areas while leaving the rest of the country more or less untouched by modernisation. To speed up the industrialisation of the interior, he suggested that new industrial facilities be located in the interior. Only by doing so, he believed, would industrial activities become more evenly distributed.

Indeed, Mao's era was marked by an unprecedented spatial redeployment of productive capacity. Thanks to its strong extractive capacity, the central government under Mao had firm control over the geographic distribution of resources. The investment policy of this period clearly favoured backward regions. While more developed provinces experienced substantial outflows of revenues, less developed provinces received enormous infusions of funds for infrastructure and industrial development.

Moreover, in the mid-1960s, out of security considerations, China began a campaign to construct the Third Front, which covered all western provinces and some parts of the central provinces. From late 1964 to 1971, dozens of large and medium-sized industrial enterprises were moved from coastal provinces to inland provinces, and hundreds more were built on site. Altogether, between 1956 and 1978, more than 2,000 large and medium-sized enterprises were established in west and central China. This shift in investment and the establishment of new industrial centres powerfully boosted industrial growth in the traditionally less developed regions. In 1965, for example, the ratio of agriculture to light industry to heavy industry for central China was 71 : 15 : 14. By the end of the Fourth Five-Year Plan period (1971–75), it had become 44 : 22 : 34. For the same period, the ratio for west China changed from 69 : 16 : 15 to 40 : 23 : 37. In addition to financing investments in less developed regions, fiscal transfers were used to reduce regional inequality in income and the provision of public goods and services (Sheng and Feng 1991: 667). Government transfers made it possible for consumption to be much more evenly distributed than output. As a result, Mao's era witnessed a strong trend toward greater equality in per capita consumption across the country.

In 1978, China changed its policy orientation, shifting the emphasis from equity to efficiency. The years since have marked a period of rapid economic growth and rising living standards that are unprecedented in Chinese history. Equally important, no province has been excluded from the growth club. Every one of China's provinces has experienced substantial real growth in the post-1978 period. While economic conditions have improved in all regions in absolute terms, however, performance in relative terms has varied markedly among the regions.

In the next section, I describe these regional disparities in detail and consider whether China's recent economic reform has ameliorated or contributed to regional disparity.

Changes in regional disparities since 1978

As a vast country, China has always shown significant geographical variation in economic development. In order to examine whether China's market-oriented reform has ameliorated or aggravated existing regional inequality, it is necessary first to identify the indicators of economic development, as well as the methods for measuring regional disparity in economic development.

Measurements of regional disparity

In this chapter, per capita gross domestic product (GDP) is used as the indicator of the overall level of development and well-being. GDP measures the value of the goods and services produced in a region during a given period. Through the production of goods and services, incomes are created. Therefore, the per capita GDP of a region can serve as an estimate of regional economic welfare in much the same way as the per capita GDP of a country can be used to measure national economic welfare.

CALCULATING INDICES OF REGIONAL DISPARITIES

If GDP is used as an estimate of regional welfare, we need to be able to accurately calculate and compare GDP per capita across provinces. Measuring comparative levels of GDP involves use of two indices:

1   standard deviation;
2   the coefficient of variation.

What does each index represent, and how is each calculated?
    If a country were composed of only two regions, the per capita GDP differences between regions A and B could be measured by two methods. One measures 'the absolute gap', or the difference in per capita income between A and B. The other measures 'the relative gap', or the ratio of the per capita income of A to the per capita income of B. When a country has more than two regions, as China does, then summary measures are needed to index the overall absolute and relative gaps. The standard deviation (SD) is the yardstick of the overall absolute regional inequality, and the coefficient of variation (CV) is the yardstick of the overall relative regional inequality. In both indices, a higher value means larger regional differences. The following equations describe how these measurements are calculated.
    If n ($n = 1, 2, 3 \ldots n$) denotes the number of regions and x_i the per capita GDP of the ith region, it is easy to calculate the average per capita GDP in the nation:

$$x = \Sigma x_i / n$$

Then the standard deviation is:

$$SD = [\Sigma (x_i - x)^2 / n]^{1/2}$$

And the coefficient of variation is given by the equation:

$$CV = SD/x$$

Economists normally prefer the relative measure to the absolute measure in depicting trends of regional convergence or divergence. From a political point of view, this may not be a sensible choice, because it is possible for relative disparities to narrow while absolute disparities widen. We take the view that people are more concerned about the absolute difference in economic welfare than about the relative difference. If absolute gaps indeed have a greater effect on people's perceptions of regional disparity and thereby are politically more relevant, it is essential to include an absolute measure in any study of regional disparities.

Once it is known how to measure regional disparities in both relative and absolute senses, it is easier to assess changes in inter-provincial inequality and begin to discern patterns of regional inequality.

Discerning trends of regional development and inequality from 1978 to 2004

Figure 4.1 presents data on per capita GDP in China's 30 provinces for 1978 and 2004, the starting year of the reform and the last year for which data are available, respectively.

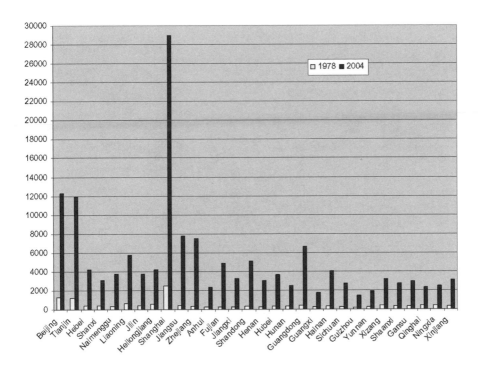

Figure 4.1 Per capita GDP, 1978 and 2004 (1978 constant price)
Source: SSB 2005

As can be gleaned from Figure 4.1, regional gaps existed even before China embarked on reforms. In 1978, per capita GDP in Guizhou, China's poorest province, amounted to only 175 yuan, less than one half of the national average. At the other end of the spectrum, per capita GDP in Shanghai, China's leading industrial centre, was almost seven times the national average and more than fourteen times that of Guizhou. Even if we exclude the three metropolitan centres (Beijing, Tianjin and Shanghai) and compare Guizhou with Liaoning, the fourth richest province, the latter's per capita GDP was still 3.87 times that of the former.

Twenty-six years after the introduction of market-oriented reforms, Shanghai and Guizhou were still China's richest and poorest areas. Moreover, the same areas remained at the very top (Shanghai, Beijing, Tianjin) and very bottom (Guizhou, Guangxi, Yunnan) of the development scale in both 1978 and 2004. However, this does not mean that the regional pattern of economic development has not changed in the intervening years. Figure 4.1 also clearly indicates that coastal provinces, such as Guangdong, Zhejiang, Jiangsu, Fujian and Shandong, were able to make much headway during the reform period. Consequently, an unmistakable geographical pattern of regional inequality has emerged: the coastal provinces are better off than the central provinces, which, in turn, have surpassed the western provinces.

Figure 4.2   Coastal, central and western regions of China

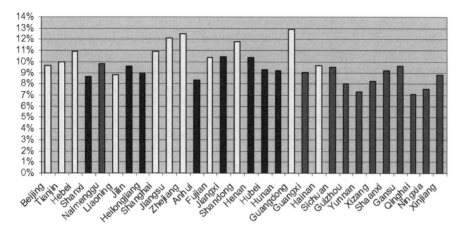

Figure 4.3 Average growth rates of per capita GDP, 1978–2004

Source: SSB 2005

Figure 4.2 categorises China's provinces into these coastal, central and western regions.

It is, of course, impossible to discern any long-term trends by looking at figures for two years, twenty-six years apart. We therefore turn from the starting and ending points of the study to looking at the whole 26-year period. Since a province's growth rate is the most important factor that affects changes in its relative position within the nation as a whole, we start with an examination of regional growth differences. The growth rates for all provinces over the 26-year period are presented in Figure 4.3.

Figure 4.3 reports the average annual growth rates of real per capita GDP in thirty provinces and municipalities from 1978 to 2004. All seem to have grown rapidly. Even the slowest-growing province, Qinghai, was able to grow at 7.04 per cent annually, a respectable growth rate for any economy. However, provincial growth rates diverge widely around the national average (9.63 per cent), varying from 7.04 to 12.93 per cent. In general, the growth rates of western provinces were relatively low. In none of them did annual growth rate exceed 10 per cent. The growth rates of most western provinces were below 9 per cent. In contrast, the fastest growth rates were all observed in coastal provinces (Zhejiang, Guangdong, Fujian, Jiangsu, Hainan and Shandong). Central provinces tended to grow more slowly than coastal provinces but faster than western provinces.

HOW IS PER CAPITA GDP DISPERSED ACROSS REGIONS?

Since our main interest in this study is changes in the distribution of per capita GDP across regions, we now turn our attention to investigating whether China's market-oriented reform has reduced the dispersion of per capita GDP. Figure 4.4 plots two measures of relative dispersion. Both are coefficients of variation (CV) of per capita GDP (in 1978 constant price).

The top and bottom curves of Figure 4.4 differ only in sample size: the former includes Beijing, Tianjin and Shanghai, whereas the latter excludes the three cities. We separate the two curves for a simple reason: although the three metropolitan areas enjoy provincial status, it would be problematic to treat them in the same way as we treat the rest of the provinces, because they are far more urbanised and industrialised than the others. As a result, they enjoy extraordinarily high levels of per capita GDP relative to the national average. For this reason, treating these metropolitan areas as ordinary provinces may greatly bias our analysis of regional disparities. In order to present an unbiased picture, it is necessary to segregate two sets of statistics – one including the three cities and the other excluding them. As Figure 4.4 reveals, changes in regional disparities display different patterns when the three cities are excluded.

The top curve represents changing coefficients of variation for the whole nation during the period 1978–2004. The time path yields a U curve. In other words, relative dispersion declined sharply between 1978 and 1990–91, but the falling trend was reversed afterwards. The years since 1991 have witnessed an upsurge in regional inequality. As noted, a higher CV means greater relative disparities.

The bottom curve (excluding figures for Beijing, Tianjin, and Shanghai) yields two noteworthy changes in coefficients of variation. First, the CV becomes much smaller. Rather than fluctuating between 0.80 and 1.05, it now oscillates in the neighbourhood of 0.35–0.45. In other words, once extreme cases are excluded, relative dispersion in per capita GDP does not appear to be alarmingly large in China. Second, the patterns of change in CV are different. Regional dispersion decreased only marginally in the initial years of reform, but the years following 1985 saw a steady increase in relative dispersion, especially after 1991. Conse-

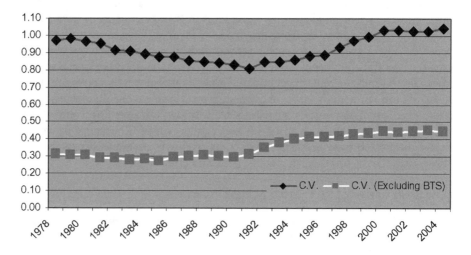

Figure 4.4 Coefficient of variance of regional per capita GDP, 1978–2004

Source: SSB 2005

quently, the CV at the end of the period was 0.14 percentage points higher than that in 1978 (increasing from 0.31 to 0.45).

Mainstream economists have long argued that regional disparity is an abnormal phenomenon that will not last. Although there is no way for them to deny the presence and persistence of spatial inequality in many parts of the world, they envision a long-term trend toward inter-regional equality. In 1965, Jeffrey Williamson published an article titled 'Regional Inequality and the Process of National Development: A Description of the Patterns'. Drawing on a large set of cross-sectional and time series data, Williamson identified 'a systematic relationship between national development levels and regional inequality', or an inverted 'U' in the national growth path; that is, regional gaps tended to increase in earlier stages of development and to diminish in later stages. Since then, the inverted-U-shaped pattern of regional development has often been called 'the Williamson law'.

China, however, does *not* support Williamson's inverted U hypothesis. Neither of the two curves in Figure 4.4 is inverted-U-shaped. Instead, they reveal that, as market forces play a bigger and bigger role in Chinese economy, regional inequality has worsened.

When relative dispersion grows, it is impossible for absolute dispersion to narrow. Figure 4.5 makes this abundantly clear. Here, the absolute dispersion of per capita GDP is measured by standard deviation (SD). The figure again plots two sets of SDs, one covering all the provinces and the other excluding Beijing, Tianjin and Shanghai. Both curves point to the same conclusion: absolute dispersion increased continuously throughout the whole period and accelerated after 1991.

To sum up the above findings, it seems fair to divide the years after 1978 into three sub-periods. Before 1985, the general trend was for relative dispersion to diminish. Even though absolute dispersion was still on the rise, it increased at a slow pace. The early trend came to a halt during the second half of the 1980s. The

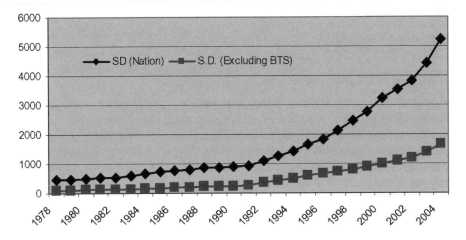

Figure 4.5 Standard deviation of per capita GDP, 1978–2004
Source: SSB 2005

overall relative dispersion continued to fall if the three centrally administered metropolises were included. However, once we controlled for the effects of the three extreme cases, a different picture emerged: the relative dispersion among the rest of the provinces began to grow, albeit only marginally. In the meantime, the absolute dispersion was increasing at a faster rate than it had been. After 1991, there was strong evidence of a secular increase in regional disparity, no matter which measure was used and whether or not the three big cities were counted. Having experienced convergence from the late 1970s to the early 1980s and stabilisation in the degree of regional inequality in the second half of the 1980s, China seems to have entered a period of divergence.

DISPARITIES BETWEEN HAN CHINESE PROVINCES AND ETHNIC MINORITY PROVINCES

Although Chapter 7 of this book is devoted to the topic of minority nationalities, a few words may be in order here about economic disparities between Han Chinese and minority nationalities. In China, five 'minority' provinces are designated as autonomous regions (Tibet, Xinjiang, Inner Mongolia, Guangxi and Ningxia). In addition, in three provinces (Yunnan, Guizhou, and Qinghai) minority nationalities comprise over one-third of the population. In 1978, among these eight provinces, only Qinghai enjoyed a level of per capita GDP higher than that of the national average. Tibet and Ningxia were below the average but came close to it. The other five were well below the national average. During the reform period, however, Qinghai and Ningxia were among the slowest growing provinces. The other minority-concentrated provinces did not do well either. Except for Xinjiang, their annual growth rates of real per capita GDP were all lower than the national average. As a result, all minority-concentrated provinces, except Xinjiang, found their relative positions in the nation worsened. And, by 2000, in none of the eight provinces was per capita GDP higher than the national average. The huge gaps between minority-concentrated areas and Han areas have led a professor at the South-Central Institute of Ethnology to conclude: 'In the final analysis, regional disparities in today's China are disparities between Han areas along the east coast and minority-concentrated areas in the west' (Yang 1996).

Intra-provincial inequality

In addition to inter-provincial differences, intra-provincial variations have been characteristic of China. In a country where a province often has the size of a territory and a population comparable to that of a middle-sized country, substantial intra-provincial inequality is to be expected. A county in a rich province, for instance, is not necessarily rich. The broad picture delineated by aggregate data may mask sharp internal variations. Thus, studying intra-provincial disparities may help us identify conditions and trends disguised by aggregate data.

To illustrate intra-provincial variations, regional variations within Guizhou and Guangdong can be analysed. Due to space and data limitations, I focus only on one year – 2000. Although Guangdong is about the same size as Guizhou, its population was more than twice as large. In its level of economic development, Guizhou fell far behind Guangdong, with total GDP reaching only 10.4 per cent of

Guangdong's. In 2000, Guizhou's per capita GDP was the lowest in China, whereas Guangdong's was among the highest.

Despite the big differences between the two provinces, Table 4.1 shows that they shared two common features. First, relative dispersion was very large *across counties* in each province. The coefficients of variation of per capita GDP were as high as 1.04 in Guizhou and 0.75 in Guangdong, both of which were higher than the corresponding CV measuring inter-provincial inequality in the same year when Beijing, Tianjin and Shanghai were excluded. The ratio of the richest county/city to the poorest county/city was approximately 23 : 1 in Guizhou and 18 : 1 in Guangdong. Second, absolute dispersion was even more striking. The standard deviation of per capita GDP was 3,144 yuan in Guizhou and 5,878 yuan in Guangdong. The difference in per capita GDP between the richest county/district and the poorest county/district was 18,618 yuan in Guizhou and 29,824 yuan in Guangdong.

The two cases reveal that significant regional inequalities may be found within poor as well as rich provinces. From the standpoint of the nation, Guangdong was one of China's most rapidly growing provinces during the period 1978–2000 and, by 2000, one of China's most affluent provinces. Yet, there were considerable variations even within such an advanced province. The two cases also hint that changes in regional disparities observed at the county level may not correspond to those at the provincial level. Therefore, anyone who studies China's regional disparities should not lose sight of the importance of intra-provincial inequalities.

Table 4.1 Intra-provincial inequality: Guizhou and Guangdong, 2000

	Guizhou	Guangdong
Number of counties/districts	87	122
Min* (yuan)	832	1 789
Max (yuan)	19 450	31 613
Mean (yuan)	3 016	7 847
SD (yuan)	3 144	5 878
CV	1.04	0.75
Max/Min	23.38	17.67
Max–Min (yuan)	18 618	29 824

Source: SSB 2001
* Here 'Min' (minimum) means the average income of the poorest county in a province. Similarly, 'Max' (maximum) means the average income of the richest country in a province.

The economic causes of uneven regional development

Regional disparities persist because growth rates of output have varied widely across regions. As shown in the last section, growth rates across China's thirty provinces exhibit tremendous variance and some regional economies have grown much faster than others. Why have growth rates differed? What have been the factors underlying differential economic growth performances among provinces? These questions are addressed in this section.

It goes without saying that economic growth is governed by many determinants – economic, social, political, and cultural. However, if these diverse factors are to affect economic growth positively, they must somehow help either increase the supply of factor inputs (mainly capital and labour) or enhance factor productivity. Thus, to arrive at an understanding of the factors behind the growth of output, we must first identify the immediate economic sources of growth. I argue that the acceleration in capital investment is the most important engine of growth for all Chinese provinces.

Proximate sources of output growth

Any explanation of growth variations in China needs to consider the cause and effect links between proximate growth and ultimate growth. What is meant by 'proximate' and 'ultimate' growth? To understand these terms, it is necessary to first assume that any growth in output is generated by growth in input, or by gains in the efficiency with which the inputs are used, or by some combination of the two. Two types of input are indispensable for output growth, labour input and physical capital input. Increases in input or gains in efficiency that result in output growth are called the 'proximate' sources of growth. In this section, we are most concerned with examining the proximate sources of growth as an explanation of differential growth in provinces. Other factors that may determine growth (such as governmental policy, religious beliefs, attitudes toward income and leisure, the international environment) enhance or hinder the proximate sources of growth. These other factors are known as the 'ultimate' causes of growth.

In the last decade or so, economists in China and elsewhere have conducted extensive research trying to break down the proximate sources of output growth and examine the contributions of labour and capital to output. They generally arrive at two principal conclusions.

First, the contribution of labour input to economic growth was insignificant in China. Here, labour input is measured not only by the total number of working persons but also by such indicators of labour quality as the age and gender composition and the educational and health profiles of the labour force. A World Bank study, for instance, attributed only about 17 per cent of growth to improvements in both quantity and quality of the labour force in the Chinese economy as a whole (World Bank 1997). An abundant labour supply may explain the relatively small contribution of labour in China. It is intuitively plausible that, in a capital-scarce and labour-abundant economy, the injection of more human resources would not increase output very significantly and rapidly.

Second, rapid capital accumulation alone can account for a very substantial part of GDP growth for each and every province of China. This finding confirms the central importance of capital accumulation for growth at early stages of economic development, a position held by such prominent economists as Domar (1947), Harrod (1948), Lewis (1955) and Rostow (1960). It is also consistent with the results of many empirical studies of economic growth. Furthermore, the role of capital in the explanation of growth in China was very similar to that found in other East Asian economies and in developing countries at large.

Figure 4.6 shows average growth rates for per capita GDP and investment for the period 1985–2004 in all provinces. Although there are some exceptions (such as in Guangxi and Yunnan), higher rates of investment generally correlate with higher GDP rates.

In addition to increasing the stock of physical capital, capital investment may generate technological progress. Given that most technological progress requires a substantial investment of resources, we would expect that an acceleration of the pace of capital accumulation, by reducing the age of the capital stock, speeds the rate at which embodied technical progress can be incorporated into production. Indeed, numerous studies have established that investment in physical capital is the principal means by which new technology enters the production process (e.g. Lau 1996; Romer 1990; Grossman and Helpman 1991; Barro and Sala-i-Martin 1994). In particular, foreign investment may embody more advanced production technology and management practice than domestic investment does.

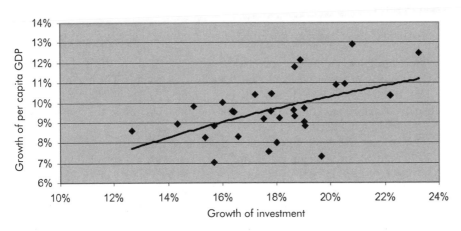

Figure 4.6 Average growth rates of per capita GDP and investment, 1985–2004

Source: SSB 2005

Sources of capital accumulation

Since capital investment is the key to economic growth, regions with greater capital mobilisation capacity are expected to grow faster. Why then has gross investment increased at much faster rates in some provinces than in others?

By China's official definition (SSB 2001), capital investment is financed from one of the following five sources of funds or their combinations:

1   state budgetary appropriation;
2   domestic bank loans;
3   self-raised funds;
4   other domestic funds;
5   foreign capital.

We may reclassify these sources of capital investment into three broad categories:

1   local capital;
2   capital inflow from, or outflow to, other provinces;
3   foreign capital.

By definition, capital investment in a province depends on its ability to mobilise local capital, to obtain capital imports from other provinces, and to attract foreign capital. If variations in capital investment between provinces are to be explained, we need to understand why some provinces are more capable of mobilising local capital and of obtaining capital inflows from other provinces and from other countries.

Local capital

Local capital refers to capital originating within the province. Data show that the volumes of investment and the volumes of saving were highly correlated in all the provinces of China. Such a high correlation suggests that domestic investments in most provinces were predominantly financed by local savings. The higher the local savings, the higher the local domestic investment. To put it differently, a high level of provincial domestic investment was not possible unless the province was able to achieve a higher level of local savings.

What were the determinants of local savings? Empirical studies found that the income level was a major predictor. There was a strong correlation between the saving rate (saving/GDP) and per capita GDP for China's provinces. As per capita GDP grew, the saving rate increased in almost all provinces. And, at any given moment, provinces with higher per capita GDP tended to enjoy higher saving rates. With both higher per capita GDP and higher savings rates, obviously, rich provinces were in a much better position to mobilise funds and to invest in their local economies.

Inter-province capital inflow/outflow

If a country is the unit of analysis, a high level of domestic investment is only possible with a commensurate high level of domestic savings. For the regions within a country, however, such a relationship is expected to be much weaker, because the central government may play a strong redistributive role, allocating funds across regions through fiscal transfers, and/or because capital movement between regions is supposed to face fewer barriers in the context of a national economy than in an international context. Thus, it is possible for a region with a relatively low level of savings to invest at a much higher level, as long as it is able to obtain and/or attract capital inflows from other regions.

In China just as in other countries, there were certainly times when capital moved from one province to another. Which provinces were 'exporters' of capital? Which provinces were recipients of capital imports? The direction of inter-provincial capital flows may be gauged by examining data on 'net export', defined as the difference between a province's total savings and the total investment in the province. If a province saves more than it invests locally, it is investing outside of the province. Conversely, if the total amount of investment in a province exceeds its total savings, it must have received capital imports from somewhere else.

Capital is expected to flow from relatively advanced provinces to less developed provinces. This was found to be true in the early years of reform. Between 1978 and 1984, the provincial ratios of net export to GDP had fairly strong correlations with their per capita GDPs, which meant that rich provinces were exporting capital to poor provinces during this period. After reform programmes were introduced into urban areas in 1984, however, the correlation between the two variables significantly weakened. By the middle and late 1990s, there was virtually no correlation between the two variables at all (Wang and Hu 1999: 162–3). In other words, although there were still capital-surplus and capital-deficit provinces, the level of development could no longer serve as a predictor of whether a province was a capital exporter or a capital recipient.

China's market-oriented reform not only changed the direction of inter-provincial capital flows but also substantially reduced its volume. When the reform started in the late 1970s, there appeared to be a massive inter-provincial movement of capital. Capital outflow from Shanghai, for instance, amounted to nearly 60 per cent of its GDP for the period 1978–80. Meanwhile, Qinghai and Ningxia received capital inflows that were equivalent to about 40 per cent of their GDPs. Inter-provincial movement of capital began to slow down in the 1980s. Proportionally, capital-surplus provinces exported much less than they used to.

Consequently, capital-deficit provinces were no longer able to obtain as much help from other provinces as before. By the early1990s, capital seemed to have become very 'sticky', tending to stay where it was originally generated. Except for Shanghai, no province now exported more than 10 per cent of its GDP to other provinces. At the same time, only five provinces were still able to receive capital imports that amounted to more than 15 per cent of their GDPs. Four of them (Tibet, Qinghai, Ningxia and Xinjiang) happened to be minority-concentrated autonomous regions (Wang and Hu 1999: 164–5).

The most important change in inter-provincial capital movement during the reform period, especially after the mid-1980s, seems to be that all provinces had become financially more independent. Rich provinces now did not have to transfer much locally generated savings to other provinces. Several rich provinces, such as Beijing and Tianjian, had actually become net recipients of capital from other provinces. With more capital left at their disposal, the rich provinces' ability to increase local investment was undoubtedly strengthened. Poor provinces were forced to become financially more self-reliant. As capital inflows from other provinces dwindled, they had to rely increasingly on local savings to finance local investments. Given their relatively low per capita GDP and low saving rates (and thereby per capita saving), poor provinces were unlikely to achieve as high rates of capital accumulation as rich provinces were.

Foreign capital

Whereas foreign capital was completely absent in pre-reform China, its role has become increasingly visible after 1978. In the early years of reform, foreign capital came mainly in the form of grants and loans from foreign governments, international organisations, and international capital markets. At that time, the central government played a dominant role in allocating foreign capital. Since the promulgation of the Provisions for the Encouragement of Foreign Investment in late 1986, foreign direct investment (FDI) has been growing continuously. Especially after 1991, China has become the largest recipient of FDI among all developing countries. As FDI inflows surpassed the combination of foreign grants and loans, the share of foreign capital channelled directly to provinces has increased sharply in the last decade.

All provinces welcomed foreign investment, because it would augment their capital and investment stocks. But not all of them were equally successful in attracting foreign investors. As Figure 4.7 shows, the spatial distribution of foreign capital in China was highly uneven.

Of the total accumulated amount of foreign capital that China's provinces received up to 2000, Guangdong Province alone took nearly 30 per cent. Fujian, Shandong, Jiangsu, Zhejiang, Shanghai and other coastal provinces were also able to attract substantial amounts of foreign capital. In contrast, the records of inland provinces were rather poor. Altogether, they received 18 per cent of foreign capital.

What were the determinants of the spatial distribution of foreign capital in China? Two factors have been identified as the most important. One is market size measured by provincial GDP. The greater the local market, the greater the opportunity for foreign investors to make profit and the higher the incentive for them to invest. The other is preferential policy. From the very beginning, China's foreign investment regime has been 'heavily slanted in favor of cities along the coast' (Broadman and Sun 1997: 8). For instance, for quite a long time, only coastal provinces were allowed to provide fiscal incentives for foreign investors. Even among coastal provinces, some (e.g. Guangdong) enjoyed a more generous package of incentives than others. Thus, it is not surprising that the provinces that can offer

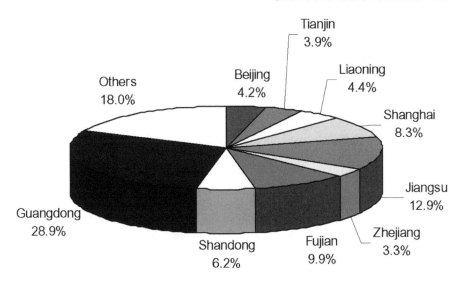

Figure 4.7 FDI distribution by region, as of 2000

Source: SSB 2001.

generous incentive programmes tend to attract more foreign capital (Wang and Hu 1999: 155–62).

In summary, in China, a province's investment depended on three sources of capital: local savings, capital inflows from (or capital outflows to) other provinces, and foreign savings. Local savings were primarily determined by the level of economic development. Therefore, advanced provinces had a decisive edge in mobilising local savings over other provinces. This advantage was discounted in the early years of reform, because at that time advanced provinces had to export substantial proportions of their local savings to relatively poor provinces. However, as reform proceeded, they were allowed to keep more and more local savings to themselves. As a result, their ability to increase local investment was strengthened at the expense of poor provinces that used to benefit from inter-provincial capital flows. Moreover, it was precisely the same provinces with relatively strong ability in mobilising local savings that were in foreign investors' good graces.

The political causes of uneven regional development

The previous section raises two crucial questions, but leaves them unanswered. Why did inter-provincial capital flows plunge in the course of economic reform? Why were coastal provinces able to find favour in the eyes of foreign investors? To answer these questions, this section turns to political factors that affected the direction of capital flows. In particular, we analyse how the central government's regional preference and extractive capacity affect the spatial distribution of investment resources and ultimately the growth potential of different provinces.

Government intervention: revenue collection vs egalitarianism

In a world where government intervention was absent, capital would presumably move across regions to seek no objective other than the maximisation of its return. And the direction of capital movement would be determined only by such economic factors as regional climate and terrain, endowment in natural resources, geographic location, infrastructure, the quality of the labour force, market size, and so on. However, no such world exists. In no country is capital mobilisation and allocation completely left to the free play of pure economic forces. Every government in the world pursues some sort of regional development policy by guiding or inducing capital investment in a certain direction. This is especially true in China, a country where central planning once prevailed. Since government plays an important role in facilitating or restraining capital mobility, any story about regional disparities in capital accumulation would be seriously incomplete without taking into consideration the role of government policies or political factors.

Although many have argued that government intervention is essential for narrowing regional disparities, it should be made clear at the outset that government intervention as such does not necessarily help to achieve that goal. In fact, government policies could result in regional convergence just as they could lead to divergence. Whether government intervention will alleviate spatial inequality depends on two variables: the government's willingness to keep regional gaps from growing, and its ability to affect capital flows moving in the direction that would benefit poor regions.

Strictly speaking, all governments want to see the narrowing of regional gaps, as long as it does not involve any cost. If it is believed that regional policies would somehow lower the overall efficiency of their economies, however, some governments may become less willing to trade more equality for less efficiency. Especially if a government subscribes to the logic of the 'trickling down' thesis, it will favour maximal aggregate economic growth and tolerate regional inequality. When the political will to promote balanced regional development is lacking, it is unlikely that the government will allocate capital investment to areas where conditions are not deemed most suitable for high growth.

Even if a government has a strong commitment to egalitarianism, it may still not be able to reduce regional inequality unless it is capable of mobilising, aggregating, and directing the requisite resources to fulfil the goal. In any society, in order to advance its chosen goals, regardless of what those goals may be, the state must overcome the resistance of various groups with competing priorities. Since revenue is an absolute requirement for formulating and implementing any policy, the bottom line is whether the government is able to extract enough resources from the population and allocate them according to its preferences in the face of societal resistance. Without such resources, governments simply cannot govern. Only with adequate resources at its disposal can the government function. The more resources are available to a state, the more options it will have, and the more capable it will become. A capable government can resolve the challenges associated with development far more effectively than a less capable government can under similar circumstances.

As far as regional development is concerned, the role of central government should be emphasised. Provincial governments may be able to reduce regional disparities within their jurisdictions. However, they cannot be entrusted with the task of narrowing gaps between provinces. If decision-making were left to provincial governments, the only possible result would be a pattern of resource allocation that simply reflects existing economic disparities. Only the central government may have an incentive to change the pattern by redistributing resources between rich and poor regions. But the central government's ability to perform the function of redistribution crucially depends on its ability to generate revenue. Its financial strength is the economic base for it to implement regional policy. If there are severe fiscal constraints on the number of transfers that the central government is able to direct, its regional policy cannot be very effective, no matter how strong its commitment to egalitarianism may be.

It is therefore worthwhile to briefly examine how alternative policy regimes have affected regional disparities.

Mao's China (1949–76)

By and large, the central government enjoyed considerable control over the distribution of resources during the Maoist era. The fiscal system was so arranged that rich provinces had to remit large proportions of their revenues to the central government, and poor provinces were allowed to retain all their revenues and receive additional direct subsidies from the central government. Acting as a redistributor, the central government could use fiscal transfers to influence the inter-regional flows of resources.

However, this image of the state strongly intervening in capital flows for the entire pre-reform period disguises the variations of central extractive capacity in these years. In fact, four sub-periods within the Mao years can be identified, based on the state's centralised extractive capacity:

1   In the early years of the People's Republic (between 1949 and 1956), the Chinese central government greatly strengthened its extractive capacity.
2   Between 1957 and 1960, Mao introduced his first decentralisation drive, which resulted in a sharp decline in central extractive capacity.
3   The period 1961–6 was one of recovery, during which Beijing recentralised fiscal power and strengthened its extractive capacity.
4   In the first two years of the Cultural Revolution (from late 1966 to the end of 1968), China was in total chaos. While Mao enjoyed absolute personal power, the state lacked the basic ability to exert social control, much less to direct economic development. Public authorities were restored in 1969. But, soon after, Mao initiated yet another decentralisation drive, which again weakened the centre's extractive capacity.

Numerous studies have established that regional disparities in China narrowed somewhat between 1953 and 1957 and in the early 1960s but widened during the Great Leap Forward (1958–60) and the Cultural Revolution (1966–76). In other words, regional inequality and central capacity were moving in precisely the opposite direction: increasing disparities coincided with declining extractive capacity while decreasing disparities were associated with growing state capacity. Such a relationship is by no means surprising. During the Maoist era, the central government pursued its regional objectives mainly through inter-regional transfers of investment resources. Only with stronger central capacity was greater flow of fiscal transfers from richer to poorer regions possible, which was essential to reduce variations in development across provinces. Conversely, decline of the central financial strength was unfavourable for controlling regional disparities.

Policy changes and regional inequality in the reform period

After Mao's death in 1976, his regional development strategy was criticised as too costly in comparative advantage, production efficiency, and national growth forgone. Underlying the reform that followed was a fundamental transformation of development philosophy. Chinese policy-makers thus gave top priority to rapid aggregate growth. This predominant concern with growth made them less willing to sacrifice growth for such goals as balance and equity. Instead, they were ready to tolerate a certain degree of inequality or widened disparity. It was believed that if certain regions were allowed to prosper first, their affluence would eventually trickle down to other regions.

Whereas in the West, believers of the 'trickle-down' theory generally hold that government should not intervene in the course of economic development, their Chinese counterparts actually advocated government intervention on behalf of more developed regions. In their view, China, as a developing country, had to make the best use of extremely scarce capital. Therefore, it was necessary for the government to concentrate investment resources where conditions were most suitable for growth.

Since the coastal provinces enjoyed considerable advantages at the beginning of the reform period (a large number of skilled workers, a high level of technology and managerial sophistication, and relatively well-developed infrastructure), these areas received the state's economic blessing. These provinces also had much easier access to foreign trade and the closest ties to overseas Chinese, an important source of capital and business know-how. Concentrating investment resources in these areas clearly offered the prospect of much more rapid aggregate growth than spreading resources thinly or investing in interior areas where the preconditions for modern growth were still lacking.

The 'gradient theory' of development

For these reasons, a so-called 'gradient theory' (*tidu lilun*) dominated the thinking of Chinese policy-makers for much of the 1980s. The theory divided China into three large geographic regions – the eastern (coastal), central, and western – and likened them to steps on a ladder. According to the 'theory', the government should capitalise on the advantages of the coast first. Only after the coast became sufficiently developed should attention be turned to the central region. The western region, however, would have to wait patiently for its turn. If this strategy had unfavourable implications for equity, its advocates advised people to consider its effects in the long term. In the long term, the 'theory' promised, the fruit of development would eventually come down to everyone in the country.

In the pre-reform period, nearly two-thirds of state capital investment went to the central and western provinces, whereas the coastal provinces received only 36 per cent. After 1979, the centre of gravity in state capital investment shifted from the interior to the coast. In the period 1979–91, for instance, the coastal region as a whole received over half of all state capital investment, while the interior's share shrank to about 43 per cent. The western region suffered the greatest loss, its share falling more than 7 per cent. At the provincial level, while the shares of nearly all coastal provinces went up, the shares of most interior provinces fell. The interior provinces whose shares did not drop tended to be minority-concentrated autonomous regions, for which the central government might have offered special assistance (Wang and Hu 1999: 175–7).

As anyone could imagine, competition for central investment among the provinces was extremely keen, as the pressure for rapid growth was building up during the reform period. The emergent distribution pattern of state capital investment, however, did not show any egalitarian strand that would narrow the gap in investment resources between needy provinces and their richer counterparts. Instead, provinces that had greater resource mobilisation capacity were placed in advantageous positions in the race for central investment. Such a location bias of central investment can be explained only by the central government's policy preference.

Preferential investment policies for coastal areas

The new leadership's growth-first strategy was also reflected in its decisions to open up certain areas along the coast to foreign investors and grant them preferential treatment in varying degrees:

- *Special Economic Zones* (SEZ). In 1980, four SEZs were created in Shenzhen, Zhuhai, and Shantou in Guangdong Province, and Xiamen in Fujian Province. In 1988, Hainan Island was separated from Guangdong Province and the entire island was designated the fifth SEZ. In 1990, Shanghai's Pudong was also granted similar special privileges enjoyed by SEZs.
- *Coastal Open Cities* (COC). In 1984, the government decided to open fourteen coastal cities to foreign investors. They included nearly all the major port cities along China's coast, stretching from Dalian in Liaoning in the north to Beihai in Guangxi in the south.
- *Economic and Technological Development Zones* (ETDZ). From 1984 to 1988, twelve ETDZs were established near some of the open cities. After 1992, an additional eighteen ETDZs were set up. All thirty ETDZs were located in coastal provinces except one each in Jilin, Heilongjiang, Hubei, Anhui and Sichuan.

- *Coastal Economic Open Zones* (CEOZ). Between 1985 and 1988, five huge CEOZs were created in the Yangzi, Pearl, and Yellow River deltas, southern Fujian and Liaodong Peninsula. Altogether, they covered 260 cities and counties.
- *Customs-Free Zones* (CFZ). From 1990 to 1993, the government approved the establishment of thirteen CFZs in Liaoning, Tianjin, Shanghai, Jiangsu, Zhejiang, Fujian, Shandong, Hainan and Guangdong.

To encourage foreign investment on the coast, the central government gave coastal areas special autonomy in a wide range of economic decisions, including the authority to approve large-scale investment projects, the freedom to grant tax concessions to foreign investors, and the right to retain a higher proportion of earned foreign exchange. These privileges enabled coastal areas to offer more incentives to potential investors than interior areas could achieve. Combined with the coast's naturally and historically advantaged position, these policies ensured that much of China's foreign investment took place along the coast.

In sum, the bias of the top policy-makers explained why the central government poured an increasing proportion of its own investment resources into coastal provinces and why it went out of its way to help the same provinces to lure foreign investment. The large influx of investment resources in turn made it possible for coastal provinces to grow at faster rates than others did. There is little doubt that the central government's pro-coastal bias was an important factor contributing to the worsening of regional inequality.

The central government's policy preference is indeed a fairly good predictor of changes in regional disparities in the 1980s. Although the 'growth-first' philosophy has served as China's guiding principle for development since 1978, the central government's policy has not been hard and fast. Rather, several minor and major changes occurred in the government's development strategy, which somehow coincided with changes in regional disparities depicted by the bottom curve of Figure 4.4.

The shift of regional development priority began as soon as Deng Xiaoping consolidated his power in 1978. In the last three years (1978–80) of China's Fifth Five-Year Plan, coastal provinces' shares of state investment steadily increased. During the following Sixth Five-Year Plan period (1981–5), China officially adopted a pro-coastal policy programme. Yet, old ideas died hard. The remnants of the previous balanced development strategy could still be seen in the new plan. Although its main goal was to accelerate the development of the coastal region, the importance of bringing along the interior provinces was not entirely ignored. Nevertheless, coastal provinces' shares of state investment continued to grow in the period. The same period also witnessed the introduction and expansion of the 'open-door' policy, which primarily benefited southern coastal provinces. The fast growth of these provinces rapidly narrowed the gaps between southern coastal (e.g. Guangdong and Fujian) and eastern coastal provinces (e.g. Shanghai, Jiangsu and Zhejiang) regions, thus leading to the reduction of overall regional disparities in the early 1980s.

In the second half of the 1980s, the central policy-makers' pro-coastal policy orientation became more pronounced. The 'gradient theory' discussed above became the cornerstone of China's Seventh Five-Year Plan (1986–90). For the first time, the government divided China into three regions: coastal, central and western. According to the plan, the investment priority for the rest of the twentieth century would be placed on the coast. The central region might be allocated some investment resources in energy and raw materials in so far as they were necessary for supporting the development of the coast. As far as the western region was concerned, its development would have to be 'postponed', at least for the time being. The Chinese government's pro-coastal policy orientation was further strengthened in 1988 when it announced an explicit 'coastal development strategy'. To speed up the country's aggregate growth, the government now decided to open the whole coastal strip to foreign investors. Coastal provinces were even encouraged to seek their raw materials from foreign sources and sell their products to the world market, though doing so might run a risk of severing their links with interior provinces. As is clearly shown in Figure 4.2, the central government's strong pro-coastal bias in the late part of the 1980s resulted in the worsening of regional disparities.

Policy shifts in the 1990s

The widening regional gaps gave rise to criticism of the government's pro-coastal bias in the late 1980s and early 1990s, which forced the government to adjust its policies when preparing the Eighth Five-Year Plan period (1991–5). The 'gradient theory' was quietly abandoned. Although the government still vowed to continue its pro-coastal development strategy, it began to recognise the importance of preventing regional gaps from becoming excessively large. As a result, numerous interior development zones were established, and dozens of interior cities designated as 'open cities' in the early 1990s. Another major adjustment was to switch the focus of coastal development from the south coast (Guangdong and Fujian) to the east coast (Shanghai and the Yangtze River Delta).

Deng Xiaoping endorsed the second change but viewed the first as unnecessary. During his famous 1992 tour to south China, for instance, he warned: 'Do not throw obstacles in the way of areas that can grow fast. Areas with the potential for fast growth should be encouraged to develop as rapidly as they can' (Deng 1992). In his view, it was unwise to tackle the issue of regional disparities too early. He suggested China wait until the end of this century before putting this issue on the agenda.

However, the regions that had been left behind could not wait any longer. At the annual sessions of the National People's Congress in 1993 and 1994, more representatives from interior provinces, especially those from the west, began to express their grievances with the planning bias. In 1994, a report by the State Planning Commission sounded a serious warning that if problems caused by growing regional gaps were not settled properly, they might one day become a threat to China's social stability and national unity. Facing growing pressure from interior provinces, the central government finally decided to reverse its coastal development strategy in 1995. The new guiding principle was to 'create conditions for gradually narrowing down regional gaps'. This principle was embodied in China's Ninth Five-Year Plan (1996–2000), which promised to increase central support to the less-developed regions in the central and western parts of the country. In September 1999, China formally launched the Western Development Programme (*Xibu da kaifa*).

The Western Development Programme

The Western Development Programme is aimed at gradually narrowing the socio-economic gaps between the coastal provinces and the western provinces. Given the huge existing gaps, it is unrealistic to expect that these disparities will disappear overnight. At present, the best China can do is to halt the trend of growing regional gaps. It may take several years before the trends can be reversed, and at least fifteen to thirty years before the regional gaps can be substantially reduced. The key aim of the Western Development Programme is to improve the development potential of the western region. Western provinces have been poor because many preconditions of modern growth, such as transportation and communications facilities, power and water supply, and human resources, are lacking. Thus, to promote faster economic growth in the western region, the Chinese government focuses on three things (www.chinawest.gov.cn):

1   improving infrastructure;
2   improving education;
3   facilitating factor mobility.

In the final analysis, any regional policy that cannot generate a process of self-sustaining economic growth in lagging areas should be regarded as a failure. However, indigenous development is possible only if backward regions are able to attract new economic activities. The improvement of infrastructure and education will certainly create more attractive conditions for such activities to come in, but such a change alone is hardly sufficient. External capital, for instance, will not flock to less-developed regions simply because infrastructure facilities and human resources are as good as those available in the developed areas. To facilitate the mobility of production factors (capital, technology, labour and talent) in ways beneficial to the western regions, the central and provincial governments have gone out of their way to lure Chinese and overseas business establishments to set up or relocate plants in the lagging region. Measures of inducement include, among others, locating central projects in western provinces to serve as a generator of expansion, offering preferential taxation policy to both domestic and foreign investors, creating a friendly environment for investment, and so on.

The following websites provide further information on the Western Development Programme and details of specific development and investment projects in the western provinces:

- www.chinawest.gov.cn
- www.xbdkf.com
- www.tdctrade.com/gowest

Declining central extractive capacity

At this point in the discussion it is worth pondering the following: why, despite a re-orientation of the Party's regional development strategy, has there been no sign that regional inequality is narrowing? To answer this question, we have to look at the other key factor that affects spatial distribution of resources: central capacity.

Central extractive capacity is relevant and important in this context because, as the only institution responsible for redistributing resources between regions, the central government must control an adequate amount of revenue before it can conduct any redistributive policy. Strong central extractive capacity may not be a sufficient condition for inter-regional redistribution, as there are instances of governments with strong extractive capacity not doing much redistribution. Nonetheless, it is a necessary condition, because no other institutions, provincial governments included, have incentives to pursue inter-regional redistributive policies.

The Chinese central government's extractive capacity has been critically enfeebled during the course of economic reforms. At the core of Deng Xiaoping's reform programme was decentralisation. While no one denies that the decentralisation of decision-making has been instrumental in generating high economic growth in China over the past two decades, many agree that it has probably gone too far, significantly weakening the central government's capacity to perform functions it is expected to perform, including the movement of investment resources from rich to poor provinces. As Figure 4.8 reveals, despite its 'miraculous' record of GDP growth, China's ratio of overall government revenue to GDP decreased from 31 per cent in 1978 to less than 11 per cent in 1995 and 1996. Although the ratio has rebounded somewhat since 1997, it is still relatively low compared with that of most countries in the world.

As the government share of national income shrank, it was not possible for the government to have much to spare for capital investment. In the pre-reform period, the government budget was used to finance the bulk of capital investments. Not any more. In fact, the deepest cuts to be made to the government budget during the reform era have been made in capital investment. Between 1981 and 1996–7, the share of China's total fixed investment financed by state budget declined sharply, from nearly 30 per cent to almost a negligible 2.7 per cent (see Figure 4.9). It was only after 1997 that the proportion of state appropriations to total investment began to bounce back, albeit marginally.

If we compare Figures 4.8 and 4.9, it is clear that there is a strong and positive correlation between the state share of national income and the budgetary share of investment.

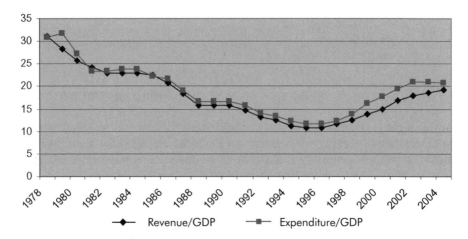

Figure 4.8 Government revenue and expenditure as % of GDP, 1978–2004

Source: SSB 2005

Of course, the central government still enjoys some control over investments financed by other means, such as bank loans, self-raised funds and so on. Economic planning, investment quotas, and project review and approval are some of the instruments that the central government might use to influence the level, structure and direction of investment. However, even if we take into consideration all those factors, central control over investment still appears small and declining, which means that there is less leeway for the central government to redistribute investment resources from rich to poor provinces. A central government with weak extractive capacity cannot be expected to do much in the way of fighting against regional inequality, no matter how committed it is to achieving this goal.

Although since the mid-1990s the Chinese government has somewhat re-oriented its regional investment preferences, hoping to mitigate tensions caused by growing regional gaps, regional disparities have showed no sign of narrowing. This is so because the decentralisation unleashed by reforms has significantly weakened the capability of the central government to mobilise and redistribute resources. Unable to extract large surpluses from rich provinces as it did before, the central government finds it difficult to make large subsidies to poor provinces. Voluntary movement of capital from rich to poor regions has also proved minimal. While the concentration of investment resources in economically prosperous provinces has allowed them to gain a good lead in growth, the lack of investment resources has dampened the growth potential of the backward provinces. The result is the continued worsening of regional inequality up to now, despite the re-orientation of central government preferences. Unless the central government is able to regain control over the redistribution of resources, the trend of divergence we have observed in the last decade or so is unlikely to be reversed.

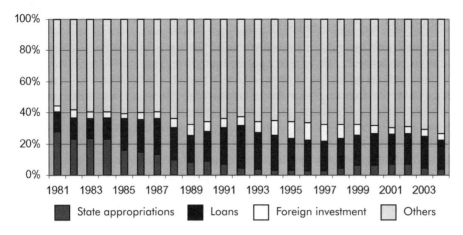

Figure 4.9 Investment by sources, 1981–2004

Source: SSB 2005

Options for addressing regional disparity

If the growing regional inequality in China is the result of biased state policies and enfeebled state capacity that can be altered, then China has no reason to fatalistically let inequalities mount. Equitable growth is not only desirable but also attainable. To achieve more equitable growth in China, the Chinese government must do two things:

1   redress the coastal bias;
2   rebuild its extractive capacity.

Redressing the coastal bias

The development bias towards coastal regions is based on the mistaken 'gradient theory' which is morally more outrageous than the infamous 'trickle-down' theory. Whereas the trickle-down theory only opposes government intervention on behalf of the poor, the gradient theory actually advocates government intervention on behalf of the rich. Unless this development bias is removed, interior provinces will have no chance to catch up with coastal provinces. At present, the Chinese government appears to be shifting its attention to the issue of distributive justice, with the aim of narrowing regional gaps. However, 'getting the policies right' is not enough. A strategy for reducing regional disparities must focus not only on what types of policy are needed but also on how to ensure that these types of policy will be enacted and implemented. Institutional changes are needed to guarantee that the new policies will be implemented and that they will not be later reversed.

Rebuilding extractive capacity

A government's commitment to distributive justice is by itself not sufficient for bringing about real changes. For a government to achieve its desired policy goals, whatever those goals may be, it must be able to mobilise requisite resources from society in the face of resistance by various groups with competing priorities. Without such resources at its disposal, the government may not be able to survive, let alone fulfil its chosen policy objectives (Levi 1988). In general, it can be said that governments with strong extractive capacity are able to pursue their policy goals far more effectively than less capable governments do under similar circumstances. For this reason, we believe that state capacity matters a great deal with regard to income distribution.

In the early decades of the People's Republic, China addressed the problem of regional inequality with some success through inter-regional transfers (Lardy 1980). In recent years, however, such transfers shrank considerably because, unable to mobilise enough resources under an excessively decentralised fiscal system, the central government simply did not have much to spare. When all regions moved toward a higher degree of self-financing, regional disparities were further aggravated. To iron out the variations in average income levels across provinces, the Chinese government must rebuild its extractive capacity so that it can again play a significant redistributive role in the economy. Only when the central government is able to extract large surpluses from rich regions and make large transfers to poor regions can the effects of the initial unequal distribution of resources be offset.

Conclusion

In the first decade of the post-Mao era, when everyone was benefiting from the fast-growing economy and the level of inequality was relatively low, the issue of regional economic egalitarianism almost never arose in China. However, concerns over the distributive effects of the post-Mao reforms began to emerge in the late 1980s. By the mid-1990s, increasing inequality and its possible consequences for social and political instability became a major issue of policy debate and of scholarly research.

This chapter has essentially focused on one type of inequality – inter-provincial. It has examined changes in regional disparities and explored why these changes have occurred. The data presented in the preceding sections point to a conclusion: inter-provincial inequality has been widening. The Chinese economy converged briefly in the early years of reforms, but the trend was soon reversed. Disparity in per capita GDP between China's coastal and interior provinces has been on the rise since 1983. And what is worse, the divergent trend has accelerated since 1990.

Mainstream economists have predicted that, coupled with economic growth, the operation of the free market tends to bring convergence of regional income. According to their theory, in an economy that allows for free factor mobility, capitalists will maximise profits by locating their investments in areas of high labour availability and low labour cost, and workers will maximise wages by moving between regions in response to differences in employment prospects and income levels. Thus, labour tends to migrate from regions of high unemployment and low income to regions of low unemployment and high income, whereas capital tends to migrate in the opposite direction. The two contrasting movements will lower the capital–labour ratio in places with initially high ratios and increase the capital–labour ratio in places with initially low ratios. In short, these economists expect regional inequality to be temporary, as long as market forces are unhampered. Eventually, equilibrium will be reached at which returns to factors, or income, are equalised among regions.

The case of China challenges this view. Were the mainstream economic hypothesis correct, the rate of convergence would have sped up in the 1990s, since many restrictions on capital and labour mobility were removed during this decade. The experience of China, however, has revealed that such blind faith in the magic power of markets is nothing but an illusion. Neither capital nor high-human-capital labour seems to have moved in the directions predicted by main-stream economic theory. Instead, market forces have led to the clustering of scarce resources (e.g. capital, high-human-capital labour, information, technology, and the like) in advanced areas. The limited advantages of backward regions (such as cheap labour) are insufficient to offset these agglomeration advantages. This does not mean that convergence is not a possibility. But, if anything, the case of China suggests that convergence is by no means automatic.

Should China's policy-makers be concerned about the ominous trend of growing regional inequality? Absolutely. Regional inequality is a politically divisive issue. For one thing, widespread senses of frustration and deprivation might surface in regions where incomes are noticeably lower than in other parts of the country. The residents of those regions might come to view an insufficiently sympathetic central government as partly responsible for their plight. Also, more developed regions might regard any central redistributive intervention as unfair drainage of their resources. Conflicting interests between regions could generate adverse effects on the political unity of the nation. This is not to suggest that China is already on the edge of national disintegration. Nevertheless, Chinese leaders should never treat this danger lightly. As long as building a 'socialist' market economy is still their professed goal, and 'stability' (*wending*) and 'development' (*fazhan*) are still their top priorities, they should handle the issue of inequality with great caution. Some degree of inequality may be inevitable in any society. The government may be able to persuade people that some regions must get rich first so that every region will eventually get rich. But, if it fails to distribute the gains from reforms more or less evenly and the gap between those who flourish and those who stagnate becomes unacceptably large, then people's patience with growing inequality could wear thin and their frustration will sooner or later reach a crisis point. Experience elsewhere suggests that few political regimes can maintain political stability under conditions of severe economic disparity. For this reason, China now has to make the reduction of regional disparities a top national priority.

To confront growing regional disparities, the Chinese government first has to change its skewed regional policies. Unless its development bias towards coastal provinces is removed, interior provinces will have no chance to catch up with coastal provinces that enjoy tremendous natural and human capital advantages to begin with. Meanwhile, for the Chinese government to be able to effect equalisation across regions, it also has to rebuild its extractive capacity by overhauling the country's fiscal system. Only when the central government is able to extract large surpluses from rich provinces and make large transfers to poor provinces can the effects of the initial unequal distribution of resources be offset.

References

Barro, R. and Sala-i-Martin, X. (1994) *Economic Growth*, Cambridge, MA: McGraw-Hill.

Bo, Y. B. (1991) *Ruogan zhongda juece yu shijian de huigu (Recollections of certain major decisions and events)*, Beijing: Zhongyang dangxiao chubanshe.

Broadman, H. G. and Sun, X. (1997) 'The Distribution of Foreign Direct Investment in China', *World Bank Policy Research Working Paper*, No. 1720.

Deng Xiaoping (1992) 'Excerpts from Talks given in Wuchang, Shenzhen, Zhuhai and Shanghai (January 18 – February 21, 1992)', *Selected Works of Deng Xiaoping*, vol. 3. Accessed 13 November 2005, at english.peopledaily.com.cn/dengxp/vol3/text/d1200.html.

Domar, E. (1947) 'Expansion and Employment', *American Economic Review* 37: 34–55.

Grossman, G. and Helpman, E. (1991) *Innovation and Growth in the Global Economy*, Cambridge, MA: MIT Press.

Harrod, R. F. (1948) *Towards a Dynamic Economics*, London: Macmillan.

Lardy, N. R. (1980) 'Regional Growth and Income Distribution in China', in R. F. Dernberger (ed.), *China's Development Experience in Comparative Perspective*, Cambridge, MA: Harvard University Press.

Lau, L. J. (1996) 'The Sources of Long-term Economic Growth: Observations from the Experience of Developed and Developing Countries', in R. Landau, T. Taylor and G. Wright (eds), *The Mosaic of Economic Growth*, Stanford, CA: Stanford University Press, pp. 63–91.

Levi, M. (1988) *Of Rule and Revenue*, Berkeley: University of California Press.

Lewis, A. (1955) *The Theory of Economic Growth*, London: Allen and Unwin.

Romer, P. (1990) 'Endogenous Technological Change', *Journal of Political Economy* 98: 71–102.

Rostow, W. W. (1960) *The Stages of Economic Growth*, Cambridge: Cambridge University Press.

Sheng, B. and Feng, L. (1991) *Zhongguo guoqing baogao (Condition of the Nation of China)*, Shenyang: Liaoning People's Publishing House.

SSB (State Statistical Bureau) (comp.) (2001, 2005) *Zhongguo tongji nianjian (China Statistical Yearbook)*, CD-ROM, Beijing: China Statistical Press.

Wang, S. G. and Hu, A. G. (1999) *The Political Economy of Uneven Development: The Case of China*, Armonk, NY: M. E. Sharpe.

Williamson, J. (1965) 'Regional Inequality and the Process of National Development: a Description of the Patterns', *Economic Development and Cultural Changes* 13: 4.

World Bank (1997) *China 2020: Development Challenges in the New Century*, Washington, DC: World Bank.

Yang, Q. (1996) 'Narrowing the East-West Gaps and Developing the Western Minority-Concentrated Regions', *International Conference on Coordinated Development among Regions in China's Economic Reform and Social Development*. City University of Hong Kong, 11–12 December 1996.

Further reading

Armstrong, H. and Taylor, J. (1993) *Regional Economics and Policy*, New York: Harvester Wheatsheaf.

Keidel, A. (1995) *China: Regional Disparities*, Washington, DC: World Bank.

Lai, H. H. (2002) 'China's western development program: its rationale, implementation, and prospects', *Modern China* 28/4: 432–66.

Larsen, K. A. (1992) *Regional Policy of China, 1949–85*, Manila: Journal of Contemporary Asia Publishers.

Rae, D. (1981) *Equalities*, Cambridge, MA: Harvard University Press.

5

China's environmental problems

RICHARD LOUIS EDMONDS

Introduction

Environmental degradation in China remains serious despite major efforts at conservation and clean-up in recent years. Some rivers are unable to sustain any form of life. Air pollution during the winter in northern cities has caused the sky to go black. China's carbon emissions are climbing rapidly. Noise levels in cities remain extremely high.

This chapter examines China's environmental problems. Specifically, it assesses the seriousness of pollution and land degradation in China, discusses the causes of these problems, and examines some of their social, economic and political effects.

The chapter begins by putting environmental problems in a historical context and examining the evolution of environmental degradation in China, up to the reform era. It then addresses the causes of current environmental problems. China's population exerts tremendous pressure on resources such as land, food, water and sources of energy and the nation's environmental problems are made worse by the fact that the population is heavily concentrated in the southeastern part of the country, whereas some of the energy and mineral resources can only be found in remote parts of the country. Population and resource scarcity have indeed contributed to China's degradation, but there has been a tendency for Chinese scientists – especially before the 1990s – to conclude that natural conditions and overpopulation were the predominant causes of China's environmental problems. Outside writers, however, tend to see mismanagement by the government as responsible for the country's environmental woes.

This chapter also looks in detail at various forms of pollution that affect China. China is one of the few areas in the developing world with major acid pollution (acid rain) problems. Water pollution in major rivers is serious, and polluted sections are not confined to urban areas. Pollution associated with solid wastes is also a concern for China. This category of pollution includes domestic landfill waste and hazardous waste from industry. We consider the issues of China's air quality and noise pollution, and evaluate some proposed measures for reducing and controlling various forms of pollution.

Since it straddles humid and arid zones, agricultural and pastoral regions, inland and external draining river basins, forested lands and grasslands, and has the greatest elevation variation of any country in the world, China is particularly susceptible to a great variety of forms of ecosystem degradation. Fragile transitional environments now occupy almost 10 per cent of the total area. As a poor agricultural society now transforming into an open developed economy, China is facing a double threat. On the one hand are the problems we expect to find in an underdeveloped and overpopulated society, such as soil erosion, deforestation, and desertification. On the other hand, the rapidly developing industrial sector produces widespread and sophisticated pollution problems and regional imbalance.

This chapter tries to assess the seriousness of China's resource degradation and offer an evaluation. It concludes by briefly examining some of the social, political and economic effects of environmental degradation.

Historical background to environmental problems in China

China has been facing environmental problems for centuries. In this section, I argue that a good agricultural environment has always been important to China. As a consequence, China learned to deal with some of these problems. At the same time, modern China has inherited some of its degradation from the past.

Environmental problems in early Chinese history

Several aspects of the country's physical geography have conditioned the Chinese peoples' impact on their environment. A scarcity of arable land relative to population necessitated relatively intensive integration of cultivation, animal husbandry and forestry, and encouraged the use of sloping land for cultivation. The nature of China's terrain, soils and climate has made it very easy for degradation to occur in many parts of the country. Inevitably, the intensive, successive use of land throughout the centuries has led to a reduction in vegetation cover that in turn has facilitated soil erosion, flooding and increased silt loads in rivers. Problems of mudflows, landslides, desertification, gullying and lowering of the groundwater table are not new.

At times, warfare, famine and disease reduced populations in parts of China, and this had mixed consequences for the environment. Often, lack of management of human-made facilities led to degradation, such as when irrigation systems fell into disrepair after wars in arid parts of China, leading to desertification. At other times, such as when nomadic peoples invaded northern fringe settlements, the grasslands regenerated as a result of the reduction in farming. The rich canon of Chinese literature shows us ample examples of historical regeneration and degradation (Elvin and Liu 1998). Some of this change appears to have been induced by natural causes. Other changes, such as deforestation resulting from the need for wood to build cities, palaces, temples and vessels, or the use of bad agricultural practices, demonstrate pre-industrial negative human effects on forests.

Knowledge of the need to control human activity or modify it to reduce environmental degradation existed early in China. Chinese classics demonstrate that people were aware of the relationship between forest cover and levels of precipitation by 500 BCE. In some places, farmers' knowledge of how to improve soils means that some soils today are better off because of careful organic farming undertaken in the past. Overall, however, the Chinese environment has seen its worst degradation in the last 400 years, and it has been in the last 50 years in which the most damage has occurred.

Environmental problems and policy from 1949 to 1978

With the rise of the Chinese Communist Party and the establishment of the People's Republic in 1949, the environmental damage caused by the Second World War and the Civil War between the Communists and the Nationalists came to an end. However, a philosophy that urged the conquest of nature (armed with the thoughts of Chairman Mao Zedong, and emphasising population growth) was to put the Chinese landscape under a great strain.

As the Maoist state was totalitarian, environmental policy was closely tied to the views of the central Party leadership. Most writings on China's environment by Western scholars noted the strong role of Stalinist-style central planning found in Communist China in the 1950s and the first half of the 1960s. When the disastrous results of the Great Leap Forward (a policy in effect from 1958 to 1961 which stressed rapid industrial growth at all costs) became apparent, the Chinese tried to rectify some of the environmental damage. However, the trend towards regulation of environmental degradation was again cut short during the Cultural Revolution (1966–76) and there was little policy of any sort from 1966 until the early 1970s. Instead, the various political movements and factional infighting led to considerable neglect of the environment. Those who were aware of the damage done were in no position to speak out during this reign of terror.

As China opened up in the 1970s, the government began to link environmental protection with economic development. In 1973, a document entitled 'Some Regulations Concerning Environmental Protection and Improvement' was formulated. This was China's first all-round environmental protection regulation. In 1974, the State Council set up the Leading Group of Environmental Protection. This was China's first organ responsible for environmental policy.

In 1978, China adopted a new constitution. Article 11 stipulated that the government had a duty to protect the environment. After the establishment of the Chinese Environmental Science Association and the promulgation of the Environmental Protection Law of the People's Republic of China (for trial implementation) in 1979, all areas of the People's Republic except Tibet went about setting up environmental research institutes and central monitoring stations. This date marks the substantive beginning of environmental protection in China.

Overall, environmental policy from the late 1970s began to move away from the bureaucratic centrist approach whereby decisions were made by the top of the bureaucracy and passed down to the local level. From the early 1980s, market-based policy incentives slowly began to appear: for example, the polluter-pays policy of fines, the sale of licences to pollute, and payment of labourers to undertake conservation work. Involvement in international accords such as China's entry into the Convention on International Trade in Endangered Species of Wild Fauna and Flora (1980) and international funding also increased markedly. In line with this, China increasingly applied international norms to its environmental policies.

Environmental policy from 1949 to 1978

Between 1949 and the beginning of the reform era in 1978 environmental policy was characterised by the following features:

- The strong influence of the Soviet government on the organisation of the bureaucracy and research institutes continued – even after the Sino-Soviet split in 1963.

- There was an emphasis on production output growth with little regard to environmental costs.
- Rapid policy reversals led to much degradation of the environment and wasted effort – especially during the Great Leap Forward and the Cultural Revolution.
- Policy emphasis was on pollution control rather than conservation of natural resources. Natural resources were viewed as something to be exploited for the benefit of society and without much non-economic value. Water pollution control was emphasised because of its perceived direct impact upon human health.
- Population policy generally was not supportive of family planning, although at times planning was attempted. Famine in the early 1960s was the major check on rapid population growth.
- Efforts were directed mostly at control of local sources of pollution in the eastern part of the country near urban areas. More effort was put into maintaining waterworks and other functional aspects of the environment.

What causes China's environmental problems?

Many authors suggest that the solution to environmental problems lies in changes of management techniques or increased technological expertise. However, solving environmental problems is not just a matter of correcting or reducing the effects of environmental degradation by changes in management or the adoption of high technology, although the political structure and culture/education are crucial. The severity of environmental degradation in China also is related to the ratio of population and natural resources and the geographical distribution of the population and those natural resources.

Population pressure

China's population at the last census in 2000 was recorded at 1,295,330,000. As Chapter 6 notes, population has been growing rapidly since 1949 and is projected to continue to grow for some time, despite control policies enacted in China in the 1970s and 1980s. From an environmental point of view, the key issue in relation to population is the question of what population China can sustain.

What population can China support?

A series of conferences held in China in 1979 and 1980 concluded that the optimum desirable carrying capacity of the land (i.e. the number of people that Chinese agriculture and the environment can support) was a population of 700 million, a figure that China has exceeded by 600 million. In 1996, experts were saying that 500 million would be the ideal population and that the number must be kept below 1,000 million. One has to be careful about carrying capacity estimates,

Table 5.1 Demographic and land data for China 1949–2025, with a comparison to global figures for 1989

Year	Population (millions)	Total arable land (million ha)	Arable land per capita (ha)	Total forest store capacity per capita (cu m)[a]
Figures for China				
1949	570	108	0.19	n/a
1957		112		
1982	1 031	99	0.10	n/a
1994	1 200	95	0.08	9.3
Official released figures				
1995	1 200	122.2[b]	0.09	n/a
2000	1 295	127.5	0.101	8.7
Estimates				
2020	1 500	90	0.06	8.0
2025	n/a	89	n/a	n/a
World figures for 1989				
	5 201	1 373	0.26	59.6

Source: Data from Chen and Edmonds 1989: 2; various statistical yearbooks.
[a] Total forest store capacity per capita means the potential cumulative yield for timber and non-timber products per capita. Calculations are based on figures for closest years to 1989 available. These figures are likely to be the result of aggregations from various sources based on different definitions and can only be considered approximations.
[b] The arable figures since 1995 are based on newer survey techniques and are considered to be more accurate than earlier figures.

since the needs of people in the future are impossible to predict. Yet, by today's standards, most experts in China see the country as overpopulated.

A big worry of the 'overpopulation problem' is food. Problems related to food production and population are discussed in Chapter 6. It is important to note that the problem of the food-to-population ratio also depends on the maintenance of good quality cultivated land, as well as population levels. If China pushes its resource base to the limit, it is thought that the country can feed and keep warm 1,600 million people at sustenance level. Even with stringent population control measures, China should reach this perceived optimum population around 2030.

Population distribution

As discussed in Chapters 4 and 6, population distribution is a general problem for Chinese development. Most of the population is crowded into the southeastern half of the country. The west is often cited as the region with the most potential to absorb in-migrants, yet the number of people that this fragile area can absorb is so small that migration to the western border areas has little effect on the congestion of the east.

Shortage of natural resources

Although China is not particularly deficient in natural resources, the shortages that the country experiences are severe because of the low per capita level of available resources. China's per capita levels of land, total forest store capacity (amount of timber on standing trees) and water resources are only 36 per cent, 13 per cent and 25 per cent of the estimated world per capita levels.

'Land loss'

As just under 60 per cent of the Chinese people live in rural areas, shortage of agricultural land is an acute problem. China is currently supporting 22 per cent of the world's population on 7 per cent of the world's total farmland. Cropland accounts for only 10 per cent of China's total area, and the total quantity of arable land is more likely to decrease than grow. The amount of arable land per capita halved between 1949 and 2000 (see Table 5.1). There is some consolation in the fact that the pace of arable area reduction appears to have slowed down since the 1990s. Moreover, some of this 'land loss' is actually conversion of cropland to fishponds, orchards, and other equally productive uses. Whether these statistics are reliable or not, the amount of arable land available per capita is already far below the world average and will more than likely worsen at a faster rate in China than the world average for some time to come.

China will experience considerable urbanisation in the near future. One estimate is that China will be 60 per cent urban by 2030. This represents a massive increase in urban population from the 2005 levels (43 per cent) and will lead to loss of good suburban farmland.

The potential for development of new agricultural lands is limited. Even with optimum development of potential lands for cultivation, China's arable land area will not reach 1949 levels. Most of the good quality land in easily accessible locations with favourable climatic conditions has been used up, and the amount of productivity that can be attained from what remains for agricultural development is not high.

Deterioration of land quality

The soil nutritional base on which China's agricultural development is to take place is not that strong. The average organic matter content of soil for China is less than 1.5 per cent compared to 3–4.5 per cent for Canada and 2.5–4 per cent for the

USA. Over 59 per cent of China's agricultural land is estimated as lacking in phosphorus, over 22 per cent is lacking in potassium, and 14 per cent is lacking in both; over 60 per cent of China's soils lack zinc, manganese and other trace elements. Moreover, soil surveys suggest that overall soil fertility is dropping, although independent research by Peter Lindert (2000) suggests that phosphorus and potassium levels may actually be increasing but confirms drops in nitrogen and organic matter in eastern China. In part, the drop in fertility results from reductions of fallow times.

In some instances, salinisation and waterlogging accompany drops in soil fertility. Farmers can induce salinisation-alkalisation through improper or excessive irrigation. If too much water is left on the land for extended periods, or saline water is constantly in use, evaporation will eventually leave salts that are not adequately leached out of the soils. Costs to rectify salinisation are high as proper drainage systems must be built and the salts must be washed out of the land or reduced by other means such as planting of salt absorbent grasses. Gleisation is a natural process affecting soils in cold moist climates or a process caused by triple cropping of paddies without proper soil maintenance in the south, where a gleyed layer is formed in the soil horizon restricting water penetration. The result is that plants are drowned and the soil quality further deteriorates because of waterlogging. In addition to problems of soil quality, soil erosion, desertification and pollution are threatening the quality of some agricultural land.

Deforestation is a worldwide problem which can lead to soil erosion, laterisation or the formation of an impenetrable reddish clayey iron and aluminium oxide layer in tropical soils and increased water runoff which in turn leads to water shortages. Although afforestation can reverse much of this trend, loss of flora and fauna variety can be very difficult to reverse.

Water shortages

Water is in short supply, and the amount of water available per capita is growing smaller. China generally has lower levels of precipitation than developed countries, which limits the ability of water to cleanse the environment. Even in the relatively water-abundant provinces of the east, the precipitation level is less than two-thirds of that in Japan. The overall levels of precipitation for the north and the northeast of China are far poorer. As a consequence, dust and other forms of air pollution, as well as water pollution, remain in the Chinese environment longer than they do in many developed countries.

Energy and mineral shortages

Energy and mineral shortages exist on a per capita basis. China's power-generating capacity and the quantity of power generated per capita as of 2000 was only between one-tenth and one-sixth of the figures found in developed countries. China's reserves of coal are only 40 per cent of the world average in immediately exploitable coal reserves on a per capita basis. The picture for oil and natural gas is worse. Although there is considerable hydroelectric potential, it is generally found far away from industrial centres, and its development is likely to cause additional environmental problems. Despite efforts, increasing energy shortages will take place during a period of growing expectations for higher energy consumption levels. It is partially this urgent need for energy that is responsible for the Chinese government's construction of the controversial Sanxia (Three Gorges) Dam on the Chang (Yangtze) River.

Government planning, policy and management

Just as the environments in various parts of China are different, the environmental problems in different regions are also different. This means that a state such as China, which has been ruled largely from Beijing, has had troubles devising one central policy for dealing with disparate environmental problems. In the Maoist era, the policy of regional self-sufficiency meant that all regions of the country were to produce their own food and manufacture their own goods. Central planning often tried to devise standards for what each province or city should possess to be self-sufficient. Although this policy did have some positive results – for instance it reduced the strain on China's then feeble transport network – it also led to irrational economic activity. For example, more wealth could have been generated by planting crops that were more suited to the climate and soils in one region and then trading the surplus to another region, rather than growing crops that were not suitable just so the region could be self-sufficient. Sometimes a town could not buy goods available in a nearby town across a provincial border but had to buy from a factory in a remote part of its own province. Today this problem is nowhere near as great as it used to be.

How serious is pollution in China?

Environmental problems can be divided into two broad classes: resource degradation and pollution. To some degree, policy organs for these two sets of problems have been slightly different in China. The former National Environmental Protection Agency concentrated most of its efforts on pollution control, whereas land degradation was often the remit of various governmental ministries such as Agriculture or Forestry. Restructuring after 1998 brought more degradation issues under the management of the renamed State Environmental Protection Administration. In this section, I focus on issues related to pollution and attempt to evaluate measures that the Chinese government has (and has not) taken to address pollution.

Water pollution

Water pollution is a function of the number of pollutants released into the water, the volume of the water body, and the ability of the water to clean or disperse those pollutants. The number of pollutants released is influenced by population density and type of economic development. The ability of existing water bodies to cope with wastewater effluent is influenced by the size of the water body, its existing chemical composition and temperature, the flora and fauna in the area, and by precipitation, tributaries and lakes which feed rivers, and their flow rate.

Developed countries are increasingly controlling point source pollution (pollution coming from a particular factory) so that heavy metal and other industrial pollutant output that potentially flows into a water source is reduced. However, pesticides, organic wastes and pollutants coming from storm sewers continue to increase, and these create a heavier mix of organic pollution and eutrophication of lakes (the process by which a body of water becomes rich in dissolved nutrients, thereby encouraging the growth and decomposition of oxygen-depleting plant life which results in harm to other organisms). In developing countries, the number of industrial pollution sources and general sewage is still increasing, resulting in a rapid increase in both organic and inorganic water pollution.

Water pollution became more serious in China in the 1970s as industry expanded and the population increased. The Chinese made progress in wastewater treatment during the 1990s and the nature of water pollution changed as the proportion of municipal wastewater increased and industrial wastewater dropped. Treatment of both municipal and industrial wastewater has increased markedly. Even so, in urban areas 80 per cent of surface water is still polluted, with ammonia and nitrogen as the main pollutants, and 50 per cent of China's potable water is polluted. Sadly, water pollution has been reported to still be threatening the health of hundreds of cities. There is variation in the level of water treatment provided for large cities, but the proportion of industrial water treated in smaller cities generally is much lower.

All main rivers and many branch tributaries are polluted to some degree, with organic water pollution being universal. Pollution generally is more serious in northern China's rivers than in the south because rivers in the north generally have lower flow rates. There is some variation in the types of waste found in various rivers. For example, the major pollutants found in the Huang (Yellow) River in the north include ammonia, potassium permanganate, organic oxygen-demanding wastes, and petroleum, whereas the Zhu (Pearl) River in the south contains large amounts of ammonia nitrogen, suspended matter, and nitrite nitrogen. Despite the general consensus that river pollution is at its worst in the north, problems with rivers seem to have increased most in the south since the 1990s. Water pollution is also more serious in eastern China than in the west, because of the higher concentration of population in the east. Water quality is generally at its best in sparsely populated portions of the southwest.

Most lakes around cities have become dumping grounds for large quantities of untreated urban sewage and industrial wastes. In general, only lakes and reservoirs that are drinking-water sources have been protected. The volume of wastewater entering large lakes can be quite staggering. However, it is in small lakes near large industrial areas that pollution is at its worst. Problems of inland water body quality have become more serious as many lakes shrink. The filling in of lakes was a prominent policy during the Mao era.

Although pollution of the coastal seas is not as serious a problem as pollution of rivers and lakes, some alarming developments have occurred in recent years. Serious pollution from organic chemicals and heavy metals has been found in the Bohai Bay and at the mouth of the Zhu River in Guangdong. In general, the situation along the northern coast has improved since the late 1990s, but the southern coast continues to worsen. Red tides, which are caused by the build up of red algae in coastal waters, have been common since the late 1980s. Red tides emit toxins that can kill marine life, resulting in serious ecological damage and loss of income. As a result of growing knowledge about coastal pollution, the National Marine Ministry has begun to issue more regulations in recent years regarding oil exploration and dumping at sea.

Water pollution is not limited to surface water bodies. The underground water beneath most cities has been polluted to some extent. Wells have had to be shut down in some cases, because the water pollution levels have exceeded drinking water quality standards. In some instances, the dropping water tables around coastal cities have led to pollution of drinking water by salt water.

Solid wastes

Improper disposal of solid wastes can lead to loss of valuable land, air and water pollution, and the spread of disease. The sight and smell of dumps can have negative psychological effects on residents and affect the migrating habits of some animals. In developed countries, a tremendous amount of solid waste is produced per capita, but the facilities to treat many of these wastes exist. In less developed countries, the production of the more dangerous wastes per capita is much lower. However, facilities to treat even common organic wastes are often lacking.

The rate of rubbish growth in China has been considerable and as elsewhere has been greatest in periods of economic growth. Levels of heavy metals found in the rubbish of Shanghai have reached those found in developed countries. Industrial solid waste emissions more or less stabilised in the 1990s, and real progress has been made in controlling industrial solid waste from large and medium urban enterprises. In 2000, the Ministry of Construction began selecting a number of pilot sites to experiment with the assorted disposal of urban waste. However, as of 2000, 90 per cent of urban waste was just buried. Industrial solid wastes are growing annually by about 7 per cent and urban solid wastes by about 4 per cent.

Chinese urban refuse, especially in northern China, contains a large amount of coal ash. Coal ash alone also accounts for the majority of waste produced by industry. The high proportion of ash in northern China's urban refuse has led to a poorer quality of composting material, making farmers uninterested in using urban compost. A shift away from solid fuels to gas should reduce daily per capita rubbish output as well as lower air pollution levels. However, natural gas production has been weak. Therefore, it will be difficult for Chinese cities to move away from coal in the near future. Kitchen wastes make up a considerable portion of China's urban refuse, especially in south China. Most of this is vegetable matter, which means that China's urban refuse has a high humidity, making it difficult to incinerate. Better marketing has helped China to decrease vegetable wastage since the late 1980s, although more vegetables now are packed in plastic, thus adding a worry to China's growing refuse problem.

'White pollution'

On 1 July 1996, railway stations and passenger trains banned the use of non-biodegradable styrofoam meal boxes in an attempt to minimise the environmental impact of the millions of containers thrown from trains each year. The new boxes are made of paper and polypropylene, a kind of biodegradable plastic. As of 1996, 7,500 million boxes were produced a year, of which about 400 to 500 million were discarded onto the railways. Meal boxes carelessly thrown out by passengers created a serious 'white pollution' problem near railway lines. These old meal boxes require 200 years to decompose, even when buried, and are potentially poisonous to animals. The paper boxes are environmentally safer but cost more than the old boxes.

Recycling and waste disposal

Recycling of metal, scrap and other solid wastes was not very successful in the early 1980s, because pricing, marketing and recycling technology were all inadequate. Industrial inefficiency, presumably a result of the lack of environmental considerations in production planning and pricing of materials, also ensured that more solid waste was being generated by industry than was necessary. Today, there remains a shortage of incinerators and lining systems. As an example, the city of Beijing was surrounded by 7,000 landfills and more than 500 ha of farmland was covered by rubbish as of 1997.

By 2000, official statistics stated that China discharged 2 million tons of untreated hazardous waste. Pollutants in this category include used electric cells, chemical fluids, organic solutions, electroplating liquids, solid chemical wastes, preservatives and materials from surgical operations. Authorities even have discovered that some unscrupulous profiteers collected and processed contaminated bandages to use as stuffing for quilts and coats. The Chinese government set 2005 as the date by which all of China's hazardous waste was to be properly treated and disposed of. However, over 264 million tones of dangerous wastes accumulated in storage between 1996 and 2002 so that it will take a long time to erase the accumulated impact of hazardous waste. Domestic nuclear waste so far is minimal.

Today, fines for importing wastes not allowed are severe, and businesses can be shut down. Even if entrepreneurs are kept in line, it appears that the Chinese government is interested in storing foreign toxic wastes for cash in government-approved sites. Cases have been reported of radioactive waste being imported from the US and neighbouring central Asian republics.

Air pollution is generally thought of as the contribution to the atmosphere resulting from the activities of humans that have a negative effect on ecosystems or particular forms of life. Air pollution can harm humans by directly inducing respiratory diseases including cancers, and by affecting their skin and eyes. Ultimately it can cause harm to plants as well as animals, and damage to buildings and other objects. Air pollution becomes more serious when a mix of pollutants combines to form new chemical compounds. Excessive release of certain gases is also thought to be responsible for global warming (chlorofluorocarbons or CFCs, carbon dioxide, methane and nitrogen oxides) and destruction of the ozone layer (CFCs).

Greenhouse gases

The World Bank's high growth scenario says that coal use for energy in China will triple between 1995 and 2020. China already accounts for 10 per cent of world energy use and 82 per cent of the greenhouse gases generated in China come from energy consumption. Of the big energy-use countries with potential to produce greenhouse gases, China is the most likely to have its energy use grow over the next half century. Chinese agriculture is also responsible for much of the methane (CH_4) which is the second largest greenhouse gas produced in China, accounting for 13 per cent of total greenhouse gas emissions. Flooded paddies, flatulent animals and organic wastes account for the majority of agricultural methane produced in China. Fertilisers are one of the big emitters of the third major greenhouse gas – nitrous oxide (N_2O).

China's ecology is likely to be seriously affected by climate change. If oceans rise by one metre, it is predicted that China's coastal areas below four metres above current sea level would be flooded (an area the size of Portugal) resulting in the loss of much good agricultural land as well as submerging major cities like Shanghai and Guangzhou. The effect of global warming on Chinese agriculture would no doubt be mixed. Warmer temperatures could mean that growing seasons would be lengthened. It is possible that in many places precipitation would increase. However, so would evaporation, making soil drier, reducing yields and increasing soil erosion potential, so overall, water supply could decline. Pests and weeds as well as more severe storms could also reduce yields in many places.

Particulate pollution

Particulate pollution (total suspended particulates or TSP is the major air pollutant in Chinese cities, particularly industrial centres of the north. A report by the World Resources Institute in 1999 stated that nine of the ten most polluted cities in the world, in TSP levels, are in China. Table 5.2 provides a comparison of pollution in China's main cities and that in other large world cities.

Although most major particulate air pollutants are regulated, Chinese threshold particulate values are frequently exceeded. Vaclav Smil (1993) estimates 200 million Chinese are exposed to annual TSP concentration of above 300 micrograms per cubic metre ($\mu g/m^3$). For short-term exposure, the lowest

Table 5.2 Air pollution comparison of world cities, 1990s

Country	City	Population (thousands)	Total suspended particles ($\mu g/m^3$)	SO_2 ($\mu g/m^3$)	CO_2 ($\mu g/m^3$)
China	Shanghai	13 584	246	53	73
	Beijing	11 299	377	90	122
	Tianjin	9 415	306	82	50
Australia	Sydney	3 590	54	28	n/a
Austria	Vienna	2 060	47	14	42
Brazil	Rio de Janeiro	10 181	139	129	n/a
Canada	Toronto	4 319	36	17	43
US	New York	16 332	n/a	26	79
	Los Angeles	12 460	n/a	9	74
	Chicago	6 844	n/a	14	57
Singapore	Singapore	2 848	n/a	20	30
Spain	Madrid	4 072	42	11	25
France	Paris	9 523	14	14	57
Germany	Frankfurt	3 606	36	11	45
	Berlin	3 317	50	18	26
India	Delhi	9 948	415	24	41

Source: World Bank, World Development Indicators 1998: 162

daily average concentration that might produce a physiological effect is in the range of 220–420 $\mu g/m^3$ for TSP. For long-term exposure, the lowest daily average concentration that might produce a physiological effect is 110–180 $\mu g/m^3$ for particulates. Coal combustion is responsible for over two-thirds of China's particulate emissions. Much of this coal is not washed (has not had dust removed), and the problem is further aggravated by the fact that much of the coal is consumed directly and burned in small to medium-sized furnaces. Particulate emissions began to decrease from the late 1980s. However, unmeasured particulate releases in rural areas probably mean that the total particulate release has not dropped as rapidly as Table 5.3 suggests.

The percentage of household particulate emissions recovered is much lower than in industry. The particulate problem is more serious in the cities of northern China than in the south. Northern cities often have temperature inversions in winter that increase the severity of air pollution. Greater levels of dust in the north

Table 5.3 Annual emission totals for various air pollutants, 1982–2003 (million tons)

Year	Total particulate emissions	Sulphur dioxide
1982	14.6	12.7
1985	26.0	13.0
1990	21.05	14.94
1995	17.31	23.70
1997	18.73	23.46
1998	14.55	20.91
1999	11.59	18.57
2000	11.65	19.95
2003	10.48	21.87
2004	10.94	22.54

Source: Data from Cao 1989; NBS 1991: 798; 1992: 818–20; 1994: 668; 1995: 692; Qu and Li 1992: 136; *Report on the State of the Environment in China 1994* 2 1998: 2000

Note: Figures for sulphur dioxide before 1997 are likely to have been exclusively from industry

also account for a considerable part of the difference in particulate levels between north and south.

As China has industrialised, various elements have been added to the particulate pollution mix. For example, lead pollution has become more serious as the amount of petrol consumed by automobiles has increased. Lead in the air can lead to cardiovascular diseases and affect the liver, kidney and nervous system. Today, all petroleum enterprises in China are supposed to produce lead-free petrol only, and car-manufacturing enterprises must make models suitable for use with lead-free petrol.

Sulphur dioxide and acid rain

Sulphur dioxide is created when burned sulphur combines with oxygen to form a pungent gas. An analysis done in 2000 of sulphur emissions over the last 200 years shows that China now leads the world in sulphur pollution levels. Complaints about acid rain in Indochina, Japan and Korea, mostly due to Chinese sulphur emissions, are increasing.

As with particulates, levels of sulphur dioxide are more severe during winter in northern Chinese cities than in the south. Beijing, Xi'an and Shenyang have been listed among the world's ten worst cities for sulphur dioxide concentrations. However, in the summer months, certain southern cities such as Chongqing and Guiyang can have higher sulphur dioxide levels than most northern cities. All

Chinese city centres have emission levels that exceed the legal limits. In 2002, the State Environmental Protection Administration introduced a sulphur dioxide quota in some provincial-level units. When an industry exceeds its quota, it will have to buy some of the quota from its counterparts or the market.

Coal combustion is also responsible for about two-thirds of the nitrogen oxides emitted in China. Nitrogen dioxide is largely the result of burning coal, whereas nitrogen monoxide is primarily caused by the exhaust fumes of motor vehicles. Nitrogen oxide pollution is not yet serious when compared with particulates and sulphur dioxide. Plants are more susceptible to harmful effects of NO_x than are animals. The increasing number of motor vehicles and use of fossil fuels suggests an increase in future levels of carbon monoxide, hydrocarbons and nitrogen oxides.

Southern China is one of the developing areas of the world most susceptible to acid pollution, also known as acid rain or acidification. About one-third of China's territory is experiencing acid pollution. In southwest China, forests are thought to have died from acid rain. Although it is often difficult to assign damage directly, cities in the southwest have metal, concrete and stone that show signs of rapid and severe corrosion.

Air pollution has other serious consequences. Soot and dust are the main sources of polycyclic aromatic hydrocarbons that have cancer-producing capabilities. Sulphur dioxide reduces lung function and can aggravate existing respiratory diseases. Respiratory related diseases due to air pollution include lung cancer, cardiovascular disease, chronic bronchitis and nose and throat infections, as well as silicosis in mining areas. The conditions for miners in virtually unregulated small mines are unhealthy, and larger mining sites are often heavily polluted. Research in China shows rises in the incidence of malignant tumours and of respiratory disease in both urban and rural areas. However, efficient stove programmes have reduced biomass consumption for energy as well as improved rural indoor air quality.

Noise pollution

Higher levels of noise are subtler in their effects, but they can result in loss of sleep and increased stress with all its side effects. Because of all the other pollution problems facing China, noise pollution has taken a back seat. In 1979, a work place noise standard was implemented and a wider range of urban and construction noise standards was formally published in 1982. The recommended maximum residential and road noise levels in China do not vary greatly from those found elsewhere. Even today, the differences in noise levels inside and outside most rooms are often not that great. Industrial noise pollution can be very serious as many factories produce noise on a 24-hour basis, whereas transportation noise and household-generated noise levels tend to drop off during the evenings.

Surveys on the effects of noise pollution among 150,000 people in Beijing, Tianjin, and Shanghai found that transport was perceived as the largest single cause of noise disturbance. Narrow streets and poor quality buildings heighten the congestion and noise levels. Social noise is a problem in cities, because families are crowded close together in homes that have often been subdivided or in housing blocks with poor acoustics. Industry and transport noise have fallen in the perception of China's urban residents during the last decade. This suggests that attempts to control factory noise have been better than attempts to control household noise.

Government responses to China's environmental problems

Much of the government's master plan for pollution management deals with resource degradation rather than with pollution, and as mentioned previously, the problem of water pollution is given a high place largely because water resources are seen as critical. Feasible solutions to the various types of pollution described above are complex and must be filtered through China's political patronage systems and the limited funds allocated. Proper development of proposed pollution alleviation programmes also require funding being spent on poverty alleviation, education, and health care.

Foreign aid also influences the government's priorities. For instance, early Japanese aid was targeted at clearing up air pollution in the northeast, particularly Liaoning Province, in part, because the air blows out over Japan. While such aid frees up national funds for pollution programmes in other parts of the country, it can also dictate what problems are addressed and what regions are given priority.

How serious is the resource degradation found in China?

When we assess the extent to which China's resources have been degrading, we must approach official statistics with even more caution than we do statistics on pollution. Figures on degradation (and even definitions of what constitutes degraded land) can be changed to suit political needs, as occurred when the 1986 Forestry Law defined grassland and woodland as forest resources with only 30 per cent canopy cover rather than 40 per cent, as it had previously. This change raised China's forested land area from 273 million to 287 million hectares in one stroke. In recent years, statistics indicating the qualities of China's degradation are increasing and provide better quality information. In this section of the chapter, we evaluate the extent to which resources such as forests and soil have been degraded. Although overall vegetation cover appears to have stopped decreasing in recent years, soil erosion, desertification, and depletion of water resources continue to be growing problems.

Deforestation

Vegetation cover in China is far below world averages and generally has been decreasing both totally and per capita since 1949, although there are claims of improvement since about 1990. National statistics hide the unbalanced distribution and structure of China's forests. The state timber industry is heavily concentrated in the northeast and the southwest. What natural forests remain today appear to have been saved largely by inaccessibility.

The conversion of forested land into fields was catalysed by changes in land use rights since 1978 that in some cases led to the reduction of forests on farmsteads. In recent years, more trees have been cut than were originally planned. Fuel wood demand grew throughout the 1990s. There is a considerable latent demand as plant stalks are still used as fuel in some places. Estimates also suggest that illegal felling, fire, and disease loss is large but not excessive when compared with similar forests in Russia and Canada.

Afforestation projects

It seems highly unlikely that the country will have sufficient timber resources in the near future. Because of the pressures of population, the growing need for farmland and the effects of acid rain and other forms of pollution on forestland, the government has increasingly recognised the need to protect and increase China's forest resources. As a result, the Chinese government has instituted several afforestation programmes. The 2003 major afforestation project categories were:

- the so-called Three Norths (*sanbei*) Shelterbelt Project and the Chang River Middle and Upper Reaches Protective Forest Construction Project (75 per cent of area planted);
- grain for green projects (10 per cent of area planted);
- sustainable forestry development projects (8.4 per cent of area planted);
- harnessing wind and dust around Beijing and Tianjin (6.5 per cent of area planted);
- Continual Production Timber Forest Base Construction Project (0.02 per cent of area planted);
- key grassland conservation projects (technically not afforestation but grass planting projects).

These projects have included measures such as the following: the planting of street trees and shrubs that have tolerance to air pollution; the integration of tree planting with agriculture; the planting of tree belts and grasslands along the desert fringes of northern China; the planting of trees to reduce soil erosion and river silting; and the creation of fuel wood forests, timber forests and plantations of so-called 'economic' trees (i.e. fruit trees).

China is one of the countries that have vast areas affected by arid land degradation. Over 40 per cent of the arid, semi-arid, and sub-humid tillage is desertified and 56.6 per cent of the pasture degraded, affecting 400 million people in 471 counties of eighteen provinces and autonomous regions. Recently, the government has taken the initiative of encouraging people to convert farmland (on steep slopes or marginal lands) back to forests, in order to reduce desertification.

Soil erosion

Erosion is a naturally occurring process. Under conditions in which an ecosystem is not under stress, various land building processes generally offset erosion. Therefore, when we talk about a soil erosion problem, it is really a situation in which the rate of erosion has increased far beyond the rate of soil build-up. Removal of vegetation cover is the primary human-induced cause of soil erosion. Aside from exposing bare topsoil to the effect of rain and hail, removal of vegetation increases the rate of evaporation, which renders the topsoil less stable and aids aeolian erosion. Microclimate, site aspect, soil conditions and vegetation types all combine to determine varying rates of erosion. Although it is difficult to verify, some authors state that China has the most serious soil erosion problem in the world. According to one Chinese definition, over one-third of China's total land area is affected by soil erosion. The common assumption is that soil erosion is serious for agriculture, although there are studies suggesting that the relationship is far from direct. In any event, China has pledged to have nearly two million square kilometres of eroded land under fundamental control between 2002 and 2052. To some degree, such policies are politically motivated.

Silting in the Huang and Chang River valleys

The most serious erosion found in China is in the Huang (Yellow) River Valley. The Huang River carries 1,200 million to 1,600 million tonnes of silt from the eastern edge of the Loess Plateau in central China to its mouth annually. Only the Ganges River of Bangladesh and India with 1,450 million tonnes of silt comes close. Deposition of eroded sediment in the lower course of the Huang creates a considerable amount of new delta land in years of adequate flow. Most data suggest the erosion problem has been getting worse since 1950. However, some sources indicate that sediment loads in the Valley have been decreasing since the early 1970s. Reductions are said to be a result of decreased precipitation and control measures – in particular, reservoir construction.

Because of the relatively high human-to-land ratio in the Huang River area, many slope lands that should not be farmed are cultivated. As moving peasants off the sloping lands is impossible on much of the plateau, measures must be taken to reduce the amount of erosion and water loss caused by agricultural activities. These include the construction of high-quality level terraces, reduction of ploughing and adjusting planting cycles, increased use of chemical fertilizers in combination with organic fertilizers and selection of profitable crop varieties that can grow in dry conditions and will help stabilise the soil, if at all possible.

Better vegetation cover and a milder climate than is found in the Huang River Valley have meant soil erosion in the Chang (Yangtze) River Valley has been less severe. In addition, the thinner layers of soil in the upper Chang River Valley mean that gullying is less common than on the Loess Plateau. The bedrock in the upper Chang Basin is very thin. Therefore, much of the Chang River Valley has the potential for serious soil shortages. Population increases in the basin have meant that more people have been cultivating the previously uncultivated moun-

Provinces with rainfall less
than 600 millimeters annually

Figure 5.1 China's arid lands

tainous areas. As more and more flat land is being taken over for urban uses and
the population is increasing, more steep slopes are being cultivated, with disastrous consequences. Soil erosion in the southwest can often take the form of a
landslide or mudflow.

Since 1980, new economic policies led to new erosion problems resulting
from conflict between short-term profit and soil conservation. Programmes were
implemented on a trial-and-error basis with little attempt to understand the
processes involved and no attempt to coordinate programmes in upland and
lowland areas.

Aridity

Figure 5.1 shows the areas of China that are arid, semi-arid or suffering from problems such as desertification and salinisation.

Arid (less than 250 mm of precipitation per annum) and semi-arid (from 250
to 500 mm per annum) lands make up approximately one-third of China's territory.
Areas with less than 25 mm per annum are referred to as extremely arid. The
extremely arid portions of China correspond to the deserts in the northwest. In
these deserts, conversion to grassland is virtually impossible. Natural vegetation

cover gradually drops from around 60 per cent in the semi-arid areas to less than 10 per cent or sometimes only 1 or 2 per cent in extremely arid areas. Within portions of the sub-humid areas (between 500 and 700 mm of precipitation per annum), we also find similar problems to those found in the arid and semi-arid lands such as so-called desertification (a degradation process which leads to a desert-like barren landscape), salinisation/alkalisation (salts or alkalis remaining in the soil) and soil erosion.

Next to soil erosion, desertification and related phenomena are probably China's most serious land resource degradation problems. A 1997 definition states that 17.6 per cent of China's territory (1.689 million sq. km) is made up of desert-affected lands.

Much of the area of the northwest arid region is desert of long standing, but there are also new signs of desertification. A second, less arid region, largely in central Inner Mongolia, Ningxia, northern Shaanxi and Shanxi provinces, contains a significant amount of land desertified within the past 100 years along with long-standing deserts. Desertification and resource degradation in the north central region is serious, but land can be reclaimed with effort. Along the western edges of the Northeast Plain and in central parts of the North China Plain, there is a less arid region composed of patches of desertified land. These sandy lands consist of large patches of semi-fixed sand dunes and contain from 30 to 90 per cent vegetation cover. If properly managed, much of this northeastern region can return to non-desert-like conditions.

Water shortages

There is a lack of fresh water in China. Compared to a world average of 10,900 m³ per capita per annum in 1997, China had only 2,220 m³, and the figure should drop over the next several decades. According to one commonly accepted standard, a nation that has below 1,700 m³ of water per capita is considered desperately short of water resources. As mentioned, China's inland water resources are unevenly distributed. In the arid regions of the west there is a serious shortage of water, a water resource imbalance that persists despite the creation of hundreds of thousands of reservoirs and dams since 1949.

The vast majority of China's total water use is for irrigation. However, although the irrigated area grew modestly in the 1990s, the water balance has continued to decline dramatically. The shortage is compounded by inefficiency in agricultural water.

Urbanisation and industrialisation are also responsible for the increasing water shortage. As of 2002, some 110 Chinese cities were suffering from severe water shortages, especially large cities, because of worsening water pollution and shortage of water. Some cities in northern China are forced to ration their water supply, and provinces in central China are faced with a shortage of electric power caused by low levels of river water. Where the water level in urban areas is shallow, the water is often is too polluted for human consumption.

Many cities face serious subsidence problems. As Shanghai is undergoing a building boom, subsidence has increased the potential for flooding. In Suzhou, ground subsidence has led to the collapse of bridges, whereas in Xi'an and Datong surface fissures have been reported. Ground subsidence has caused underground pipes to break and houses to collapse. Combined with possible sea level rises due to global warming and river bed level rises due to siltation, many of China's major cities have something to worry about.

In many parts of China, rivers, lakes and reservoirs are shrinking and in some cases have even dried up. The reduction of water has even led to a reduction in the length of China's inland waterways.

In agriculture, a lot of irrigation water is lost through evaporation and seepage in transit. One result of the depletion of water resources on the North China Plain has been the increasing difficulty of growing rice, even in traditional rice-farming areas. To combat shortages in the north, many water diversion projects were completed. It is still possible that greater savings in agricultural water use could fill the gap in industrial and urban water needs for the immediate future. China is desperately looking for more water-saving technology to combat this problem. Otherwise, the only solutions will be to encourage more dryland farming on the North China Plain, make up for reductions in yields from other parts of the country or by importing foodstuffs, or develop interbasin water transfer from south China.

Over the years, a dozen plans have been put forward for water transfer from the south to the north. There is opposition that argues that groundwater estimates

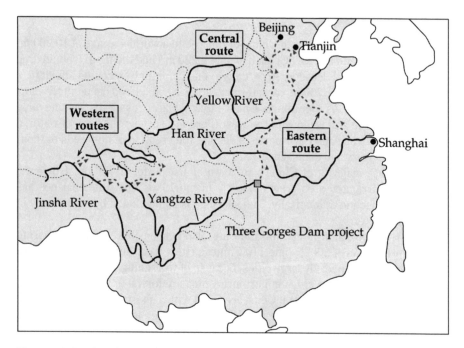

Figure 5.2   South–north water diversion routes

may be too low, and saving from more efficient use of water on the North China Plain could be significant. Yet most experts agree that sooner or later, north China is going to run out of water no matter what water saving efforts are made. Of all the water transfer plans, three were eventually selected for implementation, and formal approval came in 2002. These three water transfer plans are shown in Figure 5.2.

The eastern plan pumping water north through the Grand Canal can be implemented faster and initial investment would be lower, although in the long run it will require one million kilowatts of electric pumping capacity at thirteen pumping stations. As one would expect, the eastern route has the approval of the richer downstream provinces through which it passes. The central route is to divert water from the Danjiangkou Reservoir via a 1,236 km canal, the water moving exclusively by gravity through numerous tunnels. The central route has been favoured, as it links nicely with irrigation plans for water from the Danjiangkou Dam project and uses water from the Sanxia or Three Gorges project. The central route also links nicely with economic development plans along the Beijing–Guangzhou Railway. The western plan is to divert water from tributaries of the Chang River on the Qinghai-Tibetan Plateau. This route is the least likely to be completed.

As with the Sanxia Dam, many individuals and ministries worry that such a massive water transfer project will tie up funds better used for smaller projects and will have unforeseen ecological consequences. Many have urged that large-scale water transfer projects should be dropped in favour of less expensive remedies such as tube well development, use of less water-demanding crops (such as soybeans and sorghum), and concentration of irrigation water on high-quality lands.

How is nature conservation managed in China?

Nature conservation in one region benefits the entire earth and its inhabitants. Preserving habitats such as forest cover can mitigate the effects of pollution and land degradation, and protecting species helps to maintain the balance of ecosystems. However, in China, as in other parts of the world, the protection given to wildlife and to seed banks and nature reserves is erratic and often inadequate. In addition, finding disease-resistant plants and crops is becoming more and more difficult, and the extinction of species is a regularly occurring natural phenomenon. The loss of one species can trigger the death of dependent species and set off a chain reaction of extinction. In this section, I review China's nature conservation policies. I begin by briefly looking at China's natural heritage and assessing conservation management during the Mao years and the early reform years. I then examine the rise in nature reserves that occurred in the 1980s and 1990s and look at some of the laws and agencies that have been created to support conservation in China. Using the case of the giant panda, I try to illustrate some of the threats to China's flora and fauna and to highlight some of the protective measures that have been put in place.

China's flora and wildlife

China is known as a treasure house of rare species of wildlife. Official statistics indicate that China has more than 2,100 kinds of terrestrial vertebrate including 1,186 birds, 450 mammals, 320 reptiles, and 210 amphibians. Several hundreds of these animals are native to China, the most famous being the giant panda (*Ailuropoda melanoleuca*), the lesser panda (*Ailurus fulgens*) and the Yangzi crocodile (*Alligator sinensis*). China also is home to 14 per cent of the world's existing 9,000 species of birds and about one-fifth of the world's reptilian species. A mapping exercise of 2,980 genera found in China shows a substantial number of uniquely Chinese flora.

Conservation during the Mao years

In the early 1950s, environmental conservation was far from the minds of most people. Little nature conservation was undertaken before the completion of the First Five-Year plan in 1957. The first nature reserve, Dinghu Shan near Zhaoqing in Guangdong province, was established in 1956. Between 1957 and 1975 China became preoccupied with political movements. The Great Leap Forward (1958–61) and the three bad years (1959–61) during which there was widespread famine left China little time to heed nature conservation. However, as the famine was partly caused by environmental degradation, the government began to think more about nature conservation in the early 1960s. In 1963, new proposals on nature conservation work were put before the National People's Congress, and it looked as if nature preservation was beginning to make considerable progress. The beginning of the Cultural Revolution in 1966 meant that these laws and proposals were never put into effect, and little was accomplished for most of the following decade.

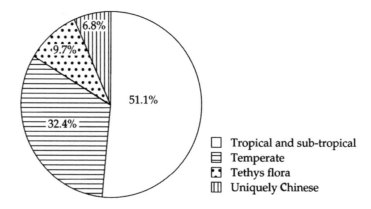

Figure 5.3 A typology of 2,980 genera of flora found in China
Source: Zhongguo Kexueyuan 1985: 20

The establishment of nature reserves

China began to establish nature reserves in earnest in the early 1980s. However, by 1980 it was probably too late for many nearly extinct animals including the wild horse (*Equus przewalskii*; now reintroduced), the long-nosed antelope (*Saiga tatarica*), the Xinjiang tiger (*Panthera uncia*), the rhinoceros (*Rhinoceros sondaicus*), the white-headed leaf monkey (*Presbytis leucocephalus*), the hog deer (*Cervus porcinus*), the Oriental ibis (*Threskiornis melanocephalus*), the white crane (*Grus leucogeranus*), Cabot's tragopan (*Tragopan caboti*), and Swinhoe's pheasant (*Lophura swinhoii*). With its total area of nature reserves equalling only 0.17 per cent of national territory in 1980, China was way behind the leading nations.

As the country began to embark on new economic policies in the 1980s, nature reserves were often seen as burdens on local budgets. In particular, people living around the reserve areas felt burdened, as the state did little to compensate them for their loss of resources when a reserve was established. Indigenous peoples from minority groups were largely ignored and given little or no compensation when reserves in the 1980s were established. From the 1990s, a wider socioeconomic view of reserve management began to develop, and more attention was given to the effect of reserves on indigenous groups.

In general, the land and the resources in China's nature reserves are state-owned. However, the administration of nature reserves in China was not uniform until 1998, and before 1998 only a minority of reserves was directly administrated by the national government. Today, the system is undergoing consolidation and the state now coordinates and administrates all of China's reserves. Official accounts state that China had 14.8 per cent of its land territory set aside as nature reserves as of 2004. However, such numbers are meaningless if there is little or no enforcement of conservation measures within these reserves.

Nature conservation was largely assisted by foreign funding and foreign expertise in the 1980s and early 1990s. However, foreign money and participation was often concentrated in only a few reserves in particular areas of the country. Certain animals and plants became favoured for protection because of their public image among foreign populations. The giant panda is the classic example. Consequently, the preservation of some species was given less priority. This led to the development of a few world-class quality reserves, whereas other reserves were reserves in name only.

Often, officials had to destroy part of what they were to protect in order to pay for protection of the rest of a reserve. Even in some reserves today, officials often must maximise income from all their lands. Forestry officials have been known to ignore regulations and allow safaris to enter their forests in exchange for shooting fees and the sale of trophy heads. Many Chinese argue for increased investment in nature conservation by pointing out the long-term economic value of such a policy. This is the only benefit they can stress when faced with a poor, pragmatic and, at times and in some places, corrupt government.

Government responses to endangered wildlife

One cannot talk about Chinese wildlife without mentioning the giant panda. Today the territory of the panda has shrunk considerably to six small discontinuous areas in southern Shaanxi and Sichuan provinces. The areal range of the animal had decreased from about 20,000 sq. km in 1970 to 10,000 sq. km in 1990. During 1975 and 1976, 138 giant pandas died in areas along the Sichuan–Gansu border due to the deterioration of the bamboo groves that provide their food. This stimulated the beginning of attempts to preserve the panda's habitat. In 1983, several dozen pandas died from starvation. A considerable rescue effort was organised and many pandas were saved. In 1994 and 1995, cold weather and another shortage of arrow bamboo necessitated the rescue of nine pandas near starvation. The total giant panda population of China is estimated to be above 1,000 in the wild as of 2001, but dozens more have been bred through artificial insemination. The Wolong Nature Reserve in Sichuan is by far the largest reserve. The World Wildlife Fund has funded studies of the panda at Wolong since 1981.

At present, some other animals are receiving similar protection to the panda, and others are not. Many authors have noted the absence of birds, finfish and crustaceans. In many ways, it is this reduction in numbers of common wildlife that is most disturbing and difficult to combat. Pollution and increased economic activity are largely responsible. In order to increase marine food production, for example, larvae of certain aquatic animals such as crabs and carp have been stocked in lakes, leading to a reduction of indigenous species. Problems with coastal fishing have also become serious. The government has only recently responded to some of these alarming situations. For example, in 1999, China announced a policy of no further increases in fish catches.

Trade in endangered species

Profit-making is also taking its toll in other forms. China has been among the top exporters of cat skins in the world. China has also contributed to reductions in animal populations in other countries. For example, Hong Kong, the People's Republic of China and Taiwan were all among the top ten ivory-importing polities in the last two decades, and at times they have been accused of ignoring bans on the trade in rhinoceros horns.

What are the effects of environmental degradation?

To conclude this chapter, we now briefly look at some of the social, political and economic effects of environmental degradation in China.

Worsening conditions for the urban poor

There are clear links between environmental degradation and poverty in China. In rural areas, this is reflected in data on soil erosion and income. In urban areas of China, as in everywhere else I know of, poor people tend to live in the most polluted districts. Some of this is institutionalised by the *hukou* or household registration system. Rural in-migrants used to be effectively kept out of cities through the Communist rationing system and people without an urban *hukou* had to share rations of rice, eggs and other things that belonged to their relatives or friends, as there was no other way they could get these basic foods. Today, rationing in Chinese cities is minimal, which means that rural people can move to the urban areas where they can find menial or illegal jobs that pay better than farming or working in rural enterprises. These people end up living in the parts of cities with the worst services and the most pollution, since rent is cheap and their presence is tolerated. The potential for social disturbances in these urban ghettos is large, and in recent years we have seen protest, although most of it is tied to wage discrimination rather than to the local environment. It appears that *hukou* regulations are being freed up, so rural in-migrants may have more rights in urban China in the future.

Increasing political commitment to environmental issues

Politically, the environment is slowly moving up the agenda. Since the late 1990s, environmental organs within various levels of government have been upgraded, and local offices are getting assigned environmental targets as part of their responsibility system. The latter means that environmental clean-up and management is tied to job retention or promotion. Campaigns for environmental education mean that Chinese youth are now more aware of the environmental consequences of their actions. So far, it appears most of the impact has been on the urban élite, but environmental education is filtering down to rural areas. Green semi-governmental organisations (GONGOs) are being tolerated; so too are non-governmental organisations, as long as their work appears to stay out of the political arena. As noted in the conservation section, foreign involvement has been greatest in the establishment of nature reserves and the protection of favoured species.

Environmental diplomacy

The environment has also played a role in diplomacy. The earliest example was so-called 'panda diplomacy', in which the Chinese under Chairman Mao Zedong gave pandas to zoos in favoured foreign countries. Later, foreign countries and China saw the environment as an easy way to negotiate exchanges of aid. Whereas foreign organisations can get criticised by non-governmental organisations for funding development projects or aiding development of the Chinese government, environmental aid frees up Chinese government capital for less politically correct investment. Some countries have been very pragmatic in their aid packages, such as Japan, the largest donor to China. In the early days, the Japanese gave considerable sums of money for pollution clean-up in the northeast. In part, the reason was that Japan had colonised this area and was familiar with it. Also, the wind from this area blows directly over Japan most of the year. Today, the Japanese have changed their focus and are investing in much more altruistic poverty alleviation programmes in the interior. We have also seen some competition among various groups such as Japan, the European Union, and the United States to contribute environmental aid. To a limited degree, the Chinese have offered aid to other countries – most notably in combating arid land degradation and in training about biogas (marsh gas) production in rural areas. Biogas is produced by fermenting straw, faeces, and other wastes. The biogas then can be used for cooking and heating.

Conclusion

Environmental problems in China are serious and clearly pose a dilemma for the government. In some parts of China, particularly but not exclusively the west, poverty makes it difficult for people to not harm their natural environment in order to survive. At the same time, more prosperous areas of the country have developed the ability to pollute as a get-rich-quick philosophy has dominated – particularly at the local level.

Although much progress has been made in the last twenty years in correcting mistakes of the past, new environmental problems have arisen as the population of China continues to grow and as the country shifts towards a market-oriented economy. Thus the two keys to China's future environment are the ability of the Chinese state and economy to regulate and manage environmental problems in a rapidly changing society, and the ability of China's natural environment to cope with a continuing growth of population and demands of that population for more consumption.

There is no easy answer to these problems, but certain measures will help.

Although political transparency and growth of non-governmental organisations can be harmful, particularly if non-governmental groups are not armed with proper information or the ability to analyse the situation properly, they are absolutely necessary to keep a check on officials and enterprises determined to achieve economic growth at any environmental cost.

Education can be very helpful for increasing environmental awareness and thus reducing environmental degradation as well as improving the above-mentioned pressure on the government and enterprises.

Continued opening to the outside world introduces environmental problems such as the development of the private automobile industry and social problems such as increased instability that could affect the environment. But these introductions can be seen as an inevitable trade-off, since further environmental information and other resources from outside the country are helping to halt environmental degradation in many areas.

Finally, there is a need for China, as well as the rest of the world, to properly cost environmental degradation into the economy and to give environmental protection a major role in government policy. Although this appears to be easier to do for pollution than resource degradation, it must be done for both in order for some sort of balance to be reached which will stop the country from suffering much loss of life and beauty.

References

Edmonds, R. L. (1992) 'The Sanxia (Three Gorges) Project: the Environmental Argument Surrounding China's Super Dam', *Global Ecology and Biogeography Letters* 4/2: 105–25.

—— (1999) 'China's Environmental Problems', in R. E. Gamer (ed.), *Understanding Contemporary China*, London: Lynne Rienner, pp. 237–65.

Elvin, M. and Liu, T. J. (eds) (1998) *Sediments of Time: Environment and Society in Chinese History*, Cambridge: Cambridge University Press.

Lindert, P. H. (2000) *Shifting Ground: The Changing Agricultural Soils of China and Indonesia*, Cambridge, MA: MIT Press.

NBS (National Bureau of Statistics) (1991, 1992, 1994, 1995) Beijing: China Statistics Press.

NBS (National Bureau of Statistics) (1985, 1987, 1990) *Zhongguo tongji nianjian* (China statistical yearbook), Beijing: China Statistics Press.

Smil, V. (1993) *China's Environmental Crisis: An Inquiry into the Limits of National Development*, Armonk, NY: M. E. Sharpe.

Zhongguo Kexueyuan (ed.) (1985) *Zhongguo ziran dili*.

Further reading

Brown, L. (1994) *Who Will Feed China? Wake-up Call for a Small Planet*, London: Earthscan.

Cannon, T. (ed.) (2000) *China's Economic Growth: Impact on Regions, Migration and Environment*, Basingstoke: Macmillan.

Day, K. A. (2005) *China's Environment and the Challenge of Sustainable Development*, Armonk, NY: M. E. Sharpe.

Economy, E. C. (2004) *The River Runs Black: The Environmental Challenge to China's Future*, Ithaca, NY: Cornell University Press.

Edmonds, R. L. (1999) 'China's environmental problems', in R. E. Gamer (ed.), *Understanding Contemporary China*, London: Lynne Rienner, pp. 237–65.

Edmonds, R. L. (ed.) (2000) *Managing the Chinese Environment*, Oxford: Oxford University Press.

—— (1994) *Patterns of China's Lost Harmony: A Survey of the Country's Environmental Degradation and Protection*, London: Routledge.

Johnson, T. M., Liu F. and Newfarmer, R. (1997) *Clear Water, Blue Skies: China's Environment in the New Century*, Washington: World Bank.

Lee, J. C. K. and Tilbury, D. (1998) 'The Challenge for Environmental Education in China', *Geography* 83/3: 227–36.

Lindert, P. H. (2000) *Shifting Ground: The Changing Agricultural Soils of China and Indonesia*, Cambridge, MA: MIT Press.

Livernash, R. T. (ed.) (2001) *China: Air, Land, and Water*, London: World Bank.

Ma, X. and Ortolano, L. (2000) *Environmental Regulation in China*, Lanham, MD: Rowman & Littlefield.

McCormack, G. (2001) 'Water Margins: Competing Paradigms in China', *Critical Asian Studies* 33/1: 5–30.

McElroy, M. B., Neilson, C. P. and Lydon, P. (eds) (1999) *Emerging China: Reconciling Environmental Protection and Economic Growth*, Cambridge, MA: Harvard University Press.

Murphey, R. (1967) 'Man and Nature in China', *Modern Asian Studies* 1/4: 313–33.

Sinkule, B. J. and Ortolano, L. (1995) *Implementing Environmental Policy in China*, Westport, CT: Praeger.

Smil, V. (1995) 'Who Will Feed China?', *China Quarterly*, 143: 801–13.

Smil, V. and Mao, Y. (coordinators) (1998) *The Economic Costs of China's Environmental Degradation*, Cambridge, MA: American Academy of Arts and Sciences.

Sun, H. D. (1995) 'Nature Reserves Gain Ground Step by Step', *China Environment News*, 15 August: 4.

6

Population change and food security in China

ROBERT FAIRBANKS ASH

Introduction

Since the end of the eighteenth century, when Thomas Malthus published his *Essay on Population*, anxiety has been expressed that continuing population growth will eventually place an unsustainable pressure on food supplies. This doomsday scenario has not been realised, although some warn that it could yet happen. However, even if global production of food remains more than sufficient to meet everyone's needs, hunger, malnourishment and starvation still affect hundreds of millions of people throughout the world – especially in sub-Saharan Africa.

The fact that widespread hunger and malnutrition exist despite global food output having reached a level capable of feeding the world's population highlights the critical importance of distribution policies. Producing enough food is one thing; ensuring that available supplies are shared among the world's population in such a way as to reduce, or eliminate, hunger is quite another. In the late 1970s and early 1980s, intense competition among major cereal exporters – the United States, Canada and the European Union – resulted in major increases in grain stocks. Storing large amounts of cereals is a costly operation, and a short-term consequence of the rise in stocks was a sharp rise in cereal aid to poor countries. At the same time, the gluts caused international grain prices to fall. This encouraged exporting countries to reduce the area of land planted under cereals, either by cutting subsidies previously paid to farmers or by deliberately paying them not to plant cereals – the so-called 'set aside' policy. This longer-term response helped protect farmers in developed countries, but at the expense of the populations of developing countries who depended on imports of cheap food.

Maintaining a balance between food and population is the core economic issue that has faced China throughout its history. Historical evidence suggests that in normal conditions, farmers were capable of producing enough basic food (i.e. grain) to provide China's population with sufficient energy to keep it reasonably healthy and productive. But the cushion above subsistence was a narrow one. Indeed, not until the 1980s did grain output growth overtake population growth by a sufficiently wide margin to guarantee China's basic food security. In the past, natural disasters – especially floods and drought – often caused famine. A survey conducted during the early 1930s revealed that, on average, three famines had occurred within the memory of informants. In the years since 1949, the most serious lapse in food security reflected a man-made disaster – that of the collapse of the 'Great Leap Forward' – which precipitated a catastrophic famine that led, between 1959 and 1961, to the deaths of up to 30 million people.

Following this disaster, the Chinese government coined a slogan which stated that 'agriculture is the foundation of the economy; grain is the cornerstone of that foundation'. In the context of that time, with farming in a state of collapse and millions of peasants dead from starvation, the imperative of prioritising agriculture and restoring food production commanded obvious logic. But even today agricultural and food issues are still major preoccupations of the central government. For Chinese leaders, mindful of the catastrophic famine of forty years ago and nervous of reliance on imported food supplies, the old slogan remains relevant, even though grain output growth has generated a comfortable cushion above subsistence needs. This is the background to the Chinese government's commitment to maintaining basic domestic food self-sufficiency.

China is so large, both in terms of its geographical size and its population, that emerging demographic trends promise to have a significant impact on associated global trends. By the same token, China's changing involvement in international grain trade is also likely to have a significance that transcends its own borders. Much of the concern that has, in recent years, been expressed in some quarters about China's grain economy derives from a powerful international dimension that attaches to the so-called 'grain problem' facing China. If China cannot feed itself, it will have to turn to external sources of supply and become a grain importer. China's growing inability to maintain grain self-sufficiency could, it has been argued, raise its imports to such levels as to cause world food prices to rise dramatically, to the detriment of many low-income, food-importing countries (above all, in sub-Saharan Africa). Hence, the spectre of China squeezing out other countries competing for exportable supplies, and 'starving the world'.

This chapter examines the issues of population changes and food security in China. It first examines changes to China's demographic profile since 1949, and official attitudes towards these changes. It then analyses the rationale and effect of official policies towards the food sector in order to investigate to what extent domestic food supplies have been able to accommodate China's growing population over the last half-century. Later in the chapter, I suggest that, at the beginning of the twenty-first century, the importance of population change has been overtaken by rising per capita income as a main determinant of food demand. The chapter concludes with an assessment of China's food security for the short-term future.

Demographic trends in China since 1949

In September 1949, Mao Zedong made the following remark:

> It is a very good thing that China has a big population. Even if China's population multiplies many times, she is fully capable of finding a solution ... Of all the things in the world, people are the most precious. Under the leadership of the Communist Party, as long as there are people, every kind of miracle can be performed ... (Mao 1961: 453–4)

The sanguine tone of these remarks reflect Mao's view that man, in a generic sense, was the instrument of economic, social and political transformation. As Figure 6.1 shows, China's total population has, in fact, more than doubled since 1949.

Concealed in this figure are estimates of the average annual rate of growth of total population, which are shown in Table 6.1.

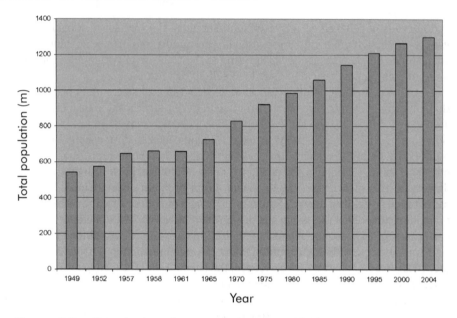

Figure 6.1   China's changing population since 1949

Sources: National Bureau of Statistics (NBS), *Xin Zhongguo wushi nian tongji ziliao huibian* (Compendium of Statistical Materials on Fifty Years of New China) (Beijing: Zhongguo tongji chubanshe, 1999); NBS, *Zhongguo tongji nianjian* (China Statistical Yearbook) (Beijing: Zhongguo tongji chubanshe, various issues); NBS, *Zhongguo tongji zhaiyao 2005* (China Statistical Abstract), (Beijing: Zhongguo tongji chubanshe), p. 39.

The years since 1949 divide themselves into two main periods. Except for a major interruption associated with the Great Leap Forward (1958–62), from the early 1950s until the early 1970s, China's population growth was rapid, averaging over 2 per cent per annum. By contrast, from 1972 down to the present day, the government has had unprecedented success in limiting population growth. In less than two decades, the rate of natural increase was more than halved. As a result, by the end of the twentieth century, China had completed its demographic transition. Although not literally unprecedented in modern times (South Korea and Taiwan also achieved spectacular declines in population growth in a short period of time), the Chinese achievement is remarkable, bearing in mind the country's physical and demographic size.

In interpreting official Chinese population figures, it must be remembered that the quality of official estimates has steadily improved since the 1950s. Even so, the scale of the task of measuring demographic change remains formidable, requiring the involvement of 6 million 'on-the-spot' investigators during the most recent (2000) National Census. Quite apart from temptations by parents to conceal births or by officials to falsify data to show a 'better' result, in recent years efforts to track population change have been made more difficult by the loosening of household registration controls (the *hukou* system) and the associated mass

Table 6.1 Population growth (selected periods, 1949–2003)

Period	Average rate of natural increase (% p.a.)
1949–72	2.1
1972–2004	1.3
1953–7	2.4
1958–62	0.8
1963–5	2.5
1966–72	1.5
1973–7	1.5
1978–85	1.2
1985–90	1.6
1990–5	1.2

Sources: National Bureau of Statistics (NBS), *Xin Zhongguo wushi nian tongji ziliao huibian* (Compendium of Statistical Materials on Fifty Years of New China) (Beijing: Zhongguo tongji chubanshe, 1999); NBS, Zhongguo tongji nianjian (China Statistical Yearbook) (Beijing: Zhongguo tongji chubanshe, various issues); NBS, *Zhongguo tongji zhaiyao 2005* (China Statistical Abstract) (Beijing: Zhongguo tongji chubanshe), p. 39.

movement of migrants around the country (for more on the quality of China's demographic data, see Banister 1987: 12–49, and Scharping 2003: 202–7).

Because of differences in income and tastes (incomes in urban areas have traditionally been higher than in rural areas), the changing distribution of population between countryside and cities is a structural demographic feature that has influenced food demand and consumption. From this perspective, two important observations may be made. The first is that during the Mao era, the Chinese government pursued a deliberately anti-urbanisation strategy (especially after the Great Leap Forward). This not only embraced controls to prevent peasants from entering cities but also involved the implementation of measures designed to send urban residents (especially unemployed young people) to the country-side – a process described by Banister (1987: 342) as an attempt to 'ruralise' China. By contrast, this process was reversed from the 1980s. As a result, the post-1978 years have seen an accelerated process of urbanisation taking place. Thus, between 1978 and 2004, the urban share of total population rose from 17.9 to 41.8 per cent (see the sources for Table 6.1 for more details).

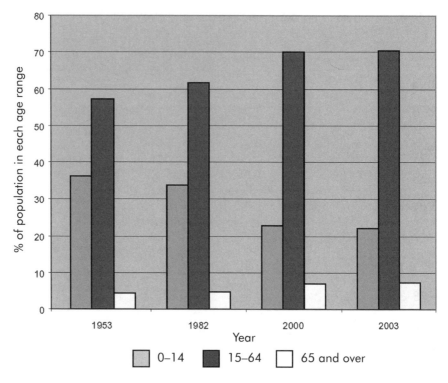

Figure 6.2   Changing age structure of China's population

Sources: National Bureau of Statistics (NBS), *Xin Zhongguo wushi nian tongji ziliao huibian* (Compendium of Statistical Materials on Fifty Years of New China); NBS, *Zhongguo tongji nianjian* (China Statistical Yearbook), (Beijing: Zhongguo tongji chubanshe, various issues).

The age structure of a population is an important determinant of food demand. If infants and children are to grow healthily, their caloric and nutritional needs have to be met. The same principle applies to pregnant and lactating women. Studies show that, in general, grain requirements rise by about 70 per cent between the 0–14 and 15–44 age groups, before declining as middle and old age set in. These are important considerations to bear in mind in interpreting the changing age structure of China's population since 1953, when the first official census was taken.

Since 1953 there has been a steady increase in the share of people of working age (15–64 years) in China's total population. This has been offset by a steady decline in the proportion of young dependents (0–14), especially under the impact of strict family planning policies during the 1980s and 1990s. Although recent years have seen a quite significant rise in the share of the 65s and over, the problem of an ageing population has yet to emerge in China. It will do so after 2010, as increasing numbers of workers reach retirement and pensionable age. By the 2020s, the burden of looking after a rapidly ageing population will start to become acute. For the time being, however, China remains in a demographic 'Golden Age', characterised by a relatively low dependency ratio – especially in terms of elderly dependents. The favourable age profile of the population offers China a window of opportunity during which the government can formulate policies to anticipate the challenges associated with a less propitious future age structure.

Population policies in China

Before 1949, China's crude death rate was about 25 per thousand, its infant mortality rate was some 200 per thousand, and life expectancy at birth was a mere 35 years – conditions typical of a poor country (Hao 2000: 34). Subsequently, with the establishment of a strong government capable of implementing simple but effective improvements in basic health and hygiene, the crude death rate fell sharply (from 20 to 10.8 per thousand, 1949–57). By contrast, however, the crude birth rate increased significantly, and by 1957 the total fertility rate had reached 6.2. The outcome was a surge in the rate of natural increase to well over 2 per cent annually.

In part, the maintenance of a high and rising birth rate had its origins in China's young age structure, including a high share of fertile females of child-bearing ages. But population was also an ideological issue, and the absence of population control measures reflected a deliberately pro-natalist policy that favoured more, not fewer births. During the first decade of the PRC, powerful anti-Malthusian sentiment informed official attitudes towards population. Those who dissented from this view were attacked as 'rightists' and such was the strength of official opposition to them that by 1957, 'not only were the views of the anti-natalists condemned, but so also was the profession of demography' (Howe and Walker 1977: 260). Although the findings of China's first scientific census in 1953 revealed a population that was much larger than had been assumed, the First Five-Year Plan document, published in 1955, contained no discussion of population issues.

By the late 1950s, the central government's earlier pro-natalist policy had given way to rising concern about accelerating population growth. However, nascent population policy initiatives were overtaken by the events of the Great Leap Forward, which precipitated a demographic catastrophe, reflected in a rapid rise in mortality, side by side with a falling birth rate (between 1958 and 1961 the crude death rate rose from 12 to 33 per thousand, while the birth rate fell from 29 to 18 per thousand). The outcome was a famine that took the lives of up to 30 million people between 1959 and 1961.

With recovery from the Great Leap under way by the early 1960s, the renewed urgency of demographic pressures was again recognised by government policies through a variety of policy initiatives. Their impact was, however, minimal. The chaos of the early and most radical years of the Cultural Revolution made long-term population planning impossible, and as a result, fertility remained high. Indeed, until the early 1970s, China still had no effective population policy and the rate of natural increase remained very high. As a result, large annual increments continued to be added to total population.

It was not until 1972 that the government began to implement effective family planning policies, the policy thrust of which was to control births by attempting to restrict family size through late marriages, and spaced and fewer births. In 1970, the CCP Central Committee and State Council first formally proposed an optimum of two children per family. For the first time, key population growth targets were included in the Fourth Five-Year Plan (1971–5). These and other goals were pursued at local levels through the creation of birth control committees, which were responsible for formulating local population growth targets.

Until the late 1970s, the two-child family was propagated through slogans, such as 'one isn't too few; two is good; three is too many'. At first, cities were the focus of the two-child campaign, but later it spread to the countryside. Gradually too, the voluntary nature of the family planning programme began to weaken as material rewards and sanctions were introduced in an effort to check the excessive growth of families. In any case, from around 1972, a sharp decline in fertility and population growth, especially in cities, began to be observable.

The watershed Third Plenum of the Eleventh CCP Central Committee (December 1978) was symbolic of a shift from a development strategy centred on ideology to one centred on growth and economic development. The new emphasis was reflected in a change in the thrust of family planning policy from late marriages and spaced births to stricter control of family size. Early in 1979, a new policy decision was announced – propagated under a new slogan: 'one is best, at most two, but never a third' – whereby each married couple was encouraged to have only one child. At first, the one-child policy, which was advocated in both urban and rural sectors, was voluntary. Couples freely decided whether or not to sign a 'one-child pledge'. Those who fulfilled the pledge received a cash reward, as well as other benefits, such as extra maternity leave, better housing, higher pensions, free education and health, and priority access to jobs. But by 1982, a much more coercive system was in place, with increasingly severe penalties imposed on couples who contravened official regulations. The severity of such penalties is suggested in Judith Banister's comment that 'any second or higher order births that happened in spite of government pressure were met with escalating punishments designed to impoverish the offending couple for at least fourteen years if not for life' (1987: 191).

The policy met with strong resistance from couples whose first child was a baby girl, especially in the countryside, where a strong preference for boys – for both practical and cultural reasons – persisted. Resistance took various forms. One was to under-report female births or use adoption as a device to enable couples to have a second child. Another was pregnant women's use of ultra-sound scans to determine the sex of the child they were carrying, giving them the opportunity to have an abortion if the child was female. Most terrible of all was the temporary increase in the incidence of female infanticide. According to the 2000 Census, the national average male : female ratio was 120 : 100 among newborn babies; in Jiangxi, Guangdong and Henan, it exceeded 130 : 100. (The male : female ratio across China was considerably higher than in the 1990 Census, when it was *c.* 111 : 100. International norms are between 103 : 100 and 107 : 100.)

Neither the coercion nor the literal implementation of a one-child policy lasted. To some extent, the shift towards a more relaxed policy interpretation reflected the unforeseen consequences of coercion. By the second half of the 1980s, exceptions to the one-child policy were introduced, allowing rural couples to have a second baby if the first child had been a girl. Such exemptions have remained in force and been extended in most, if not all, provinces. Interestingly, this more relaxed approach has *not* been accompanied by a rise in the birth rate. On the contrary, fertility has continued to decline, although this has been assisted by a fall in the number of young women of child-bearing age. Chinese officials claim that in the absence of strict family control policies, there would have been some 250 million more births in the last quarter of the twentieth century. China's total fertility rate has also already fallen below the current average level of developed countries.

Food production in China

In China, food has traditionally been classified into staples and non-staples. 'Staples' include foods considered essential to the human diet. Broadly speaking, they coincide with the Chinese definition of food grains: namely, cereals (rice, wheat and maize), non-cereal grain, and grain equivalents (such as beans, pulses, tubers and potatoes). Access to staple foods holds the key to subsistence and the maintenance of basic health and productivity. 'Non-staples' – or 'supplementary foodstuffs' (*fushipin*) – refer to vegetables, fruit, meat, eggs, milk and other foods, which, although not essential to the fulfilment of basic nutritional requirements, are important additional sources of protein and fat.

Historically, both the production and consumption of food in China were dominated by cereals and coarse grains (including potatoes). The exception was among nomadic minorities working as pastoral farmers in remote border regions, who enjoyed a diet based more on meat, cheese and milk. But until the end of the Mao era, the diet of most Chinese – and virtually all of those living in the countryside – was overwhelmingly dependent on the direct consumption of grain crops. For example, a famous farm survey conducted throughout China during 1929–33 revealed that 87 per cent of the energy (calorie) intake of peasants, representing 90 per cent of the population, came from grain and potatoes. Legumes (mainly beans) added a further 7 per cent of calories. By contrast, little more than 3 per cent of peasants' energy intake came from vegetables (including vegetable oil), and animal products accounted for barely 2 per cent. Sugar and fruit made up the tiny – less than 1 per cent – remaining balance (Buck 1937: 411).

Until as recently as the early 1980s, China's low-income economy was still significantly driven by an agriculture in which grain farming predominated; and household budgets were dominated by spending on food. Population growth was the principal source of increased demand for food, and only after 1978 did the aspirations of a more affluent population – especially in cities and coastal provinces – for a more varied diet generate an increasingly diversified structure of food output and the rapid expansion of production of meat, fish and dairy produce. In turn, farmers came under increasing pressure to provide more grain for indirect use – above all, to feed livestock.

The Mao era

In 1949 average per capita grain output in China was around 209 kg – well below the 270 kg minimum necessary to meet basic subsistence requirements. A 1950 report by the US Central Intelligence Agency (CIA) indicated that food shortages were sufficiently serious to cause widespread famine, especially in North China. (The report was titled 'The Food Outlook for Communist China', dated 3 February 1950 and was made public on 7 May 2004. It can be can be accessed via the CIA website at www.foia.cia.gov.) By 1952, however, economic recovery from depressed pre-1949 levels of production had raised total grain production by 45 per cent, enabling per capita output to reach a level sufficient to meet the subsistence needs of the population. Increases in the output of other foodstuffs were even more impressive, although their nutritional impact was less significant, since grain remained by far the most important source of energy and nutrition.

Before the process of agricultural collectivisation got under way in the 1950s, on average, almost 80 per cent of all the grain consumed by peasants was supplied from their own farms. For legumes, vegetables and fruit, the corresponding figure was in excess of two-thirds. By contrast, two-thirds of vegetable oils, animal products and sugar consumed by farmers were bought in local markets. But there were marked regional variations. In particular, in areas where the expansion of the rail network had encouraged a higher degree of commercialisation, the opportunity to specialise in lucrative cash crop production resulted in a higher level of off-farm purchases of all foodstuffs.

In 1953, the government introduced a monopoly procurement system in order to control the acquisition and distribution of essential foodstuffs. Its principal effect was to make the state the monopoly buyer and seller of all grains – a role it retained until the economic reforms of the 1980s, when retail markets began to play an increasingly significant role in distribution. Surplus grain, as calculated by the government in excess of peasants' requirements for taxes, rations, animal feed and seed, was purchased at prices set by the state. Most of this was reserved for sales to urban households, although a significant proportion was re-sold to peasants in order to combat poverty and provide disaster relief, as well as meet the food needs of non-grain farmers. Farmers were, however, allowed to retain small private plots, which became important sources of supplies of non-grain foods (especially vegetables, pork and poultry).

During the 1950s, farm policy was dominated by the view that institutional change was a sufficient condition of farm growth. If only the government could get the institutions 'right', agricultural growth would follow. 'Right' in this context meant the pursuit of fully socialist agricultural collectivisation – a process that had originally been expected to take place over a fifteen-year period (1953–67), but which was largely carried out in little more than a year as a result of an astonishing 'high tide' of collectivisation between July 1955 and the autumn of 1956. Less than two years later, a second surge of institutional change took place, when, in summer 1958 China's farmers were incorporated into large-scale rural people's communes. By the end of the 1950s, a highly centralised and tightly controlled framework was in place in the Chinese countryside, which lasted virtually intact until the early 1980s.

The consensus view is that even allowing for some benefits – for example, tighter control over the farm labour force, the ability to undertake rural capital formation and a greater capacity to combat natural disasters – the net economic impact of these institutional changes on agriculture was negative. Above all, the downgrading of material incentives and the tenuous connection between effort and reward under the income distribution system in the collective framework were both detrimental to agricultural and grain output growth.

Meanwhile, other important aspects of agricultural policy were neglected. Despite increased emphasis on extending irrigation facilities and, after the Great Leap Forward, on introducing modern inputs (especially chemical fertilisers), investment remained inadequate. Indeed, apart from 1963–5, when farm investment rose to a much higher level in response to the deep agricultural crisis precipitated by the Great Leap Forward, the farm sector's share of capital construction and other relevant forms of state investment was consistently barely more than 10 per cent between 1958–62 and 1976–80. Meanwhile, the net barter terms of trade between agriculture and industry continued to move against the countryside.

During the Mao era, some progress was made towards improving farm technology, especially through the development of higher yielding varieties of rice, wheat, maize and sorghum. Indeed, as an analyst has commented, 'China's … breeding

Table 6.2 Sown area, output and yield of grain in China

	Total sown area (m. ha)	Total output (m. tons)	Average yield (kg per ha)
1949	109.96	113.20	1 029.47
1952	114.41	163.90	1 432.57
1957	133.63	195.05	1 459.63
1965	119.63	194.55	1 626.26
1970	119.26	239.95	2 011.99
1975	121.06	284.50	2 350.07
1978	120.59	304.75	2 527.16

Source: NBS, *Zhongguo nongcun jingji tongji daquan (1949–1986) (Statistical Almanac of China's Rural Economy)* (Beijing: Nongye chubanshe, 1989), pp. 148–9.

community became a formidable practical scientific force' (Stone 1993: 326). However, from the mid-1950s until the end of the 1970s, China achieved only modest rises in real income per head. Accordingly, the main burden on the food sector was to secure sufficient increases in the output of essential foodstuffs – above all, grain – to sustain the rising population. The performance of the grain sector during this period is summarised in Table 6.2.

Following China's economic rehabilitation (1949–52), grain output growth under the First Five-Year Plan (1953–7) was rapid (3.5 per cent p.a.), significantly exceeding population expansion. But such growth overwhelmingly reflected the expansion of the sown area, which rose by almost 18 per cent, in contrast to average yields which changed hardly at all. Between 1957 and 1965, however, the sown area under grain fell sharply, even though it subsequently stabilised. The inference is that during the 1960s and 1970s, grain output growth derived mainly from improvements in land productivity – a more secure basis of output growth in a country like China, where arable land is scarce.

Concealed in Table 6.2's deliberately brief résumé of post-1957 trends are the extraordinary events of the Great Leap Forward and its aftermath. The Leap was an attempt to accelerate farm output growth (especially grain production) without sacrificing the growth of industry (especially heavy industry). It sought to fulfil this goal mainly by mobilising farmers on an unprecedented scale by incorporating them into huge rural people's communes. These were intended to provide more effective control over the agricultural labour force, as well as to generate benefits from an even larger scale of farming than was already available in the collectives. However, the Leap was more of a vision than a carefully thought-out economic plan. As politics and ideology took precedence over objective economic considerations, production targets were raised to impossible levels. Such was the pressure on cadres to fulfil these goals that they were unable to admit failure. As reports of the 1958 grain harvest filtered upwards, the statistical claims became increasingly exaggerated. Meanwhile, early reports of a bumper harvest of 375 million tons – twice that of 1957 – were accepted in Beijing, where the government responded by adjusting grain distribution and other policies in such a way as to exacerbate a situation in which, in truth, 1958 output had risen by a mere 1.3 per cent. As output continued to fall and requisitions from villages increased, famine ensued. Between 1958 and 1960, average per capita grain output declined from 303 to 217 kg; by the end of 1961, some 30 million excess deaths had occurred. Although recovery got under way in 1962, even in 1965, when total grain production had re-attained the 1957 level, per capita output – 268 kg – was still at the very margin of subsistence.

Throughout the Mao years, farm policy was dominated by what the central government in Beijing regarded as the strategic imperative of maximising grain production. This preoccupation was understandable, given the innate poverty of China and the consequent need to maintain people's basic health and well-being through the provision of adequate energy and nutritional supplies. In turn, the grain imperative was reflected in the virtual absence of farm diversification during these years.

During the Cultural Revolution (1966–76), a cornerstone of China's farm policy was strong advocacy of grain self-sufficiency. Interpreted literally, national self-sufficiency in grain was not attained during this period, although China came very close to fulfilling the goal. Between 1966 and 1976, China was consistently a net importer of grain, the volume of such shipments fluctuating from a minimum of 0.6 million tons (1971) to a high of 4.5 million tons (1974). But in no year did such imports account for more than 1.6 per cent of domestic production.

In the end, the most telling indicator of the disappointing performance of China's grain sector is revealed by a comparison of average per capita grain output between the last three years of the First Five-Year Plan period and the final three years of Mao's life. During this nineteen-year period, average grain production per head remained virtually unchanged. In 1955–7 it averaged 302.6 kg; in 1974–6 the corresponding figure was 305.5 kg – less than a percentage point higher (estimates of total grain production for every year from 1949 until 1999 can be found in NBS 2000: 37). In terms of its welfare implications, this finding is a serious indictment of Chinese food policies in China under Mao Zedong.

China's continental scope is such that the regional dimensions of national trends always deserve consideration. An important regional finding is concealed in the foregoing analysis. It is that throughout the Mao era, the centre of gravity in terms of grain production was the southern half of the country. Detailed analysis has shown that during the period of the First Five-Year Plan (1953–7), only the existence of significant grain surpluses in northwest and southwest China prevented a national deficit from emerging (Walker 1984: 89). My calculations reveal that what, in 1957, had been a combined surplus in the northwest and southwest of just over 4 million tons was transformed into a deficit of 6.2 million tons. By contrast, however, an astonishing achievement was the emergence from deficit status in the 1950s to large surpluses by both eastern China (8 million tons), and the northeast (11.3 million tons).

The reform era

Since 1979, the reformist strategy of the Chinese government has generated rapid rises in income in both urban and rural sectors. Although the urban population and those living in China's coastal areas have benefited disproportionately from the economic reforms, it is a reasonable generalisation that in almost all regions increasing prosperity has overtaken population growth to become the single most important determinant of food demand.

Table 6.3 summarises China's grain performance between 1978 and 2004. The selection of years shown in the table is intended to draw attention to important aspects of Chinese farmers' supply response to the structural changes in demand taking place. An important watershed was reached in 1984, when average per capita grain output reached around 400 kg – a level commensurate with the provision at existing income levels of significant amounts of animal protein in addition to meeting basic direct grain consumption needs. It is noteworthy, however, that this level was not re-attained until 1990. In the first half of the 1990s, annual fluctuations in total production were quite marked, although at the end of the 1990s a series of record harvests showed the ability of the grain sector to reach levels of per capita output in

Table 6.3 Total and per capita output of grain in China since 1978

	Total output (m. tons)	Average output per head of total population (kg)
1978	304.8	316.6
1984	407.3	390.3
1985	379.1	358.1
1989	407.6	361.6
1990	446.2	390.3
1995	466.6	385.3
1996	504.5	412.2
1997	494.2	399.8
1998	512.3	410.5
1999	508.4	403.8
2000	462.2	365.1
2001	452.6	354.7
2002	457.1	355.8
2003	430.7	333.3
2004	469.5	361.2
2005	484.0	370.2

Sources: *Zhongguo tongji nianjian*, op. cit., various issues; *Zhongguo tongji zhaiyao*, 2005, op. cit.

excess of 400 kg. But the dangers of extrapolating from just a few years' harvests are highlighted in the finding that after 1999, total and per capita output declined sharply. A comparison of two four-year periods makes the point dramatically. Whereas during 1996–9 grain output averaged 505 million tons p.a., in 2000–3 the corresponding figure was little more than 450 million tons. The average annual shortfall – 55 million tons – would have been sufficient to feed almost 140 million people.

Not shown in Table 6.3 is the fact that post-1978 output growth has been based entirely on improvements in average yield. During these years, the grain sown area has shown a trend decline, falling from 120.6 (1978) to 101.6 million hectares (2004). In the same period, the average yield rose from 2,527 to 4,620 kg per hectare – an average annual rate of growth of 2.3 per cent (almost twice the rate of population growth).

To a much greater extent than in the past, post-1978 grain output growth was driven by a coherent package of policies, embracing economic, institutional and technological measures. These have included price incentives for grain farmers, as well as technological initiatives – the dissemination of hybrid seeds has been particularly important, while progress in developing genetically modified (GM) strains of rice, maize and soya beans has recently also highlighted the potential gains from biotechnology. After 1978 too, there was a major increase in the use of agricultural chemicals, including a remarkable acceleration in the rate of use of chemical fertilisers, as well as in thte provision of fertilisers with a more appropriate nutrient mix.

Meanwhile, the productivity-improving effects of institutional change were most evident in the early 1980s, when the Maoist strategy of collectivisation was reversed in favour of decollectivisation and the near-universal adoption of so-called contractual 'production responsibility systems'. That these had a favourable impact on farmers' incentives is beyond doubt. Until the early 1990s, however, for grain farmers the gains were limited by the continued imposition of quotas in a context in which China's grain economy was still far from being fully marketised. Nor indeed did later market reforms unambiguously benefit these farmers, sometimes exposing them to sharp falls in prices. In particular, adverse terms of trade resulted in many grain farmers facing income stagnation, or even real declines in income, between 1997 and 2003. At the time of writing, there is evidence that proactive measures to support farmers during 2004 and 2005 have reversed this decline, although it remains to be seen to what extent this improvement can be maintained into the future.

To suggest that post-1978 farm policies have been successful is not to deny that serious policy-related problems have persisted. The most worrying problem of all is the fact that, since the 1990s, grain farmers – traditionally the poorest farming group, given the status of grain cultivation as the lowest-return farming activity – have been exposed to increasing exploitation, especially by local government officials. One early form of harassment was the practice of issuing 'IOUs' instead of cash for grain delivered to the state under contract. This practice has since largely disappeared, but it has been replaced by an even more serious problem – that of the exaction of illegal taxes and levies, imposed in order to finance local, extra-budgetary non-agricultural development projects or simply to fill local cadres' pockets. Against this background, it is not surprising that many farmers have tried to move out of grain cultivation into other more lucrative pursuits, both inside and outside farming. No less is it surprising that social discontent within the farming community has reached a crisis level in some areas, leading to demonstrations and outbreaks of serious violence. Such conditions explain why a cornerstone of economic policy in 2004–5 was the urgent need to improve economic and social conditions within the grain sector. Major initiatives to this end included improvements in land management, reductions in farm taxes and the unprecedented extension of direct subsidies – together worth 45 billion yuan in 2004 – to grain farmers. Such measures have halted the downward spiral of grain, although their impact has so far been to generate recovery rather than to promote net growth.

Reference has already been made to the importance of the regional dimensions of the national performance of the grain sector. The grain sector is one context in which a knowledge of regional developments is critical to understanding changes that have taken place under the impact of reform. In particular, in the early 1980s a remarkable transformation began to take place, associated with a major shift in the regional 'centre of gravity' of grain production. By the mid-1990s, the huge grain surplus enjoyed by central and eastern provinces a decade earlier had all but been eliminated, while large deficits had emerged in other southern areas. Only thanks to the above-average performance of the northern half of the country – above all, the three north-eastern provinces of Liaoning, Jilin and Heilongjiang – was the emergence of a sizeable national deficit avoided. One major reason for declining grain production in southern China was the encroachment on the grain-sown area by urban and industrial developments, especially in booming coastal regions, while another was structural change within the crop sector itself, as more and more farmers converted grain land to fishponds, orchards and other agricultural uses.

The erosion of the grain base in southern coastal provinces was part of the background against which, in the mid-1990s, the government instituted a 'provincial grain responsibility system'. From the perspective of the late 1990s, the impact of this initiative seemed to have been positive. Whereas between the second half of the 1980s and first half of the 1990s, almost 80 per cent of the increase in China's total grain output came from the north, after 1995 the corresponding figure was closer to 60 per cent. This readjustment should, however, be viewed cautiously, for there is evidence that partial recovery has since taken place in some central and eastern provinces. Moreover, it seems certain that northern China will carry the main burden of future grain output growth and remain the principal source of exports to other parts of the country.

From food production to food consumption: feeding the Chinese population

The burden that China faces in feeding its enormous population is well captured in the juxtaposition of two statistics. They reveal that China has about 7 per cent of the world's arable land, on which it seeks to support 21 per cent of global population. One of the most remarkable achievements of post-1949 Chinese governments has been the basic fulfilment of this goal.

During the Mao era, access to grain – as good an indicator of welfare as any in a poor country – barely changed for most Chinese. By contrast, an analysis of food consumption trends since 1978 reveals that throughout the urban sector and in many parts of the countryside, significant nutritional and dietary improvements have taken place in the wake of rapid rises in per capita incomes. The result has been a decline in the direct consumption of grain and vegetables in favour of a more varied diet, based on higher consumption of meat, fish and dairy produce. By the end of the period of the First Five-Year Plan (1953–7), average per capita grain production in China had reached around 300 kg, although sugar, meat and fish output (averaging respectively a mere 18, 6 and 5 kg per head of total population) remained depressed. Consumption of such non-staple foods in any case strongly favoured urban residents.

Food adequacy is most simply defined in terms of a diet that offers sufficient food energy, measured in calories, the underlying belief being that a diet that

Table 6.4 Nutritional standards in China before 1978

	Food adequacy requirements		Actual availability		Availability as % of requirements	
	Energy (cal)	Protein (kg)	Energy (cal)	Protein (kg)	Energy (cal)	Protein (kg)
1950	2,069	39.5	1,742	48.5	84.2	122.8
1953	2,083	39.7	2,048	56.9	98.3	143.2
1957	2,102	40.0	2,217	59.3	105.5	148.5
1958	2,107	40.0	2,248	58.0	106.7	145.0
1959	2,111	40.1	1,854	49.0	87.7	122.3
1961	2,116	40.1	1,578	41.4	74.6	103.1
1961	2,121	40.2	1,763	46.0	83.1	114.5
1965	2,139	40.5	2,021	52.8	94.5	130.5
1970	2,156	40.9	2,192	56.2	101.6	137.6
1975	2,191	41.7	2,266	57.9	103.4	138.8
1978	2,227	42.7	2,413	60.4	108.3	141.4

Source: Adapted from Alan Piazza, *Food Consumption and Nutritional Status in the PRC* (Boulder, CO, and London: Westview Press Inc., 1986), p. 92.

provides enough energy is also likely to provide enough protein. As for what constitutes sufficient energy, detailed calculations made by the Food and Agriculture Organisation point to an average requirement of around 2,400 calories. This is simplistic to the extent that it ignores the additional protein needs of special categories of persons, such as young children, and pregnant and lactating women, as well as differences based on age and sex. But it remains a useful rule of thumb.

Table 6.4 presents estimates of calorie and nutritional adequacy in China for selected years up to 1978. Following a steady improvement in energy and protein intake between 1950 and 1958, such was the effect of the 'Great Famine' (1959–61), as well as continuing rapid population growth, that even by the mid-1970s energy intakes had not re-attained the levels of 1957–8. It is worth noting that the figures shown in Table 6.4 are averages for the whole of China and fail to distinguish between urban and rural sectors, or between other groupings; nor do they distinguish between geographical regions of the country. Thus, Piazza observes:

> even during the mid-1950s when average per capita energy and protein availability exceeded requirements by a large margin, a large number of families and individuals were consuming less than average quantities of food and many of these people no doubt suffered from inadequate intake of

food energy and protein. Since income disparity at the local level was reduced during the 1950s, however, it is very likely that many low-income
households directly benefited from the increase in national average per capita nutrient availability. Thus, the proportion of households with food intake falling below minimal standards almost certainly declined (but was not
eliminated) during the 1950s. (1986: 91)

Differences between countryside and cities, as well as between different
parts of the country, were also potentially significant. In general, the nutritional
status of urban residents was higher than that of their rural counterparts. During
the famine years, starvation seems to have been a wholly rural phenomenon. It
was also in some ways a heavily localised phenomenon: one author's calculations
indicate that Sichuan alone suffered almost 6 million excess deaths during 1959–
61, while five other provinces (Anhui, Henan, Hunan, Shandong and Guizhou)
each suffered over one million deaths (Walker 1998: 109).

Table 6.5 seeks to convey changes in food consumption and diets in urban
and rural China since the 1980s. Underlying changes in food tastes emerge clearly
from these figures. They show, unambiguously, that under the impact of the
reforms, food consumption has improved, quantitatively and qualitatively, in both

Table 6.5 Changing levels and patterns of food consumption in China
(1985, 1995 and 2003)

| | Average per capita consumption (kg p.a.) | | | | | |
| | 1985 | | 1995 | | 2003 | |
	Urban	Rural	Urban	Rural	Urban	Rural
Grain	134.8	257.5	97.0	258.9	79.5	222.4
Vegetables	144.4	208.8	116.5	104.6	118.3	107.4
Edible oil	5.8	4.0	7.1	5.8	9.2	6.3
Meat	18.7	11.0	19.7	11.3	23.7	15.0
Poultry	3.2	1.0	4.0	1.8	9.2	3.2
Fresh eggs	6.8	2.1	9.7	3.2	11.2	4.8
Milk and diary	—	—	4.6	—	18.6	1.7
Fish	7.1	1.6	9.2	3.1	13.4	3.9
Fruit	—	—	45.0	—	57.8	17.5
Sugar	2.5	1.5	1.7	1.3	1.7	1.2
Alcohol	7.8	4.4	9.9	6.5	9.4	7.7

Sources: NBS 1996: 283, 309; NBS 2004: 366, 389.

cities and countryside. That grain consumption should have fallen in the urban sector is entirely consistent with growing affluence, which has enabled residents to move towards a more varied diet, involving less consumption of grain and more of non-staple foods – especially meat and poultry, fish, and eggs and dairy produce. By contrast, rural direct consumption of grain has started to fall much more recently, and consumption of non-staple foods remains well behind that of those living in cities.

Associated with the figures shown above, significant changes in nutritional standards have also taken place. In general, these changes have been beneficial, although not uniformly so. The shift towards a diet involving higher consumption of meat, fish and dairy produce has undoubtedly enhanced nutritional standards. The World Bank (1997: 10) has acknowledged the 'relatively healthy' nature of the Chinese diet, characterised by low fat (apart from fatty pork), oil and sugar intake, alongside high vegetable consumption. Less favourable developments have, however, manifested themselves in the urban sector, where the consumption of fashionable, but less healthy, snack and fast foods, and soft drinks has also rapidly risen. Such has been the pace of change of diets that new problems associated with overnutrition – obesity, diabetes and other illnesses – are beginning to emerge in China, especially among younger age groups in cities.

Declining direct grain consumption by no means implies declining aggregate grain requirements because of the offsetting increase in demand for grain for indirect consumption – for processing (e.g. to produce more beer and liquor), and, above all, for livestock feed to generate more meat, fish and dairy produce. As economic growth proceeds, the changing demand for grain for indirect consumption reflects the impact of differing income elasticities of demand for food grain and feed grain. One study suggests that in 1995–2000 the income elasticity of demand for food grain in China was –0.4, while that for feed grain was +0.3 (Wu and Findlay 1999: 74). The use of grain for animal feed has already doubled since the early 1980s and it is projected to reach over 200 million tons (34 per cent of total cereal and coarse grain requirements) by 2020 (World Bank 1997: 2)

China's food security in the twenty-first century

Since the mid-1990s, the question of China's food security has attracted considerable international attention and concern. Much of this concern has its origins in a powerful international dimension that attaches to China's so-called 'grain problem'. It stems from an acknowledgement that China's size factor is such that its increasing involvement in international grain markets could have the potential to disrupt trade patterns and raise prices to the detriment of poor countries that already face acute shortages of basic food.

Since 1949, China has experienced one catastrophic grain crisis that precipitated a collapse of its food security. Short of an eventuality such as the collapse of central government authority, the return of apocalyptic conditions such as those that existed during the famine of 1959–61 can safely be ruled out. For many years now, China has enjoyed a comfortable cushion above its subsistence needs. Indeed, in the second half of the 1990s, China's domestic production generated sufficient grain to meet the needs of its increasingly affluent population, while accumulating enormous reserves and permitting sizeable net exports of grain. Nevertheless, recent records of the grain sector counsel caution in predicting the future trajectory of grain output growth. In sharp contrast to the record harvests of 1996–9, subsequent years witnessed a sharp contraction in output, which took per capita output to a low of 333 kg in 2003 (see Table 6.3) and eventually reduced reserves to a level that necessitated (in 2004) the introduction of large-scale grain – especially wheat – imports. In 2004, domestic shortages caused grain prices to rise sharply. This, alongside the central government's implementation of income-boosting and incentive-enhancing measures, facilitated a recovery in grain production. In 2004, total grain output rose by 9 per cent – the biggest annual increase for 14 years – to reach 469.5 million tons. Even so, total production in 2004 was still some 50 million tons below annual requirements and 43 million tons below the record harvest of 1998. Nor did conditions in 2005 make up for these shortfalls.

China's farm resource endowment gives it a comparative advantage in the production of labour-intensive products, and a comparative disadvantage in that of land-intensive goods, such as cereals. But contrary to economic logic, the imperative of maintaining basic food self-sufficiency has so far led the Chinese government to resist cereal imports. Admittedly, under the impact of farm trade liberalisation associated with WTO accession, Chinese exports of some labour-intensive goods – for example, freshwater and seawater products, fruit, and fresh vegetables – have risen significantly in recent years. For example, in 2001–3 the export value of mandarins, oranges and apples more than doubled, while that of fresh vegetables rose by 50 per cent; overseas sales of fish rose by almost 30 per cent in the same period. In terms of absolute value, the single most valuable farm export category comprises freshwater and seawater products, which earned US$3.3 billion in 2003.

That China has the ability to formulate policies – institutional, economic and technological – capable of generating rapid and sustained output growth is not in question. Nor, however, are the serious constraints on future growth posed by severe water shortages and a contracting arable land base. Meanwhile, it has yet to be demonstrated that a solution has been found to the perennial problems faced by hard-pressed farmers engaged in low-return grain farming.

Disregard of the principle of comparative advantage in agricultural production has enabled China to get at least 95 per cent of its grain requirements from domestic sources throughout virtually the entire period since 1978. One of the most remarkable features of the performance of agriculture during 2000–3 is that despite suffering a cumulative shortfall of over 120 million tons below its total gain requirements, China remained a net grain *exporter*. Indeed, in 2003, net exports were 16 million tons more than in 1999, even though domestic output of cereals (rice, wheat and maize) had fallen by over 78 million tons during the same period. The ability to remain a net cereal exporter alongside contracting domestic output was made possible only by massively running down domestic cereal stocks. Between the 1999–2000 and 2003–4 trade years, China's wheat stocks fell by almost 60 per cent, and its coarse grain reserves by almost two-thirds. Only in 2004, as a result of stock depletion and continuing excess demand in domestic production, did China finally revert to the status of a net cereal importer. In 2004, China imported 7.26 million tons of wheat – a rise of 1,513 per cent that transformed it into the world's largest wheat importer. Imports of maize (2.37 million tons) and rice (0.77 million tons). Increases in wheat and maize imports are set to continue in 2005 and may reach 10 million tons.

Alongside this change to the status of net grain importer, between 2003 and 2004 China's farm sector also shifted from healthy surplus to sizeable deficit on its foreign trade account. In 2002 and 2003, China recorded annual agricultural trade surpluses of US$5.7 billion and US$2.5 billion; in 2004, this was transformed into a deficit of US$5.5 billion. China's agricultural trade account will remain in deficit in 2005, and in the longer term that deficit is likely to persist, with any rise in China's farm exports more than offset by growing imports of both land-intensive and labour-intensive agricultural products.

The Chinese government's adherence to the imperative of maintaining 'basic' – at least 95 per cent – grain self-sufficiency is driven by political and geo-strategic, not economic, reasoning. Chinese foreign policy analysts believe that dependence on imported food would increase China's vulnerability vis-à-vis a foreign supplier – for 'foreign supplier' read the United States – trying to fulfil its own competing strategic goals. A response to this argument is to point out that although its wheat production has fallen steadily since the mid-1990s, even China's sudden emergence in 2004 as the world's biggest importer of wheat conceals the reality that its purchases constituted little more than 10 per cent of domestic production. Of these imports, about half came from the United States, indicating a bilateral dependency ratio for wheat of no more than about 5 per cent. Dependency on the US for soya beans has admittedly been much higher – during 2001–3, for example, about 40 per cent of China's soya imports were supplied by the United States (in 2000 the corresponding figure was 52 per cent). Given that soya imports have at times accounted for almost 70 per cent of domestic production, the bilateral dependency ratio for soya beans vis-à-vis the USA has clearly been much greater than that for wheat. Although maize imports do not compare with those of wheat, it is not impossible that future conditions will force China to increase its purchases. If this happens, as the world's largest exporter of maize, the US will be an obvious source of imports. It is against this background that in recent years China has been actively exploring other sources of grain imports, especially in Argentina and Brazil.

Predicting the future is, however, inherently hazardous. From the perspective of 2004–5, with cereal exports slowing down and China's two state-authorised exporters reluctant to sign new contracts, it is clear that the Chinese government has shifted its focus towards supplying the domestic market, rather than the international market. In the face of continuing excess domestic demand for wheat, maize and soya – and even rice – China's involvement in international cereal markets will, in the immediate term, be that of a net importer. But to what extent its status as a net importer will persist is more difficult to predict. My guess is that even if it does so, the rise in net cereal imports will pose a significant threat neither to China's food nor to its geopolitical security.

To argue that other Asian countries have industrialised under conditions which bear some similarity to those of mainland China begs many important questions. It is true that the Chinese economy has freed itself from a close dependence on agriculture and the fate of the economy is no longer as fundamentally determined by agriculture's performance, as it was in the past. But the livelihood of many tens of millions of Chinese peasants still depends on agriculture – and, in particular, on grain farming. The grain sector remains a critical constraint not just on the country's economic health, but also on its social and political stability. It is in this sense that agriculture's role as the 'foundation of the national economy' continues to have meaning, even in the twenty-first century.

Conclusion

The attempt to maintain a healthy balance between food production and a growing population can be regarded as the central economic issue that has faced China throughout its long history. As recently as the early 1980s, the margin in excess of subsistence food requirements for many Chinese people was a narrow one. As a result, the Chinese government had no alternative but to recognise the need, from time to time, to rely on imported grain to make up for unexpected shortfalls in domestic supplies. It is true that since 1960, when the increasing severity of famine made such imports once more necessary, the level of overseas grain purchases has been small in relation to domestic grain production. But grain imports have often played a role whose importance has been disproportionate to their limited scale. In particular, they have helped meet the food demand of China's coastal urban population, thereby easing the burden on China's own grain farmers. One interpretation of such imports is that China has, at times, been dependent on foreign grain merely in order to keep its population healthy and productive.

From this perspective, one of the most outstanding economic achievements of Chinese governments since 1978 has been finally to resolve the tension between population and food supplies. Indeed, it is reasonable to suggest that, short of some cataclysmic event, China's permanent ability to provide for national food security at a subsistence level is probably now assured. Indeed, for all the vagaries of China's agricultural performance since 1978, it is noteworthy that its grain farmers have shown themselves capable not only of fulfilling subsistence requirements but also of meeting the aspirations for a higher-protein, more varied diet of a population whose living standards have for the most part improved markedly during the last two decades. No doubt, China as a whole still has a long way to go before it can match patterns of food consumption that are taken for granted in developed countries. It is, however, revealing that children living in Chinese cities today are so much better nourished and healthier than they were during the Mao era. More worrying is the finding that side by side with these undoubted improvements, new problems associated with overnutrition are simultaneously beginning to emerge.

Overall, the story that I have tried to tell in this chapter would seem to have a happy ending. It has, after all, shown how the most populous country in the world has apparently solved the most fundamental of all economic and social problems – that of feeding its population and thereby removing what for so many centuries was the perennial threat of hunger, malnutrition and starvation.

Yet despite this optimistic message, I would conclude on a cautionary note. History – especially China's history – is full of unexpected twists and turns. The unexpected has happened with surprising frequency in China, especially during the last half-century. Who could have predicted the Great Leap Forward, the Cultural Revolution or, for that matter, the violent quelling of unrest in Tiananmen Square in 1989? Nor is there much doubt that the last decade has seen a significant deterioration in social stability. As a result serious unrest has become quite a common phenomenon in both cities and the countryside – especially, in the latter area, among grain farmers whose living standards have shown little improvement in recent years.

Moreover, it has yet to be established that the growth of national grain output really has attained a new and stable path that can continue to meet the dietary aspirations of the Chinese people. Nor should we forget the implications for grain farmers of China's accession to the World Trade Organization. As Chinese agriculture is opening to international competition, there is a strong likelihood that some grain farmers will be badly hit. More generally, China's integration in the global economy and exposure to competition from more efficient farmers overseas can be expected to jeopardise the Chinese government's adherence to what hitherto has been the sacred imperative of grain self-sufficiency.

For such reasons, I would argue that, for the foreseeable future, the grain sector is likely to retain a pivotal place in the Chinese economy. By the same token, no assessment of China's economic prospects that fails to take this sector into account can be regarded as complete.

References

Banister, J. (1987) *China's Changing Population*, Stanford, CA: Stanford University Press.

Buck, J. L. (1937) *Land Utilisation in China*, Nanking: University of Nanking (reprinted by Paragon Print Reprint Corp., 1964).

Hao, H. (2000) 'Trends and geographic differentials in mortality', in X. Peng and Z. Guo (eds), *The Changing Population of China*, Oxford: Blackwell Publishers Ltd.

Howe, C. and Walker, K. (1977) 'Mao: the Economist', in D. Wilson (ed.), *Mao Tse-tung in the Scales of History*, Cambridge: Cambridge University Press.

Mao Zedong (1961) 'The bankruptcy of the idealist conception of history', in *Selected Works of Mao Tse-tung*, vol. IV, Beijing: Foreign Languages Press.

NBS (National Bureau of Statistics) (1996) *Zhongguo tongji nianjian* (China Statistical Yearbook), Beijing: China Statistics Press.

NBS (National Bureau of Statistics) (2000) *Xin Zhongguo wushi nian nongye tongji ziliao* (Agricultural Statistical Materials for the Fifty Years of New China), Beijing: Zhongguo tongji chubanshe.

NBS (National Bureau of Statistics) (2004) *Zhongguo tongji nianjian* (China Statistical Year-book), Beijing: Zhongguo tongji chubanshe.

Piazza, A. (1986) *Food Consumption and Nutritional Status in the PRC*, Boulder, CO, and London: Westview Press Inc.

Scharping, T. (2003) *Birth Control in China, 1949–2000: Population Policy and Demographic Development*, London: RoutledgeCurzon.

Stone, B. (1993) 'Basic Agricultural Technology Under Reform', in Y. Y. Kueh and R. Ash (eds), *Economic Trends in Chinese Agriculture: The Impact of Post-Mao Reforms*, Oxford: Clarendon Press.

Walker, K. R. (1984) *Food Grain Procurement and Consumption in China*, Cambridge: Cambridge University Press.

—— (1998) 'Food and Mortality in China During the Great Leap Forward, 1958–1961', in R. Ash (ed.), *Agricultural Development in China, 1949–1989: The Collected Papers of Kenneth R. Walker (1931–1989)*, Oxford: Oxford University Press, 1998.

World Bank (1997) *China 2020: At China's Table*, Washington, DC: World Bank.

Wu, H. X. and Findlay, C. (1999) 'Grain Demand', in C. Findlay and A. Watson (eds), *Food Security and Economic Reform: The Challenges Facing China's Grain Marketing System*, Basingstoke, Hants: Macmillan Press Ltd.

7

Ethnic minorities

COLIN MACKERRAS

Introduction

In China, the overwhelming majority of the people belong to a nationality called the Han. The Chinese state recognises 55 minority 'nationalities', which take up about five-eighths of China's territory, making their importance out of all proportion to their population. The ethnic minorities range from the Koreans of the northeast, who are culturally identical to the Koreans of Korea, to the Muslim Turkic minorities of Xinjiang in the far northwest, such as the Uygurs (sometimes also referred to as the Uighurs) and Kazaks, who are much more like the Turks of Turkey than the Chinese. Other than the Koreans, several ethnic minorities have co-nationals running their own state on the other side of borders, such as the Mongolians, Kazaks and Kirgiz.

On the whole, China's ethnic minorities enjoy reasonably harmonious relations both with each other and with the Han. Yet most of them are less prosperous economically than the Han and inequalities went from bad to worse between 1990 and 2005. Economic disparity breeds cultural and social inequality, which spawns tensions that that can lead to violence. Despite the inequalities, most of China's minorities appear happy to remain part of China. However, there are several ethnic groups with significant secessionist movements. Of these, the Tibetans, with their Dalai Lama, and the Uygurs from Xinjiang are the best-known cases. The Uygurs have been more in the news since 11 September 2001, because the Chinese government has tried to link them with Osama bin Laden and his al-Qaeda network, claiming that some Uygur terrorists and separatists have taken formal instruction in al-Qaeda schools.

China has a tradition of national unity. Yet its borders have by no means been constant over the centuries. Could it fall into civil strife, war and confusion over ethnic questions, as has happened in other countries? I believe China is unlikely to fall apart, as did Yugoslavia or the Soviet Union. But it would be a foolhardy leader that struck out the possibility and refused to recognise the sensitivity and critical importance of ethnic questions.

After a brief historical overview of policies on ethnic minorities since 1949, this chapter analyses key policy issues, specifically those related to economics, population and religion, with a focus on the period since 1990. The chapter concludes by looking at the relationship between the ethnic issues in China and China's territorial integrity, as well as the role of ethnic problems in Beijing's relations with foreign powers.

Policies on minorities 1949–90

The CCP came to power in China in October 1949, establishing the People's Republic of China (PRC). Among numerous leaders, two have stood out for dominating the Chinese political scene in the second half of the twentieth century: Mao Zedong and Deng Xiaoping.

Mao's policies on ethnic minorities

Mao had basically three policies on ethnic minorities, which he summed up with the slogan 'equality and unity'. They were first formally enunciated in the Common Programme, the interim Constitution adopted on 29 September 1949, and incorporated into the PRC's first Constitution (1954). Mao's policies can be summarised as follows:

1   His government dictated that all nationalities were equal in theory, although this was not realised in practice.
2   Ethnic minorities were allowed some autonomy, meaning they could use their own languages, follow their own religions and customs, and have their own people in at least some government positions.
3   Ethnic minorities must remain part of the PRC. Mao's regime suppressed all attempts to secede.

Mao denounced 'great Han chauvinism', a phrase meaning that the Han people would look down on the ethnic minorities and treat them as inferiors. He hated 'local nationalism' even more. That phrase meant that local ethnic groups would find leaders who would try to set themselves and their peoples up as separate from China.

The worst period for the ethnic minorities during the Mao era was the Cultural Revolution. The autonomy principle was still in force – in theory. In practice, all notions of autonomy were discarded. Red Guards loyal to Mao smashed anything traditional, including monasteries, mosques, and precious works of art. They persecuted clerics and other people representing traditional beliefs, torturing and killing quite a few of them. Even now, older people in the ethnic areas speak about this period as of a nightmare, yet different from a nightmare in its ghastly reality.

The Tibetan uprising

Between 1949 and 1976, the most dramatic events in the ethnic areas were in Tibet. In 1950, Chinese troops took over much of Tibet, arguing that it was part of China. An appeal by the local Tibetan government to the United Nations went unanswered. On 23 May 1951, the local Tibetan government and the central Chinese government reached an agreement 'for the Peaceful Liberation of Tibet'. Under this agreement, Tibet would become part of the PRC, but the Tibetan people would enjoy some degree of autonomy. In September Chinese troops arrived in Lhasa, the capital of Tibet.

At first things went quite well. The young man who in the old days had been both the spiritual and temporal head of Tibet, the fourteenth Dalai Lama, accepted the agreement. In 1955, the Chinese set up a provisional committee to run Tibet as an autonomous region, and appointed him as the chair. However, in March 1959 there was a major uprising in Lhasa against Chinese rule. It was quickly suppressed, and the Dalai Lama fled to India. He immediately denounced the 1951 agreement and set up a government in exile. Meanwhile in Tibet itself, the Chinese rejected the 1951 agreement and carried out a 'democratic reform', including the emancipation of serfs. They uprooted the old administrative system and in September 1965 set up the Tibetan Autonomous Region. Despite its name, it was not nearly as autonomous as it had been in the 1950s. During the Cultural Revolution, Tibetan and Han Red Guards carried out destruction of traditional cultural objects and buildings as severe as any that occurred in China during those terrible years.

Ethnic minorities under Deng Xiaoping

Deng's regime returned to the idea of autonomy for ethnic minorities. The 1982 PRC Constitution and the 1984 Law on Regional Autonomy of 1984 were the major documents spelling out the details of this policy. The Constitution included the provision that the head of the government of all autonomous places must belong to the ethnic minority or minorities implementing autonomy. Consequently, the head of the Tibetan government had to be a Tibetan. However, it did not require the regional head of the CCP to belong to the relevant minority. This was a severe restriction on autonomy, because, as was discussed in Chapter 2, the CCP is actually a much more important power-holder than the government in China.

Still, the revival of autonomy did bring with it much greater freedom than Mao had allowed. Traditions came back, both among the Han and the minorities. Religion returned to a position far better than it had occupied at any time under Mao. Old mosques and monasteries damaged or destroyed during the Cultural Revolution were rebuilt, and new ones were erected in large numbers. Old arts and customs also returned.

Deng Xiaoping also implemented a set of preferential policies towards the minorities. These were designed to increase the educational and professional levels among the minorities and to make them feel much more part of the Chinese success. For instance, quotas ensured that a good number of ethnic minority students entered universities, even if their marks were lower than those of Han students. The government also increased efforts to train ethnic police, administrators, lawyers and teachers.

Tibet during the reform period

Just as under Mao, it was Tibet of all the ethnic regions that caused the Deng Xiaoping government the biggest headaches. In May 1980, the then CCP General Secretary Hu Yaobang (1915–89) visited Tibet and was shocked at what he found. He demanded that the Tibetans be given more control over their own situation, outlining policies to try and increase the number of Tibetan administrators and professionals. He also instituted tax relief and took special measures to improve the Tibetan economy. These measures certainly improved the situation. However, in 1987 separatist movements (which are considered further in the section on 'The question of national unity') led the government to adopt a far harsher policy on Tibet.

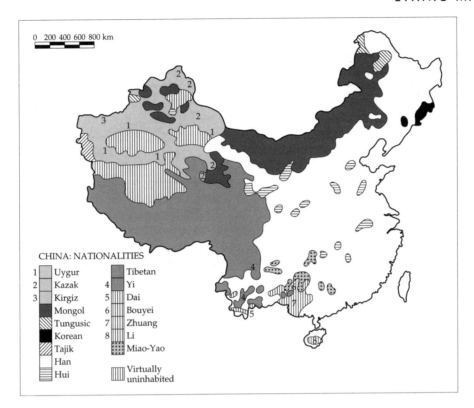

Figure 7.1 China's nationalities

What is a 'minority nationality'?

Ethnicity is a highly contested area and has assumed a higher profile in world politics since the fall of the Soviet Union took away the main basis of global ideological division. No longer was it sensible to divide the world's main powers into communist and liberal democratic, as many had done during the Cold War.

A range of terms describes people of a single ethnicity who constitute a minority in the nation-state where they live, including 'ethnic minority'. In the PRC, the term used is 'minority nationality'. This is a literal translation of the term *shaoshu minzu*. So what is a 'minority nationality'? Ever since the CCP came to power, state representatives have adopted Stalin's 1913 definition of 'nationality': 'a historically constituted, stable community of people, formed on the basis of a common language, territory, economic life, and psychological make-up manifested in a common culture' (Stalin 1953: 307). A minority nationality is one that is not a majority, which in China means all except the Han.

Western scholars generally consider this definition inadequate. Dru Gladney (1991: ix) believes that the theory limits an understanding of the dynamism of minority identities because of the 'overemphasis upon nationality identification

Table 7.1 Census populations of China's largest nationalities

Nationality	1953 Census	1964 Census	1982 Census	1990 Census	2000 Census
Han	42 824 056	651 296 368	936 674 944	1 039 187 548	1 137 386 112
Zhuang	6 864 585	8 386 140	13 383 086	15 555 820	16 178 811
Manchus	2 399 228	2 695 675	4 304 981	9 846 776	10 682 262
Hui	3 530 498	4 473 147	7 228 398	8 612 001	9 816 805
Miao	2 490 874	2 782 088	5 021 175	7 383 622	8 940 116
Uygurs	3 610 462	3 996 311	5 963 491	7 207 024	8 399 393
Tujia	—	524 755	2 836 814	5 725 049	8 028 133
Yi	3 227 750	3 380 960	5 453 564	6 578 524	7 762 272
Mongolians	1 451 035	1 965 766	3 411 367	4 802 407	5 813 947
Tibetans	2 753 081	2 501 174	3 847 875	4 593 072	5 416 021
Bouyei	1 237 714	1 348 055	2 119 345	2 548 294	2 971 460
Dong	712 802	836 123	1 426 400	2 508 624	2 960 293
Yao	665 933	857 265	1 411 967	2 137 033	2 637 421
Koreans	1 111 275	1 339 569	1 765 204	1 923 361	1 923 842

Source: Mackerras 2001: 252 for the first four censuses, and China Population Information and Research Center, Beijing, for the census of 2000.

programmes' it implies. Chinese scholars, on the other hand, have accepted Stalin's definition. Official thinking still regards it as valid. One typical account concludes that it is 'a complete and scientific definition' (Wu *et al*. 1999: 7).

We can pursue Gladney's point further by discussing the identification process. The CCP's announcement that all nationalities were equal attracted the minorities, who were used to being considered inferior. The result was that by 1955 over 400 groups registered themselves as nationalities. The next year, the government set up sixteen investigation teams, sending them to all regions with minorities. Their task was to apply Stalin's definition and come up with a reasonably objective statement of which groups had a genuine claim to be regarded as 'minority nationalities'.

Since 1979, the official count of the number of minority nationalities has been 55. Including the majority Han, the total number of state-recognised nationalities in the PRC is 56. These figures do not include minorities in Taiwan, Hong Kong or Macau. Figure 7.1 illustrates where China's key nationalities live.

As can be seen from census figures in Table 7.1, the identifications have changed slightly over the years. For instance, the 1953 gave no place to the Tujia, among several others, but later censuses have recognised them. The Jinuo were recognised as a nationality in 1979, and since then no others have been accepted as a nationality.

As Dru Gladney (op. cit.) notes, Chinese state representatives have used census figures to identify nationalities. Whether Gladney's criticism of the 'overemphasis upon nationality identification programmes' is appropriate or not depends on one's viewpoint. What concerns me here, however, is to discuss the processes and results of the state's intervention in ethnic affairs. Since most Chinese statistics assume the officially adopted ethnic identifications, they are very useful for practical purposes.

While I therefore accept Stalin's definition of ethnic minorities for teaching and scholarship purposes, I can see weaknesses and problems with it. One example illustrating these weaknesses concerns the Manchus. They once had their own script and language, but both script and language are all but extinct nowadays and Manchus use Chinese. The number of people who still speak Manchu as their background language is vanishingly small, and still declining. Perhaps they were, as Stalin defines, 'formed on the basis of a common language', but that language no longer has any meaning for them.

Another example illustrating the problems of Stalin's definition is the Hui, who are Sinic Muslims. They are very similar ethnically and culturally to the Han majority, except that they are Muslims. Indeed, Gladney (1991: 262) has even found some communities who no longer believe in Islam nor follow Islamic practices such as abstention from pork. They do not have their own language, and are Chinese-speaking. There are Hui communities all over China. Although there are some places where Hui are concentrated, it would be incorrect to say that they were formed on the basis of a common territory, one of the aspects of Stalin's definition. In essence, they are a nationality that depends on a particular religion for their existence.

Ethnic consciousness

An important feature of Stalin's definition is that it does not mention consciousness, a factor emphasised in much of the world. However, although most members of ethnic minorities appear to me to accept the identification the state has given them, ethnic consciousness is a rising phenomenon in contemporary China.

One scholar who carried out research in an area of western Hunan Province, where the locals are classified as basically Tujia with some Miao, came to the conclusion that in such places 'ethnicity means more to a visitor, who may be a government official, a journalist or an anthropologist, than to the local' (Shih 2001: 74). However, the fact is that there are many people who think it is in their interests for various reasons to belong to a minority nationality. Numerous people and groups re-registered as members of minorities in the last decades of the twentieth century. The point of re-registration will become clearer when we discuss population in relation to minorities later in this chapter.

There are also branches of ethnic minorities with members who would like to be classified as separate nationalities. When I attended a festival gathering of Miao people in 1990 in Chong'an, southern Guizhou, I found that in fact many of the people present regarded themselves as Gejia, not Miao at all. Similarly, there are many people called Hmong in China, as well as Thailand, Laos and several other countries of Southeast Asia. The Chinese state classifies them as a branch of the Miao, but many Hmong people are very insistent that they are not Miao at all, but Hmong. One scholar of the Hmong criticises the Chinese state's classification of nationalities as 'arbitrary' for its failure to differentiate between Hmong and Miao, while at the same time picking out some largely acculturated groups like the Manchus as separate ethnic minorities (Tapp 2001: 31).

Recent policy towards ethnic minorities

The crises in Tibet in the late 1980s and the student protests in Beijing in 1989 forced the CCP leadership to think about how it should react to dissent. They thought the Tibetans would welcome the improved conditions of the 1980s. The riots in Tibet from 1987 to 1989 demonstrated with crystal clarity that this had not happened. The causes the rioters put forward were independence for Tibet and condemnation of Chinese rule there. The reasons why they occurred in the late 1980s are complex, but it cannot be accidental that the Dalai Lama addressed two United States Congressional bodies and denounced Chinese policies and actions in Tibet on 21 September 1987, just a few days before the first riots began.

The end of 1989 saw a shift in CCP policy in Tibet. Melvyn Goldstein puts it admirably:

> The general feeling among the leadership was that the measures Beijing had taken to liberalise conditions within Tibet had neither produced greater appreciation from the Lhasan masses nor convinced them that

their interests could best be met as part of China. To the contrary, they had increased nationalistic aspirations and had yielded disturbances and riots that actually weakened China's position in Tibet. This failure prompted Beijing to focus on a strategy to enhance their security in Tibet in ways that did not depend on having to win over the large segment of Tibet's current adult generation who were considered hopelessly reactionary. (1997: 92)

Economic development and the suppression of separatism

Accordingly, the leadership decided to give considerably greater weight to the economy and education in the hope of winning over the young. At the same time, they attempted to improve the system of autonomy by getting more Tibetans into the system as CCP members, entrepreneurs, and 'cadres', namely administrators and professionals. Despite these reforms, the government would not tolerate secessionist activities. It carried out several 'patriotic' campaigns in Tibet, with the aim of making people more loyal to China.

In April 1990, ethnic trouble flared in Akto, southwest Xinjiang, an issue that I shall discuss in more detail later in this chapter (in the section 'The question of national unity'). Here I note that this ethnic trouble caused the government to adopt a policy rather similar to the one they had already implemented in Tibet: the carrot of economic prosperity coupled with the stick of suppressing separatism.

A turning point in CCP minorities policy came in 1996, with two highly significant domestic events. A confidential message from the CCP Central Committee to the authorities in Xinjiang, dated 19 March, demanded that the local authorities take firmer action to stop the burgeoning threat of ethnic separatism and conflict. It charged that 'Groups are fomenting trouble, assaulting Party and government structures, bombing and committing terrorist attacks. Some organisations have already turned from underground to semi-public, to the point of openly confronting the government' (Becquelin 2000: 87). In May 1996, the Xinjiang CCP held a conference in the capital Ürümqi to discuss the stability of the region. Delegates repeated the arguments that separatists were organising riots, terrorist activities and bombings, and that many were being fomented from outside China. The meeting called for several measures to solve the problems caused by riots, terrorist activities and bombings, especially to improve the economy and to strengthen CCP control by reorganising 'weak and lax' branches (especially those dominated by Muslims), and training cadres better.

Autonomy and affirmative action

Although the Chinese state signalled beyond any doubt that it would not tolerate any attempts at secession in any of China's ethnic areas, it also showed it wanted the minorities to be satisfied with their lives. It did not intend to abandon the autonomy policy and tried to raise the proportion of ethnic minority cadres. In February 2001, the government issued an amended Law on Regional Autonomy. The

Table 7.2 Economic indicators of ethnic areas

Indicator	1952	1965	1978	1986	1990	1999	2003
Grain (millions of tonnes)	15.82	22.17	31.24	40.65	53.73	68.62	64.8
Cotton (thousands of tonnes)	31.4	88.7	59.7	224.0	470.0	1361.0	1610.0
Large livestock (millions)	24.39	33.73	38.07	49.51	52.86	56.89	57.98
Sheep and goats (millions)	40.30	85.95	95.80	99.88	113.62	130.36	148.0
Hogs (millions)	11.37	21.51	32.60	48.69	56.68	72.92	77.29
Steel (thousands of tonnes)	—	394	1285	2481	3683	6433	10823
Pig-iron (thousands of tonnes)	9	558	1682	2951	4170	6964	11569
Raw coal (millions of tonnes)	1.78	20.29	60.81	88.76	120.77	153.61	190.0
Electricity (millions of kwh)	80	3340	17 400	40 080	73 880	142 890	224 320
Railways (thousands of km)	3.787	n/a	9.018	12.60	13.10	17.5	15.0
Roads (thousands of km)	25.9	125.5	208.0	250.9	293.7	402.6	548.0
Hospital or sanatorium beds (thousands)	5.71	93.23	253.5	301.0	359.4	379.1	380.0

Source: National Bureau of Statistics, PRC 2000, 39, National Bureau of Statistics, PRC 2004, 42–5, and Mackerras 2001, 257.

new version added several clauses to the original law of 1984, and all these clauses were designed to strengthen autonomy. One specific clause asked for improved recruitment opportunities for members of local ethnic minorities in the government. The earlier 1984 version had required preferential treatment for specialised ethnic personnel and professionals in various kinds of construction in the autonomous areas. However, the requirement of affirmative action for government positions was new.

Minority membership in the CCP

Figures for minorities within the country's most powerful body, the CCP, show a rising proportion, although not reflecting the 8.41 per cent the minorities take up within China's total population. In 1990, there were 2.8 million CCP members among the minorities, or 5.7 per cent of the total membership of about 49 million. The comparable figures for 1995 were 3.19 million ethnic members, or 5.8 per cent of the total of 55 million CCP members (see Mackerras 2001: 90). Referring to June 2002, *People's Daily* (2 September 2002: 1) put the number of ethnic CCP members at 4.1 million, or 6.2 per cent of the total 66.355 million members.

There does seem to be some kind of empowerment process occurring amongst ethnic CCP members. Central authorities seem keen to promote this, provided they do not have to sacrifice their own power. However, it is not known where in the bureaucracy the ethnic cadres and CCP members are. Most of them may be in powerless positions where they simply take directions from more senior Han people. Still, the same could apply to the Han CCP and cadre members. There are nationalities institutes in China, and one of their functions is to train ethnic cadres and CCP members who will be loyal to the Chinese state. There are obviously serious shortcomings in the extent to which ethnic people really run the affairs of their own regions. Autonomy still has a long way to go before it can be said to be truly genuine, but there seems to have been some recent progress.

Minority economies

In the previous section, we saw that a policy goal of the Chinese government was to strengthen the economic development of minority groups. To understand how ethnic minorities have developed economically it is useful to examine economic indicators over time and to compare minority economic development to development in Han areas. It is also profitable to look at issues such as poverty and to assess the equity of economic development among various ethnic groups. Table 7.2 shows the economic indicators for various ethnic areas.

Table 7.2 suggests spectacular economic progress under the PRC. All indicators show very large differences between the early years of the PRC and the early twenty-first century. In all cases, the growth in the period of reform has been impressive in absolute terms, but the rates of growth have in some cases decelerated. These figures and my own explorations in ethnic areas since the early 1980s leave me in no doubt that the average minority member was very much more prosperous at the beginning of the twenty-first century than in the middle of the twentieth.

Economic policy changed drastically in the late 1970s away from the planned economy and in the direction of allowing much more play to market forces. Many aspects of economic life have been privatised. It is well known that the eastern seaboard has done much better from the economic reform policies than the western areas where most of the minorities live. Privatisation has improved services in most respects, but they may not be available to as many people. Health standards have certainly improved throughout China in the last couple of decades, including in the ethnic areas. However, the fall in the number of medical personnel in the early twenty-first century suggests serious problems in health delivery. Only in Tibet are medical services still free, and they are very basic.

One indicator that grew very rapidly in the 1990s was cotton. There is a reason for this. The government took a very clear decision to boost cotton production in Xinjiang and in production terms this has been successful. However, Becquelin (2000: 80–3) argues that it has increased government revenue and provided an impetus for massive Han immigration to Xinjiang, but not actually brought much benefit to the Uygurs, the main ethnic minority of the region. My own fieldwork in Xinjiang in 2003 suggests that many Uygurs are doing very well from cotton, which is a traditional Uygur product, but inequalities between the Han and Uygurs may well be exacerbated.

As regards transportation, the length of roads has increased greatly. However, the length of railways is less in 2003 than at the end of the twentieth century. An exception to this trend is the planned 1,100-kilometre railways from Golmud in Qinghai to the Tibetan capital Lhasa, which comes into operation in 2007.

Preferential policies

I discuss preferential policies in the areas of political participation and population elsewhere in this chapter. Here it is economic matters that concern me. Ethnic authorities have the right to control the budgets of their autonomous places. As in all other areas, there are limitations on this right, since finances in all places in China are part of the economy of the state. Still, there is some leeway for autonomy. In areas where religion is important, such as Tibet and Xinjiang, the authorities may set aside a certain proportion of their budget to promoting religion by restoring old temples or mosques or building new ones. There is some irony in a Marxist-Leninist government actually paying for religious buildings.

Another area of economic preferential policies is in taxation. Minorities can get tax exemptions or reductions for certain items of local financial income, and these tax breaks are worth noting. Early in 1992, I visited Mayang Miao Autonomous County in western Hunan, set up in April 1990. There I learned that Miao peasants had enthusiastically pushed for the establishment of the autonomous county. The reason had nothing to do with ethnic identity. It was simply that they would get reduced taxes on grain if they belonged to an autonomous county.

The state also subsidises and invests heavily in ethnic areas. It provides low-interest and interest-free loans to farmers and other producers to enable them to establish enterprises that would otherwise be out of their range of possibility, or to set up trade networks. The ethnic area to get the most investment and subsidy is Tibet. Over the several decades from the 1950s to 1998 the government invested some 40 billion yuan into Tibetan development.

These policies have certainly helped raise the standard of living of the people. Critics charge that autonomous authorities are not as sensitive as they should be to particular ethnic needs or to the wishes of the people to produce what the people of the group concerned traditionally value. There may be some validity in this accusation. Since the ethnic areas have become enmeshed in the China-wide and global system of trade, similar commodities are found everywhere. On the other hand, autonomous authorities do seek to provide articles connected with ethnic religion, to avoid local taboos, and to ensure the holding of traditional festivals. Moreover, bringing global commodities to people who have never had them before, and thereby raising their standard of living, may not be an entirely bad thing.

Inequalities

One of the main problems of economic reform in the ethnic areas has been the further widening of inequalities. This is a big subject, which is covered elsewhere, particularly in Chapter 4 of this book.

I add only two points. One concerns the Great Western Development Strategy. In 2000 the government began to implement a long-term and extensive strategy to develop the western regions of China, one of the aims being to reduce the inequalities with the rapidly developing eastern seaboard. What is interesting here is that the western regions, as defined in this strategy, include almost all the main ethnic areas in the country. The most important exceptions are the Manchu and Korean areas of China's northeast. In the first years of the twenty-first century, investment and wealth in selected parts of the minority areas have greatly increased, with inequality actually increasing between areas with significant investment and those without, between urban and rural areas and between regions. Although inequalities may eventually even out as development gathers momentum, there is currently little sign of this.

The second point on inequality that needs emphasising is that the development figures given above do not and largely cannot distinguish among ethnic groups. Railways and roads can be used by anybody, whatever their nationality. There has been much complaint from human rights activists, especially in the West, that much more of the benefits of economic growth in Tibet and Xinjiang go to Han immigrants than to the local minorities themselves. However, what strikes me as most obvious from visits both to Tibet and Xinjiang is that the main beneficiaries of development there, as everywhere in China, are the urban areas. The countryside has improved and people unquestionably value the roads that enable them to get goods from the outside world far more easily than they ever could before. However, development has been far slower in the countryside than the cities. In the ethnic areas, the Han tend to concentrate in the cities, which means that they derive far more benefit from economic growth than the local minorities.

There are very considerable disparities within ethnic groups, including the Han. With that in mind, however, I think it fair to make some generalisations about economic levels among nationalities. On the whole, the Koreans and Manchus are the most prosperous and developed of the ethnic minorities. They generally have better levels in terms of industry, education, life expectancy and standards of living than other minorities. The Mongolians and the Uygurs are behind, but not very far. At the other end of the spectrum are the smaller minorities of Yunnan and Guizhou, with the Tibetans and Miao the poorest of the more populous ethnic minorities. There is a wide range of peoples in the middle, which includes the Kazaks of Xinjiang and the Dai of Yunnan, in that order. On the whole the Han are better off than the minorities, but that does not necessarily include all of them. The Koreans are probably the most economically progressive of all China's ethnic groups, including the Han.

Poverty

A point related to inequality is poverty. There are questions of definition in this matter, because the Chinese government has a lower boundary than the World Bank for just what constitutes absolute poverty (an income of US$0.66 as opposed to US$1 per day). However, the United Nations Development Programme's *Human Development Report* 1997, which focused particular attention on poverty, summarised (p. 49) that 'In the past 45 years or so China has made impressive reductions in human poverty'. It also observed serious problems in the rural areas, such as the lack of drinking water, sanitation, health and education provisions and stated that 'The incidence of poverty in these groups [the ethnic minorities] is much higher than in the general population' (UNDP 1997: 50). In 1994, the Chinese government introduced a special programme aiming to reduce poverty in a major way all over the country.

The State Ethnic Affairs Commission held a conference on 21 October 2001, and a report about it appeared on the front page of *People's Daily* two days later. Official figures reported to the conference claimed that large government investments and World Bank aid since 1994 had reduced the poverty-stricken population in the ethnic areas from 45 million in 1994 to 14 million in 1999. On the other hand, the Director of the State Council's Poverty Alleviation Office, Lü Feijie, revealed in a speech to the conference that among China's total population suffering from absolute poverty, 36.5 per cent belonged to minority nationalities.

Lü explained the context of poverty among the minorities, and included some reasons why it was so much worse than in the general population. He said:

> Natural disasters are frequent, and the ability to fight natural disasters and the hazards of the market is not very good. The annual rate of reversion to poverty is always above 15 per cent. Because local production and liveli-

Table 7.3 Ethnic minority populations and percentages

Census year	Population of ethnic minorities	Ethnic minorities as % of total population
1953	34 013 782	5.89
1964	39 883 909	5.77
1982	66 434 341	6.62
1990	90 567 245	8.04
2000	106 456 300	8.41

Source: Mackerras 2001: 212, 251; and *People's Daily*, 29 March 2001, p. 1.

hood conditions are poor, outlays for consumption are quite high. Basic facilities are weak and there are still quite a few places without electricity or roads. Culture and education lag behind, and the level of social development is quite low. In some villages, proportions of illiteracy and semi-literacy among laborers go higher than 30 per cent.

In its May 2005 report on China (paragraph 7), the UN Economic and Social Council gave credit for the China Rural Communities Poverty Relief Programme (2001–10) but also sharply criticised the persistence of poverty in the rural areas, despite rapid economic development in China as a whole (paragraph 30). The same point can be made about the ethnic minorities, most of whom are disproportionately rural. There is no need to doubt the reductions of poverty among the ethnic minorities, but it is very clear that there is still an enormous way to go.

Population issues

Population questions are discussed extensively in Chapter 6. Here, I cover two issues related to the ethnic minorities: namely, the overall growth rate of ethnic populations, and the issue of Han Chinese moving to ethnic areas.

The PRC has held five censuses, in 1953, 1964, 1982, 1990 and 2000. Table 7.3 shows the populations of totals of ethnic minorities, and their proportion to the whole population, not including Taiwan, Hong Kong or Macau. (Table 7.1, earlier in the chapter, showed the census population of specific nationalities with a population of more than two million in 2000.)

From the figures in Tables 7.3 and 7.1, it can be seen that the populations of the ethnic minorities have grown substantially under the PRC. The proportions of the ethnic minorities to the whole national population have also grown greatly since 1964. Several reasons account for this:

• Increased economic prosperity, leading to better health and conditions.

- The one-child-per-couple policy which since the 1980s the Han have been subject to. Although there have been restrictions also for the ethnic groups, they have not been nearly as severe as for the Han.
- Quite a few people and communities re-registered when the more lenient policies came into effect in the 1980s. This explains, for instance, the enormous jump in the Manchu population between the 1982 and 1990 censuses.

Han immigration

Almost all the ethnic areas now have extensive Han populations. On the whole, Han influence tends to be far greater in the cities, where most of them concentrate, than in the countryside, and integration between Han and minorities is much more extensive. The most controversial cases of Han immigration are Tibet and Xinjiang, where many locals feel that immigrants are taking over their territory.

In the case of Tibet, the 2000 census showed a total population of 2,616,300. Of this, 92.2 per cent (2,411,100) were Tibetan, and 5.9 per cent (155,300) were Han, while 1.9 per cent (49,900) consisted of other minorities such as Hui. Although this is a rise from the 1990 census, it is very much lower than the impression given by the exiled Tibetan community led by the Dalai Lama. Although the census may ignore some floating population and the army, it is striking that the census made no attempt to disguise the large Han proportions in other ethnic areas. For instance, for Inner Mongolia the 1990 census had the Han at 80.62 per cent of a total population of about 21.5 million (see Mackerras 1994: 252).

In the case of Uygur Xinjiang, there was very extensive Han immigration from the 1950s to the 1970s, reaching a height in 1978. From then until the late 1980s, the immigration declined, but then resumed (see Mackerras 2001: 293). Official figures show that the Han population increased from 5,695,626 in the 1990 census to 7,489,919 in the 2000 census, an average annual growth of 3 per cent. At the same time, the Uygur population grew from 7,194,675 in 1990 to 8,345,622 in 2000, an average annual growth of only 1.5 per cent (see National Bureau of Statistics 2002: 78–98, and Mackerras 1994: 253). As in Tibet, the figures probably ignore some of the floating population and the army.

In both Tibet and Xinjiang there is significant immigrant rotation. In other words, Han people come for a while, carry out a task, and then leave. This may in fact give the impression of a larger Han immigration than is in fact the case. On the whole, Han do not like living in Tibet, partly because they find the high altitude distressing. In Xinjiang, there is now a significant resident population. In other words, many of the 6,871,500 Han for 1999 were born in Xinjiang and are not immigrants at all.

Chinese official sources see nothing wrong with Han going to Tibet or Xinjiang, arguing that these regions are part of China. Propaganda also argues that the Han go there to help. However, there is no doubt that both the perception and fact of immigration cause great resentment among the Tibetans and Uygurs. It has become a major issue in ethnic relations, especially in Xinjiang. The government should not ask Han residents to leave if it means leaving their home and they feel loyalty to it. However, it would seem sensible to restrict further Han immigration.

Religion

On the whole, religion is stronger among the ethnic minorities than it is with the Han. Yet this is a broad generalisation covering what is in fact enormous diversity. With many minorities, there is a strong connection between ethnicity and religion. In other words, many members of ethnic minorities believe in a religion as much as a way of expressing their ethnic identity as for the faith itself. In the past, all or almost all members of an ethnic group shared a common religion. This is much less so today, because doctrines like Marxism-Leninism and Christianity have come from foreign countries and competed for allegiance. However, the ethnicity–religion link remains strong.

The three most prominent religions among China's minorities are Islam, Buddhism and folk religions of various kinds. Though the folk religions retain some following, they are so diverse that it would require more space to cover them sensibly than is available to me here. Moreover, their influence is mostly social nowadays, not economic, let alone political. They are certainly not an issue for China. Consequently, I leave them aside in this chapter.

Islam

Islam has a following in ten minorities, most notably the Uygurs and the Hui. At the end of the twentieth century there were about 18 million Muslims in China, nearly half of them (about 8.1 million) in Xinjiang. However, there are Muslims in almost all parts of China, including Beijing and its environs. Almost all Muslims in China are Sunni.

Buddhism

There are two main Buddhist forms among China's ethnic minorities, Tibetan Buddhism and Theravada Buddhism. The most important and most ardent believers in Tibetan Buddhism are of course the Tibetans. The Mongolians were converted to Tibetan Buddhism progressively from very early days, accelerating from the sixteenth century. However, the twentieth century saw a drastic decline in Tibetan Buddhism's impact on the Mongolians. Although the fall of the Mongolian People's Republic in 1991 ushered in a revival in Mongolia itself, Tibetan Buddhism remains very weak indeed among China's Mongolians.

By far the most important ethnic group believing in Theravada Buddhism is the Dai. In Xishuangbanna, most villages still have Thai-style temples, and many boys spend time in them as young monks. However, further to the northwest, Theravada Buddhism is considerably weaker.

Religion and separatism

The PRC state tries to control religion, but allows people to practise it openly. However, if the CCP considers that religious activities are threatening its own rule or state security, it will quickly act to suppress them. Most religious practice among the minorities appears to pose very little or no problem to the state. However, there are two examples that have aroused very great ire from officials because of their connections with separatism. These are Tibetan Buddhism among the Tibetans and Islam among the Uygurs.

At the end of the twentieth century an official account of religion among the minorities said the following:

> National splittists are using religion to destroy the unity of the motherland and of its nationalities. They focus on the Dalai Lama's clique to unfurl the banner of religion in an attempt to bring about Tibetan independence. Splittists both inside Xinjiang and outside are using religion as a cover for trying to destroy the unity of the nationalities and of the motherland. (Gong 1999: 307)

The question whether it is actually religion that is causing separatism has given rise to some debate among Western observers. Many differ from the Chinese government in seeing an independent Tibet as desirable and admire Tibetan Buddhism. It has become a part of the 'new spirituality' that has grown in influence in many places since the 1980s and especially since its principal emblem, the Dalai Lama, won the Nobel Peace Prize in 1989.

Since the 1990s, Islam among the Uygurs has actually posed more of a problem to the Chinese state than Tibetan Buddhism. However, it has not attracted much sympathy from outside China. In contrast to Tibetan Buddhism, Islam does not enjoy a positive image, and there is no counterpart to the Dalai Lama.

However, some Western scholars and human rights activists deny that religion plays as strong a role in separatism as the Chinese government claims. They argue that Han immigration into Xinjiang since the 1990s and Chinese oppression of minorities are more important factors in the rise of separatism. These are certainly relevant factors. On the other hand, it was a Western journalist who heard directly from a veteran of the 1990 rebellion in Akto that what inspired the uprising's leader Zahideen Yusuf and his followers was the Muslim doctrine of the holy war (Winchester 1997: 31). While in Xinjiang in 1999, I heard from a Uygur in a position to know that Muslim clerics in southern Xinjiang frequently use their position to try to stir up hatred against the Chinese, with the aim of driving out the infidel. I have no doubt at all that religion is one of the major factors in Xinjiang Uygur separatism.

Not surprisingly, the issue of religion and separatism has gained in importance since the September 11 terrorist attacks in New York and Washington. The Chinese are very clear in insisting that Xinjiang's Uygur separatists are terrorists inspired by Islamic fundamentalism and with links to Osama bin Laden and his al-Qaeda network. This issue is discussed later in this chapter.

The question of national unity

All Chinese governments of the last century (communist, republican or imperial) have been concerned with Chinese unity. On the whole, they succeeded in keeping the country together. In the past, many very large countries and empires have disintegrated and fallen apart. Examples in recent centuries include the Turkish Ottoman Empire and the Austro-Hungarian Habsburg Empire, both of which fell apart after World War I, and, more recently, the Soviet Union. It is true that China experienced severe strain after the Qing dynasty collapsed in 1911. But, unlike the Ottoman or Habsburg Empires, which have never come together again, China did not fall apart. The PRC saw unity re-established, with the exception of Taiwan. Yet potentially separatist ethnic movements in Tibet and Xinjiang continue to pose a theoretical challenge to China's territorial unity.

Challenges to national unity

The issue of national unity is related to regionalism. If particular regions of China decide to secede from the country as a whole, they set up a challenge to the whole idea of Chinese national unity. There are several different kinds of regionalism, such as those based on one or several provinces, or economic regions.

However, the category of concern in this chapter is obviously ethnic minorities. Could one or more ethnic minorities decide to set up their own independent state? Given China's emphasis on national unity, it is not surprising that central Chinese governments have always been hostile to any secessionist behaviour. Under Mao Zedong, central government control was very tight. Authorities firmly suppressed all attempts at separating from China by ethnic minorities, the most famous example being the Tibetan uprising of 1959.

Under Deng Xiaoping, central government control has tended to weaken. Although the country has been reasonably well integrated on the whole since the late 1970s, there have been several attempts at secession. However, in only two parts of China have separatist uprisings posed a serious threat to Chinese national unity. These regions are Tibet and Xinjiang and I will devote the rest of this section to these two cases.

Tibet

In September and October 1987 a series of demonstrations by monks marked the beginning of a renewed push for a Tibetan nation-state. The central government interpreted the movement as a threat to Chinese national unity and immediately sent troops and police against it. The suppression of the movement did not take long, but resulted in quite a few casualties, though precisely how many is not clear, and estimates tend to depend on the political sympathies of the observer. Further incidents followed in 1988 and 1989. Chinese troops suppressed demonstrations for independence in Lhasa in March 1989, held to commemorate the thirtieth anniversary of the 1959 uprising. These were the most serious disturbances in Tibet since 1959 and the Chinese government imposed martial law, the first time this had happened since the PRC's establishment. Not surprisingly, this measure caused great resentment among the Tibetans, and signs of this resentment still exist today. The Chinese government claimed that the disturbances threatened Chinese unity.

During the 1990s, some disturbances took place but they were on a scale much smaller than in the late 1980s. What was striking about March 1999, the fortieth anniversary of the 1959 uprising and the tenth of the movement that had led to martial law, was how peaceful it was, with virtually no open signs of discontent. When, in May 2001, the Chinese government organised celebrations to commemorate the fiftieth anniversary of the May 1951 agreement on Tibet, there were more or less no visible signs of protest.

The conclusion this material points to is that Tibet does not pose the threat to Chinese unity that it did in the late 1980s. This is not to say, however, that the problem has been solved. Chinese authorities are likely to remain vigilant for signs of movements demanding independence, especially in the monasteries. Already they have conducted several 'patriotic education campaigns', trying to eliminate the influence of the Dalai Lama, whom they regard as a 'splittist'. He remains a highly revered figure among the Tibetan people. But he is even further away from achieving an independent Tibet than he was in the late 1980s.

Xinjiang

If Tibet has been more peaceful since the early 1990s than before, then the case in Xinjiang is precisely the opposite. The earliest of the troubles in Xinjiang occurred in April 1990 when Uygur Islamic rebels attacked a government building in Baren Township, Akto County, not far from Kashgar in the southwest of Xinjiang. Journalist Michael Winchester (1997: 31), who interviewed a participant in the underground group that led the uprising, claims that the leader Zahideen Yusuf was a strong Muslim from a poor Uygur village south of Kashgar with a long-standing history of anti-Chinese unrest. Winchester adds he learned from his informant that Zahideen had smuggled and stockpiled weapons and it was a police sweep on the village in search of such arms that sparked off the initial attack. Official Chinese sources described it as an 'armed counter-revolutionary rebellion', blaming it on a political organisation called the Islamic Party of East Turkestan, which was directly separatist in its manifesto and wanted to split the Uygurs from China, setting up their own nation-state. They sent in police and troops and these very quickly defeated the rebels. They killed Zahideen and the remnants fled into the hills to organise further unrest.

There was a series of disturbances in Xinjiang throughout the early and mid-1990s. The most serious were in Gulja (which the Chinese know as Yining) in Xinjiang's far northwest, not far from the border with Kazakhstan. It appears that, early in February 1997, police entered a mosque to arrest two religious students suspected of planning an uprising against Chinese rule. The incident soon flared into independence demonstrations, mostly by Uygurs, rioting involving assaults on Han people, and vandalisation of vehicles. By the time police quelled the riots, about sixteen people were dead and nearly 150 wounded. Over the next days, there were summary arrests and executions of Uygur separatists. Arrests, trials and executions following from those times have persisted into the twenty-first century. As usual, Chinese authorities argued that social stability and national unity were under threat.

These incidents are only a sample of the most dramatic to take place in Xinjiang since 1990. They have aroused considerable concern among human rights activists, especially since the Chinese authorities have used the September 11 incidents as a reason for cracking down even more harshly on any Uygur dissidence or attempts at separatism. Human Rights in China, for instance, issued a long report in April 2005, in which it argued that 'China's efforts to control Uighur religion are so pervasive that they appear to go beyond suppression to a level of punitive control seemingly designed to entirely refashion Uygur religious identity to the state's purposes' (2005: 7).

Numerous reasons can be advanced why separatism should have developed in the 1990s in Xinjiang. Some observers put the emphasis on Chinese oppression, arguing that the Uygurs by necessity live apart from the Han, and at a lower level. Some Uygurs regard themselves as 'strangers in their own land' (Gluckman 2001: 24–6). Other observers emphasise the factor of Han immigration as a source of resentment (for example Becquelin 2000: 89–90). The Chinese government itself apportions a large part of the blame on 'illegal religious activities', meaning Islamic fundamentalism. My own view is that all these are relevant, but were not new to Xinjiang in the early 1990s. I propose, instead, that the renewed separatism in Xinjiang is one of the flow-on effects of the Soviet Union's decline and then collapse, and the rise of ethnic nationalism in an era of globalisation. These factors are of course interrelated. But they certainly mark the 1990s out from the preceding period, and brought with them important international relations factors affecting China and Xinjiang.

An intriguing and serious question to follow from the September 11 incident in New York and Washington and the resultant war against terror is whether we can legitimately describe the Xinjiang separatists as terrorists. Observers have been less sure than the Chinese government on this score. Dru Gladney (2004: 381) acknowledges a few terrorist incidents, but doubts any organised terrorist separatist movement in Xinjiang. He goes so far as to say that among the confirmed incidents of civil unrest, bombings and so on since 1990, 'very few can be definitely traced to Uygur separatist groups or events in Xinjiang'. It probably depends on how we define terrorism and even the United Nations Millennium Summit of September 2005 could not agree on that. If it involves violence directed against civilians, then it appears to me that there have been some terrorist incidents in Xinjiang since 1990, but dwindling in number since 1997 and probably not frequent enough to warrant the very severe countermeasures against Uygurs currently being taken by the Chinese authorities.

Ethnic minorities and international relations

China's ethnic minorities have impacted on China's foreign relations. There are various reasons for this. The main one is that relations with the two main powers of the post-war world, the United States and the Soviet Union (and its principal successor state, Russia), have always involved at least some of China's minorities. Also, many of the minorities live near borders with co-nationals on the other side of the border.

Indeed, borders are relevant in other ways too. India has been concerned about the situation in Tibet and China's relations with India have depended to some extent on the situation in Tibet. The situation in Xinjiang has had a considerable bearing on relations with countries that border to the west or southwest, such as Kazakhstan and Pakistan. However, by far the most important ethnic groups with impact on China's international relations are the Tibetans and the Uygurs. The foreign countries that are most relevant here are the big ones, the United States and Russia. I would like to explore the interplay among these two ethnic groups and China's relations with these two large countries.

Tibet and the USA

When the Tibetan revolt erupted in 1959, China blamed American interference, as well as local reactionaries. At the time, Sino-American relations were very bad indeed. According to a BBC television programme, in the 1950s and 1960s, the American Central Intelligence Agency actively supplied training, money and weaponry in support of a guerilla war against the Chinese, with many thousands of casualties (Sarin and Sonam 1998). This assistance did not stop until 1974, by which time the United States wanted to improve its relations with China.

One of the effects of the 1959 uprising was that the Dalai Lama fled to India and set up a government-in-exile there. He made occasional visits overseas, the first one being to Japan in 1967. However, it was not until the 1980s that his influence began to expand and he became a truly global figure. In 1989, he won the Nobel Peace Prize, which further increased his prestige. Since that time he can claim to be one of the world's most important trendsetters. In 1997 Hollywood took him and his cause up in a big way, with several laudatory, even hagiographic films about him, featuring such stars as Brad Pitt. He visits foreign countries continually. The Chinese authorities regularly issue statements of protest about this, calling him a 'splittist'. But there is nothing they can do to prevent his trips or curb his influence. The Dalai Lama addressed two congressional bodies in Washington in September 1987, just before the independence demonstrations. Naturally the Chinese blamed him and the Americans for the disturbances. On 6 October 1989, the American Senate adopted a resolution condemning China for human rights abuses in Tibet.

The crisis of mid-1989 formed a major landmark in the development of American human rights diplomacy towards China. Americans and many others were justly appalled at the violent suppression of the student movement. Yet the

1987 developments in Tibet had cast a shadow over what had been an extremely good relationship since the two countries established formal diplomatic relations on 1 January 1979. Since that time Tibet has been a major focus of disagreement in what has become a highly volatile relationship. Yet it would be a mistake to exaggerate its significance. It is highly unlikely that the Americans would ever let Tibet interfere with its commercial relations with China, let alone assist another guerilla war, as they did in the days before diplomatic relations. Tibet cannot compete with issues like Taiwan in importance.

Xinjiang, Russia and the USA

During the years of Sino-Soviet hostility from the late 1950s to the mid-1980s, Xinjiang had an extremely sensitive border with the powerful Soviet Union. What is striking is that this hostility was based far more on vital national factors than on the rights or views of ethnic minorities. This changed when the Soviet Union declined and then collapsed at the end of 1991, and when Uygur separatism became a major threat to China in the early 1990s. It was largely in response to the threat of ethnic unrest and Islamic fundamentalism in Central Asia, including Uygur separatism, that China, Russia and the three former republics of the Soviet Union that border China to the west decided to step up mutual assistance.

In April 1996, the Presidents of China, Russia, Kazakhstan, Kyrgyzstan and Tajikistan met in Shanghai to discuss mutual problems. The presidents of the same five countries continued to meet annually, once in the main cities of all five in turn. The meeting of July 2000 set up a joint anti-terrorist centre to combat incursions by Muslim extremists and drug traffickers. In mid-June 2001, the group's meeting was back in Shanghai. This time Uzbekistan came too, and the six countries signed a formal pact, establishing the Shanghai Cooperation Organisation. They also signed a document pledging to cooperate to combat terrorism and extremism, a clear reference to Islamic fundamentalism. Both 2000 and 2001 meetings seemed to forecast the American-led war against terrorism that came soon after.

The September 11 incident of 2001 had a considerable effect on the situation in Central Asia. For the first time it brought the United States into Central Asia as a major player. China gave strong support to the war on terrorism, so Sino-American relations greatly improved, at least for the time being. On 6 December 2001 Reuters reported that in discussions with Chinese government officials, American Ambassador-at-large on terrorism Francis X. Taylor admitted that United States forces had captured 'people from Western China', in other words Uygurs, during the strikes against the Taliban and Osama bin Laden's al-Qaeda network in Afghanistan. In August 2002, the United States announced that it recognised the East Turkestan Islamic Movement as a terrorist organisation, a decision the Chinese government welcomed warmly.

Conclusion

China's ethnic minorities definitely matter for the country's future and the government has to treat them very carefully indeed. Probably the most critical of all issues related to ethnic minorities is the unity of China. Governments in many parts of the world have had great difficulty in dissuading peoples from striving for independence, without creating hatreds so deep that they last for generations. In many cases in other parts of the world, what has in fact happened is that independence movements succeed, even after violent attempts to prevent them. Occasionally wars follow, such as the one between Ethiopia and Eritrea, revealing deep-seated hatreds despite the setting up of a newly independent state. In the chapter's Introduction, I argued that China is unlikely to fall apart because of the ethnic strife, as Yugoslavia or the Soviet Union did, but it would be a mistake to dismiss such a possibility and refuse to recognise the sensitivity and importance of ethnic questions.

China has to overcome the backward economies that exist among most of the ethnic minorities. However, economic authorities must not allow disparities to become too wide as development proceeds. Based on the experience of the last decades, this balance could be very difficult to achieve. Since failure could spark social unrest, economic development in ethnic areas is therefore an extremely sensitive issue.

Religion as a whole is essential to culture among many of China's ethnic minorities. All agree that religious freedom is important, but the Chinese authorities do not want to allow religion to impede the kind of social and economic development they aim for. Traditions have shown themselves very tenacious up to now. Balance is difficult, but both necessary and possible.

A related issue of the greatest importance is how to move against terrorist actions inspired by radical Islam without appearing to be fighting against Islam itself. China shares this problem with other countries. Indeed, it is a central issue in the American-led war against terrorism.

Han immigration into certain ethnic areas, especially Xinjiang and Tibet, has been a cause of great resentment. It is also very difficult to handle. It does not seem fair to expel Han people who have already lived in the ethnic areas for years or even generations. However, the kind of immigration that has happened in some ethnic areas in the second half of the twentieth century can only create social divisions, with a potential for violence.

Some ethnic issues bear on China's foreign relations, especially Tibet and Xinjiang. It may not be possible to control the policies of countries like the United States or Russia. However, at the beginning of this new century, China appears to be successfully managing its relations with these two foreign powers. It is also most certainly possible for China to do more to enhance its relationship with both powers, for instance by improving its human rights in Tibet and elsewhere.

There are, then, many difficult balances to achieve. Failure could bring disaster for China in various forms. Sensitive and realistic policies and actions could bring great successes. The issues involving the ethnic minorities are indeed critical.

References

Becquelin, N. (2000) 'Xinjiang in the Nineties', *China Journal* 44: 65–90.

Gladney, D. C. (1991) *Muslim Chinese, Ethnic Nationalism in the People's Republic*, Cambridge, MA; London: Council on East Asian Studies, Harvard University.

—— (2004) 'Responses to Chinese Rule: Patterns of Cooperation and Opposition', in S. Frederick Starr (ed.), *Xinjiang, China's Muslim Borderland*, Armonk, NY, London, England: M. E. Sharpe, pp. 375–96.

Gluckman, R. (2001) 'Strangers in Their Own Land', *Asiaweek* 27/48: 24–6.

Goldstein, M. C. (1997) *The Snow Lion and the Dragon, China, Tibet, and the Dalai Lama*, Berkeley, Los Angeles, London: University of California Press.

Gong, X. Z. (1999) *Zongjiao wenti gailun (Introduction to problems of religion)*, Chengdu: Sichuan People's Press.

Human Rights in China (2005) 'Devastating Blows: Religious Repression of Uighurs in Xinjiang', *Human Rights Watch* 17(2C): 1–114.

Mackerras, C. (1994) *China's Minorities, Integration and Modernisation in the Twentieth Century*, Hong Kong: Oxford University Press.

—— (1995) *China's Minority Cultures, Identities and Integration Since 1912*, New York: St Martin's Press, Melbourne: Longman Australia.

—— (2001) *The New Cambridge Handbook of Contemporary China*, Cambridge: Cambridge University Press.

National Bureau of Statistics, PRC (comp.) (2000) *Zhongguo tongji nianjian 2000 (China Statistical Yearbook 2000)*, Beijing: China Statistics Press.

National Bureau of Statistics, PRC (comp.) (2004) *Zhongguo tongji nianjian 2004 (China Statistical Yearbook 2004)*, Beijing: China Statistics Press.

National Bureau of Statistics, Department of Population, Social Science and Technology Statistics (2002) *Zhongguo renkou tongji nianjian China Population Statistics Yearbook 2002*, Beijing: China Statistics Press.

Sarin, R. and Sonam, T. (directors) (1998) *Shadow Circus – The CIA in Tibet*, television documentary, London: BBC.

Shih, C. Y. (2001) 'Ethnicity as Policy Expedience: Clan Confucianism in Ethnic Tujia-Miao Yongshun', *Asian Ethnicity* 2/1: 73–88.

Stalin, J. V. (1953) 'Marxism and the National Question', *Works*, vol. II, Moscow: Foreign Languages Publishing House, pp. 300–81.

Tapp, N. (2001) *The Hmong of China, Context, Agency, and the Imaginary*, Leiden; Boston; Köln: Brill.

UNDP (United Nations Development Programme) (1997) *Human Development Report 1997*, New York; Oxford: Oxford University Press.

United Nations Economic and Social Council, Committee on Economic, Social and Cultural Rights (2005) *Concluding Observations of the Committee on Economic, Social and Cultural Rights, People's Republic of China (including Hong Kong and Macao)* 13 May.

Winchester, M. (1997) 'Beijing vs. Islam', *Asiaweek* 23/42: 30–42.

Wu, S. M., Wang, P., *et al.* (1999) *Minzu wenti gailun (Summary of Nationalities Problems)*, Chengdu: Sichuan People's Press.

Further reading

Harrell, S. (2001) *Ways of Being Ethnic in Southwest China*, Seattle, London: University of Washington Press.

Kaup, K. P. (2000) *Creating the Zhuang: Ethnic Politics in China*, Boulder, London: Lynne Rienner.

Litzinger, R. A. (2000) *Other Chinas, The Yao and the Politics of National Belonging*, Durham, London: Duke University Press.

Mackerras, C. (2003) *China's Ethnic Minorities and Globalisation*, London, New York: RoutledgeCurzon.

Schein, L. (2000) *Minority Rules: The Miao and the Feminine in China's Cultural Politics*, Durham, London: Duke University Press.

Shakya, T. (1999) *The Dragon in the Land of Snows, A History of Modern Tibet Since 1947*, London: Pimlico Press.

Starr, S. F. (ed.) (2004) *Xinjiang, China's Muslim Borderland*, Armonk, NY, London, England: M. E. Sharpe.

8

Critical social issues

COLIN MACKERRAS

Introduction

The other chapters in this book have been concerned with political, economic and demographic issues. These issues were selected for their significant impact on Chinese society. However, apart from Chapter 7's discussion of ethnic minorities, there has been very little explicit attention given to social issues and problems facing contemporary China. In this chapter, we highlight some of these issues.

All societies have some way of regulating relations among their members and almost all have a family system of some kind. However, China is famous for the importance the family occupies within society. The Confucian ethic, with its emphasis on filial piety, contributed over centuries towards keeping the family system strong. However, there seems little doubt that, amid quite strong continuity, there has also been great change in the family in modern China. In the late nineteenth and early twentieth centuries, the Confucian family ideal began to be contested. The communist revolutionaries in particular saw the family as contributing to much of China's conservative and oppressive behaviour and sought to undermine its influence on society. In more recent years, the practicalities of family planning have also altered family structures and dynamics within China. As these changes in family structure have fundamentally affected the fabric of society, China cannot be understood without some insight into its family system.

One of the criteria often taken to judge the extent of changes affecting the family is societal attitudes towards women. At the Fourth United Nations World Conference on Women held in Beijing in September 1995, Hillary Rodham Clinton, the wife of the then American President Bill Clinton, received much support when she declared that if there was one message to echo forth from the conference, it would be 'that human rights are women's rights and women's rights are human rights, once and for all'. In the contemporary world most people accept that how women fare within any specific country is a critical factor in how one evaluates that country's progress, not only because females make up about half of humanity but also because most traditional societies have discriminated against them in various ways and not given them the status they deserve. This chapter will address some of the ways that women's roles and rights have evolved in modern China.

Another critical issue is education. It is hardly necessary to emphasise the importance of education for any country. Education affects the whole of society. It promotes the population's intellectual development, helps the workforce obtain the skills necessary to develop a modern economy, and allows citizens to become more involved in debates related to the country's future development. If properly managed, education improves the quality of life of any community. It is undoubtedly an element in society that is critical for any country's future.

An equally critical issue is the country's health system, since everybody in a community gets sick or needs health delivery at some point. Like universal education, a comprehensive health delivery system is one of the features of a modern society. China has its traditional medicines, many of which are still in use. But for a radical improvement in health standards all over the country, there is no substitute for a modern, comprehensive health system.

This chapter ends with a discussion of the extent to which social inequality exists in China. One could expect that a country that terms itself a 'people's republic' and is ruled by a communist party, would strive to build an equitable society. During the Maoist period, this was indeed the case, although Mao's achievement of social equality was accompanied by the extermination of entire social classes and the pauperisation of the middle class and intelligentsia. Following the introduction of economic reforms in the late 1970s, the state no longer put a premium on social equality. Instead, it has promoted economic development, in which some – thanks to their diligence, education or connections – gained financially, while others were left behind. As a result, Chinese society has become increasingly polarised into the haves and the have-nots. This polarisation is undoubtedly a critical factor in China's social stability.

We may note also that China's new party-state leader, Hu Jintao, has placed a major premium on social harmony and the harmonious society. One Chinese observer claims that since the CCP had introduced the concept of the 'harmonious society' in September 2004, giving it the same importance as economic, political and cultural development, the term 'harmonious society' had become 'the new buzzword in media' (Huang 2005: 24). The leadership believes that rising prosperity depends on stability, which in turn requires that nobody should rock the boat too much. This emphasis on stability and harmony has clear overtones of Confucianism.

Yet the fact is that instability is serious and on the rise. Official government statistics show that in 2004 there were 74,000 riots or other significant public disturbances, the number higher than in earlier years (French 2005). We shall see in this chapter that China has experienced enormous and generally accelerating social change since the beginning of the twentieth century. Moreover, although Mao Zedong's version of socialism brought about enormous transformation in virtually all areas, modernisation may well end up being even more decisive in changing Chinese society.

Family and women

Family in traditional China

A main site of the Confucian quest for harmony in traditional China, as well as of change in modern China, is the family, which was central to traditional Chinese society. According to Hugh D. R. Baker (1979: 17), the family in traditional China was a residential and economic unit composed of males. In order to reproduce itself, it was forced to import women as brides, and it disposed of females born to it by marrying them off to other families. It placed a strong emphasis on the importance of males, while the role and contributions of women were downplayed. Apart from being an economic unit (where family members contributed through their labour to the economic well-being of the household), the family in Chinese traditional society had also important ritual or religious duties.

Confucianism identified important relationships by which man's life should be governed, the so-called 'five relationships' (*wulun*). They are:

1   ruler/minister;
2   father/son;
3   elder brother/younger brother;
4   husband/wife;
5   friend/friend.

If such relationships, arranged in order of priority and superiority/inferiority, were properly observed, there could be no conflict or friction in the Chinese society in general and the family in particular, because every member of the society and family was held tightly in check by the duty and obedience which he owed to another. Each of the relationships identified above could be extended to include a wider group. Thus, for example, the father/son relationship could be taken to include the mother/son, father/unmarried daughter and mother/unmarried daughter relationships.

The five relationships implied a pecking order within traditional Chinese society, with families governed by hierarchies in generation, age and gender. To give an idea how these principles worked, let's consider an extended family with three married sons living with their parents in one household. In such a family, everyone owed obedience to the father because he was superior in generation, age and gender. Everyone but the father owed obedience to the mother because she was senior in generation and age. The eldest son's wife owed obedience to her father-in-law because of generation and age, and her allegiance to her husband was only a secondary concern because it was founded on the less important gender superiority. The youngest son owed obedience to his elder brother's wives, his elder brothers, his mother and father. The youngest grandson had to obey all members of the family. The unmarried daughters were only temporarily members of the family until they were married off.

Women in traditional China

A woman's position in the family was low. Her main responsibilities included producing male children to continue her husband's family line, contributing to the housework and serving the males. In much of China, women worked mainly within the household and rarely engaged in other activities, for example, farm work. Baker (1979: 21–2) observes that 'in classical thought [women] were considered to be minors throughout their lives, subject first of all to the man of the family into which they were born, then on marriage to the men of their husband's family, and finally on widowhood to their sons'. These obligations were known as the *sancong* – 'three obediences' – and linked to four virtues (*side*) of morality, proper speech, modest manner and diligence in work. Even upon death, a woman's soul depended on the worship of her male descendants.

Women married patrilocally, that is, upon marriage, a bride took up residence in her husband's household (or at least in the village of her husband's parents). Marriage was traditionally 'blind', and representatives of the families of the bride and groom arranged the marriage with little or no reference to the individuals involved in the marriage. The groom's family paid a 'bride price', which symbolised the legal transfer of authority over the bride from her family of origin to that of her husband. The bride brought dowry items with her: clothing, jewellery, linen and sometimes furniture. Usually, these remained under her own control. As women were usually excluded from inheritance of land or property, the dowry could be considered as a form of inheritance, although women's 'movable property' was of much less value than their brothers' share in the parents' estate. The size of a dowry was inversely correlated with women's agricultural participation rates: the less the economic contribution to the husband's household, the higher the dowry. Bride prices, in turn, tended to be positively correlated with economic participation (the higher the price, the greater the expected labour). When male families paid large sums for brides, they could expect to exert greater pressure and control over women to recoup their investment (Johnson 1983: 12).

There were no political positions for women in traditional China, although they might exercise influence indirectly. It was an established norm in Confucian Chinese society that a virtuous woman had no political ambition and even had no exceptional abilities (Yao 2000: 183). Women were not allowed to participate in imperial exams and were barred from holding state offices. And yet, in Chinese history there are a few exceptional cases of politically powerful women at the imperial centre, perhaps the best known being Empress Dowager Cixi, who held great political power from the early 1860s until her death in 1908. Bossen (2003: 313–14) notes that women in rural rebel movements, such as the Taiping Rebellion, the Red Spears movement and the Boxer Rebellion, took an active part in public life. The Taiping Rebellion (1851–64) in particular encouraged women's participation, as it stressed sexual equality, rejected traditional patriarchy, polygamy and foot binding. With the expansion of the Taiping Rebellion, women became generals and soldiers.

The family during the Republican period

The fall of the Manchu dynasty in 1911 was a blow to Confucianism, because the court had been the main centre of Confucian ritual. But this attack strengthened with the May Fourth Movement of 1919, which opposed all the values that had been dear to Confucianism, including the traditional family system. The literature of the May Fourth period includes many criticisms of arranged marriages and other aspects of the traditional system. One specific example is the play *The Greatest Event of Her Life* (*Zhongsheng dashi*) by Hu Shi (1891–1962), who stood on the liberal rather than the radical wing of the May Fourth thinkers. Set in early twentieth-century China, it concerns the marriage of a Miss Tian. Her parents agree in their wish to prevent her marrying the man she loves, but have different reasons. Her mother is obedient to a fortune-teller and to Goddess of Mercy

Guanyin, both of whom have warned her that the pair are incompatible. Miss Tian's father is motivated by loyalty to old Confucian doctrines. In the end Miss Tian elopes, seeing no way to persuade her parents out of their foolish attitudes.

In 1931 Chiang Kai-shek's government adopted the Family and Inheritance Law, which copied much from Western and Japanese family laws. Although aiming to be 'modern', the Law retained the patrilineal and patriarchal nature of the family. The wife took her husband's surname and entered his family, and the father usually got custody of the children in cases of divorce. However, the Law specifically allowed young people to choose their own spouses. It outlawed bigamy and made no mention of concubinage or ancestor worship. A woman could be a 'family head'. Whereas in traditional times men could divorce their wives, who had no mutual rights at all, the 1931 Law gave people of either sex equal rights to divorce. Furthermore, women and men were made equal in terms of property and inheritance rights. These factors were a great advance on the past family system and appeared to reflect the influence of the May Fourth thinkers.

The PRC and family

All four PRC Constitutions lay down the protection of the family, including the one issued in 1975 under the shadow of the Cultural Revolution. Article 49 of the 1982 Constitution says that: 'Marriage, the family and mother and child are protected by the State'. There have been two marriage laws issued under the PRC, the first in May 1950, the second in September 1980. The May 1950 Marriage Law was actually the first major law enacted under the PRC, showing the importance the new rulers attached to the subject. Because the Marriage Law sought to remove the abuses of the old family system by protecting equal rights within marriage, giving women the right to divorce and the right to claim custody of their children, it has come under attack from traditionally-minded people, especially rural men, who termed it 'the divorce law' or the 'women's law' (Bossen 2003: 319). It is certainly true that Mao Zedong's government was hostile to traditional Confucian family values such as filial piety and the patriarchal forms that tended to go with it.

In some ways the traditional family has returned during the reform period. Many old values have tended to revive; Confucius and Confucianism are no longer officially discouraged or attacked; many in authority view both quite sympathetically. Yet Confucian values have certainly not returned to the levels of social importance that they enjoyed before the twentieth century. Modernisation and its values inevitably influence the way the family operates and tend to weaken its social role. Moreover, the one-child-per-couple policy has made a profound impact on the family as a system, as since the 1980s, most Chinese have not experienced having brothers or sisters and most children born in recent years do not have first cousins.

One respect in which the family has weakened under the PRC is that it does not play nearly as important an economic role as it once did. When Mao was in control he introduced rural communes, which greatly reduced the importance of the family as an economic unit, especially in the countryside. Although the period of reform has returned economic power to the family by allowing for family entre-preneurship, family-owned farms, and family-run small businesses, the economic role of family has not returned to its pre-Mao importance. At the same time, with the rise of nation-wide migration in search of better economic opportunities, the scope for individualism has begun to widen, further reducing the influence of the family as an institution (Hook 1991: 92). The implication is clear: the family is not as strong in its economic or social influence as a whole as it once was.

Changing household patterns

Further evidence of the changes noted above can be gained by looking at the number of generations and people in Chinese households. The traditional (or ideal) household pattern for well-off families was for several generations to live under one roof. The more generations there were, the more prestige the patriarch and the family in general could claim. Under the PRC, household patterns have changed enormously. The latest census in 2000 showed 275,856,754 households with one or two generations, out of a national total of 340,491,197, or 81 per cent (NBS 2002: 104).

The proportion of 'nuclear families', in other words a married couple with their unmarried children, is far greater than it was and it is continuing to rise. However, there are two factors indicating that by no means all two-generation households are nuclear families. One of them is the issue of housing. While there has been a boom in residential construction in China during the reform period, house space is still at a premium. Quite a few young married couples therefore still live with their parents in the early years after they marry, and even longer. The rise in life expectancy impacts on household size and the number of generations, because it means that more grandparents will be sharing a house with their married children than would have been the case in the past.

The number of persons per household has declined under the PRC, espe-cially in the period of reform. In traditional China, the mean household size fluctu-ated between 5.0 and 5.5, which is not too different from other pre-modern societies (Hook 1991: 92). The precise census figures for household size under the PRC are 4.33 in 1953, 4.43 in 1964, 4.41 in 1982, 3.96 in 1990, and 3.44 in 2000 (NBS 2002: 95). What is obvious from these figures is that the number of people in each household on average actually rose before the Cultural Revolution and does not seem to have begun falling until the period of reform. Since then, factors like the one-child family policy have brought about a significant fall.

Marriage

A detailed survey carried out in 1991 by the Institute of Population Studies, Chinese Academy of Social Sciences, found that old-style arranged marriages were quite rare by the 1990s, even for rural women. This suggests a very great advance in the context where arranged marriages were nearly universal in the Chinese countryside until 1949 and were only in the fairly early stages of breaking down in the cities. On the other hand it found that about 15 per cent of rural people found their own marriage partner (IPS 1994: 99–100). In the countryside it is parents who choose marriage partners for their children, but the latter have veto power, whereas in the cities it is the other way around, with spouses making their own selection, which parents may veto.

The survey also found data about the age of first marriage. The mean age of men at first marriage in the cities was 26.03 years and of women, 24.08 years. In the countryside, the figures are about three years lower, 23.05 for men and 21.56 for women (IPS 1994: 103). According to the figures given, nobody married below the age of 20. The Marriage Law of 1950 put the minimum age of marriage at 20 for men and 18 for women, but the revised 1980 law raised both ages by two years. Figures for women first marrying under the age of 18 covering all China show that the proportion was 48.3 per cent in 1950, 32 per cent in 1960, 18.6 per cent in 1970 and 4.5 per cent in 1981 (Yang *et al.* 1988, 158). It is possible that underage marriages had reached very low proportions by 1995.

Although the reform period has witnessed more equality between males and females in marriage, it does not follow that pre-modern, conservative attitudes have disappeared. A 1991 survey illustrates this point. One proposition posed to people for reaction was 'a woman should follow her husband no matter what he becomes, and never remarry'. Among urban wives over 40 years old, 18.3 per cent agreed, while the percentage of wives in their twenties was only 10.99. Rural wives, however, were more conservative, with 44.36 per cent of those over 40 agreeing to the proposition, and 32.59 per cent of those in their twenties (IPS 1994: 356).

Divorce

The CCP's Marriage Laws made divorce much easier than it had been earlier, especially if both parties wanted it. The 1950 law stated that even when one party insists on a divorce, this 'may be granted only when mediation ... has failed to bring about a reconciliation', while that of 1980 changed the emphasis when it stipulated that divorce should be granted 'in cases of complete alienation of mutual affection, and when mediation has failed' (see Mackerras *et al.* 1998: 152–3).

Despite the relative ease of divorce (implied by the Marriage Law), in practice, divorce rates in China are not particularly high, although they have risen substantially in the reform period. In 1985 there were over 18 times as many marriages as divorces, but in 2003, comparable figures showed only 6 times as many marriages as divorces (see the figures in NBS 2004: 902). A 1991 survey found the main causes of discord among married couples were problems over children and housework in the cities, but with children an issue only for wives in the countryside and husbands more concerned about money matters. Other reasons for clashes between married couples included problems with parents and other relations, poor sex life and incompatible temperament (IPS 1994: 145). While sources of discord are not the same as reasons for divorce, there is no doubt considerable overlap.

Women's role and status

The 1950 Marriage Law specifically laid down equality between male and female, and Mao Zedong's government promoted the slogan that 'women hold up half the sky'. The CCP introduced a strategy to raise women's status, which included legislating for equality, bringing women into organised labour and propagating gender equality (Croll 1983: 1). The strategy produced results in bringing women into the workforce, education, the professions, and even some power positions to an extent unprecedented in Chinese history. For example, the proportion of women in China's national parliament, the National People's Congress, rose from 12 per cent in 1954 to 22.6 per cent in 1975 (see figures in Mackerras 2001: 96). The strategy specified equal pay for equal work in production and came nearer to implementing such a concept than earlier governments. It also made them less unequal in the family. However, not even official statements were prepared to argue that the reality of equality matched the ideal. For instance, a typical discussion in 1979 (cited in Croll 1983: 4) lauded the fundamental improvement in women's lives, but was still prepared to admit that 'the attitude that men are superior to women still persists' and women's complete emancipation was not on the horizon.

The reform and modernisation period has had very mixed results for women in China. The thrust towards modernity has been good for women in some respects. But the revival of traditional family values has meant the return of some trends and practices harmful to women's interests, especially in the countryside. Just as before the reform period, women are equal to men before the law. Ellen Judd suggests (1994: 114) that the 1980 Marriage Law is 'more bilateral and gender-balanced than the preceding one' of May 1950. The 1982 Constitution's Article 48 says that women 'enjoy equal rights with men in all spheres of life, political, economic, cultural and social, including family life'. It says that the state should train and select cadres from among women and even stipulates the principle of equal pay for equal work. The 1985 Inheritance Law indicates that daughters as well as sons can inherit their parents' property, a provision in the land reform law which was made broadly inoperable as a consequence of continued patrilocal residence patterns, and the loss of individual title to land during the cooperative period. These matters became crucial once again after production responsibility systems became common in the countryside during the reform period, and field division and long-term contracting raised the issue of land-use inheritance rights. These changes were reiterated in the Law on the Protection of the Rights and Interest of Women (translated Croll 1995: 184–92), adopted at the fifth session of the Seventh National People's Congress in April 1992. The trouble is that state ideology has turned against equality in just about all spheres. It is all very well to say that male and female should be equal. But the realities of the economy and society are that equality is more and more difficult to implement, including between the sexes.

Social welfare specifically aimed at women has got much worse, just as social welfare in general has deteriorated. The reason is quite simple: society has embraced the 'user pays' principle, so that things that were once provided by the state are no longer so. Just one example will suffice to illustrate the point. Kindergartens and crèches cost much more than they did, which means that for many women it is no longer an economically viable proposition to put their children into them. So if they are going to work, they have to find some other means of getting their small child looked after. Of course, this problem is partly offset by the fact that urban and many rural women have just the one child nowadays.

Gender matters are one of the concerns of the United Nations Development Programme (UNDP), which puts out a gender-related development index (GDI). The GDI measures average achievement in three basic dimensions: a long and healthy life; knowledge; and a decent standard of living. These dimensions are adjusted to account for inequalities between men and women. The nearer the GDI is to 1, the closer the country has approached gender equality as measured by the three factors. In 2002, the United Nations Development Programme ranked China 77th in the world in terms of its GDI, with an absolute score of 0.724 (UNDP 2002: 223). In 2005, China had moved to 64th place with an absolute score of 0.754 (ibid.: 300). Both years put China well ahead of India, which came in at 105th place in 2002 with an absolute score of 0.560 (ibid.: 224) and 98th in 2005 with an absolute score of 0.586 (ibid.: 301).

On 16 December 2005, the China Country Office of the UNDP released its fourth *Human Development Report* focused exclusively on China, the first having been published in 1997. In its abstract, the report had the following to say about gender inequities in the field of employment (UNDP, China 2005: 2):

> Men and women also have different employment opportunities. China's labor market is highly segregated by gender, and fewer women work in white collar jobs than men. Layoffs in urban enterprises have affected women disproportionately, and gender-based wage differences are growing as economic reforms continue.

The record, as the UNDP measures it, does show improvements in some very important areas affecting the well-being of the female sex. As is noted in Chapter 3, in the process of China becoming wealthier and more modern, inequalities have widened in many areas, and this seems to also be the case also with gender equity. Life has got better for women, but men have gone ahead much faster than women.

Women in regular employment retire at 55, men at 60. Surveys covering the whole country for the year 2000 showed that men spent on average 6 hours and 15 minutes per day on their work or labour, while for women it was 4 hours and 35 minutes. On the other hand, women did far more housework, 4 hours and 15 minutes, as against men's 1 hour and 33 minutes. In particular, women spent 1 hour 25 minutes cooking, while men took it easy with just 25 minutes' cooking (NBS 2002, 815). Men also got more entertainment and spent more time studying than women. It seems to me that what all this shows is that there is still a strong tendency for men's work to be outside the family and women's to be much more in the home than men's.

Chapter 5's discussion of the one-child policy noted how the policy has revived the passion for sons in preference to daughters and, with it, discrimination against mothers whose only child is a girl. The November 2000 census revealed that, between November 1999 and October 2000, there had been a total of 7,606,007 male births as against 6,508,529 female, which means 116.9 boys were born for every 100 girls (DP, NBS 2002: 129), which is far more than the norm and suggests widespread selective abortion and infanticide. In the long term, some of the boys will find themselves without girls to marry. Although this could have the effect of reducing the population size, since it is the female cohort that determines the size of the next generation, the extent of pain and social dislocation will be very considerable.

The record may be mixed, but the crucial importance of women's issues is obvious. Hillary Clinton was right to draw attention to the link between women's rights and human rights in her speech of September 1995. Modern societies generally insist on some degree of gender equality and progress in that direction is critical for China to modernise fully and effectively.

The education system

Education in imperial China

One of the most important things about Chinese civilisation is its respect for education and learning. This goes back a very long way. The ancient sage Confucius (551–479 BCE) was greatly concerned with education, and emphasised its importance. He believed, for instance, that people were born the same but that those who underwent education became better people. It was education that could produce the *junzi* or superior man.

The purpose of education in imperial China was to transmit knowledge and the written culture, and to inculcate Confucian morality into the younger generation of males (women not being involved in formal schooling). The official imperial examination system, which for centuries was the gateway to the official bureaucracy, tested knowledge of Confucian classics, history, calligraphy and literature. Students were taught to memorise and recite classical texts, rather than challenge them or engage in any experimental sciences. Although Qing China did not have compulsory education and, as Woodside and Elman add (1994: 529), neither 'was there much serious premonition of the modern idea that there ought to be', the literacy rate in traditional China was relatively high. According to Evelyn Rawski (1979: 140), 'it was possible for a broad cross-section of Ch'ing [Qing] males to attain some degree of literacy in private and charitable schools'. Approximately 30 to 45 per cent of men and 2 to 10 per cent of women in China knew how to read and write. However, this group included the fully literate members of the elite and also those who only knew a few hundred characters. Thus loosely defined, there was an average of almost one literate person per family. Taking a median view of Rawski's figures and assuming that about 52 per cent of the population in the mid-nineteenth century was male, we would get about 22 per cent literacy overall. However, it is important to note that these figures do not talk about age. The 22 per cent figure exempts children below an age where they could not be expected to have acquired any literacy.

By the end of the nineteenth century, Western ideas were already permeating Chinese society. Following the eight-power foreign invasion to suppress the Boxer Rebellion in 1900, an imperial edict abolished the traditional examination system in 1905. Traditional Confucian education declined along with the disappearance of the examinations. In 1902, imperial regulations on primary schools required all children to receive seven years of education; and so began the notion of compulsory education in China. Education played an important role in the modernisation process in China in the early twentieth century, especially in the transition from the Confucian empire to the modern state. To Chinese reformers, Western education practices seemed much more effective than anything the Chinese had for creating citizens who were law-abiding, hard-working, patriotic and well behaved.

Education in the Republican period

After Chiang Kai-shek had carried out the Northern Expedition and come to power in 1927, his government's policy on education (adopted in 1929) gave a high priority to official ideology, namely, the Three Principles of the People (*sanmin zhuyi*). These principles aimed to replenish and enrich people's lives; to develop the livelihood of citizens; and to promote China as a modern nation-state. Inherent in these principles were the values of nationalism and the promotion of social harmony.

During the 1930s, the Republican government developed a comprehensive national primary, secondary and vocational system, with required standards. This was the first comprehensive education system in Chinese history. The primary curriculum consisted of standard Chinese, or *guoyu* (literally 'the national language'), citizenship, hygiene, society, nature, arithmetic, fine arts and music. The secondary curriculum added such subjects as English, a second foreign language, history, geography and mathematics. Boys took a subject with a military bent called *tongzi jun* (meaning literally 'boys' army'), while girls did first aid. The numbers of students who attended educational institutions rose significantly during the 1930s and 1940s. Official figures for primary schools in 1932 show 12,223,066 students, while the comparable figure for 1945 was 21,831,898 (cited in Mackerras 1985: 171). According to government statistics, the number of secondary school students of all kinds, including vocational and teacher training, was 627,246 in 1936–7. This fell sharply when the war with Japan began to 389,948 in 1937–8 but rose to 768,533 in 1940–1 (Kwei 1968, VI: 650).

Education under Mao Zedong

From the inception of the PRC, the state's main educational aims were to achieve mass education and literacy; to give educational preference to the peasants and poor classes; and to instil the state's version of Marxism-Leninism into the people. The figures in Table 8.1 (later in this chapter) illustrate the fact that the CCP achieved partial success in achieving mass education. The figures also suggest that more peasants and people from other poor classes were able to enter schools, although the country did not achieve truly universal education.

Mao's approach to education could be summed up by the slogan 'red and expert' (*hong er zhuan*), which meant that education should both engender a 'correct' political attitude, as well as technical or academic skills. From the late 1950s, however, 'redness' took priority and students and intellectuals were expected to spend lengthy periods of time integrating manual and mental labour. One of Mao's directives during the Cultural Revolution was that 'education must serve proletarian politics and be combined with productive labor' (quoted in Seybolt 1973: 63). In January 1967 the Central Committee of the CCP issued a 'Preliminary Opinion on Reforming the Education System', which called for raising the proportion of workers and peasants among tertiary level students and for abolition of examinations for university entrance. The disdain for examinations was pushed further in 1973, when *People's Daily* (10 August) reprinted a letter, originally published in the *Liaoning Daily* of 19 July. The author was a student called Zhang Tiesheng, who had handed in a blank examination paper because he had been working hard on his people's commune, and wanted to make a public self-justification through a letter to the press.

Even before the Cultural Revolution, Mao had encouraged students to criticise those teachers who were regarded as backward in their thinking. But during the Cultural Revolution this was taken to extremes. Teachers were paraded through their schools and universities wearing dunces' caps and were subjected to gruelling self-criticism sessions. A few were even driven to suicide.

Another of Mao's views frequently quoted during the Cultural Revolution was: 'Our educational policy must enable everyone who receives an education to develop morally, intellectually, and physically and to become a worker with both socialist consciousness and culture' (quoted in Seybolt 1973: 63). The demand for a stereotyped 'correct' view of socialist consciousness and culture was taken to unprecedented lengths, resulting in serious disruption of educational institutions at all levels, especially universities, which were closed during the Cultural Revolution. For years afterwards, people would speak of 'the lost generation' of young people forced to devote themselves to what turned out to be a futile revolution. Paradoxically, the innovations in curriculum and admissions procedures which were intended to bring greater equality, probably exacerbated inequalities, especially at the local level. This was in large measure a consequence of the lack of procedures, uncertainty on the part of local administrators of the intent of the policies, and, in some instances, abuses of the system.

Changes in education during the reform period

The education system was affected almost instantaneously by the leadership transition in the aftermath of Mao's death in September 1976. It was not long before teachers were strongly bemoaning their treatment under Mao and demanding the respect that went with the importance of their position to society.

'Less ideology and more skills'

In April 1978, Deng Xiaoping gave a speech at the opening of a National Conference on Education in Beijing, calling for improvement in the quality of education 'so as to serve socialist construction better'. He denounced the 'Gang of Four' for turning China's youth into 'illiterate hooligans'. He also thought that examinations should return, arguing that they were the best way to test whether students had really learned. On the highly important subject of politics in education he had the following to say:

> Beyond all doubt, schools should always attach first importance to a firm and correct political orientation. But this doesn't mean they should devote a great many classroom hours to ideological and political teaching. Students must indeed give top priority to a firm and correct political orientation, but that by no means implies that they should abandon the study of the sciences, social sciences and humanities. On the contrary, the higher the students' political consciousness, the more consciously and diligently they will apply themselves to the study of these subjects for the sake of the revolution. Hence the Gang of Four were not only being utterly ridiculous but were actually negating and betraying proletarian politics when they opposed efforts to improve the quality of education ... (Deng 1984: 120)

Deng wanted to use the educational system to keep the people loyal to the CCP. However, as Marianne Bastid notes (1984: 189), he thought it was equally, if not more, important for education to 'respond to the needs of the economy'. The emphasis on expertise over politics continued to grow throughout the 1980s until the crisis of mid-1989. The practice of sending university students to labour in the countryside was discontinued, as were most of the other extreme practices of the Cultural Revolution. Universities began to introduce and promote higher degrees such as doctorates, and once again encouraged academics to concentrate on research. As a result of the 1989 crisis, the schools re-emphasised the importance of students' correct political worldviews, although the various workshops or seminars on domestic and international politics that students were made to attend after the June 4th incident focused more on patriotism than Marxist-Leninist ideology, and for a few years it became considerably more difficult for any student to study abroad.

In 1985 and 1986 the authorities undertook major educational reform. The main aim of the reforms was to make the educational system better geared towards training the people for modernisation. Among the important points in the educational reform were:

- the staged introduction of compulsory education;

- the overhaul of curricula and textbooks to bring them more into line with the needs of modernisation;
- more autonomy for higher education; and
- the decentralisation of the funding of the education system.

On 21 April 1986, the government adopted a law making education compulsory for nine years in the cities and developed areas by 1990, and everywhere else by the end of the century. Among the reforms, financial decentralisation was arguably the most important, although one scholar argues that financial decentralisation as 'the core' of measures was already put into practice in many parts of the country in the late 1970s (Cheng 1995: 71). In the 1980s the government decided that townships and villages, rather than governments at higher levels, should assume financial responsibility for the construction and furnishing of school buildings. This decision was referred to as the principle of 'walking on two legs', meaning that government and community should share financial responsibility. Accordingly, central authorities left education more and more to local governments, private bodies and public fund-raising bodies.

The user-pays principle so widespread in China during the reform period meant the introduction of fees. This began in the mid-1980s, first in higher education, then lower in the system. By the beginning of the twenty-first century, virtually all education institutions required fees. These were still very low at primary level, but increased the higher up the educational ladder a student climbed. There were ways of cushioning the effects fees had on poor people. The most important was Project Hope (*Xiwang gongcheng*), designed to help school dropouts in impoverished areas. Ironically, the education system has become more privatised at the same time that the government has demanded compulsory education.

As a result of these reforms, China does not spend much on education in terms of a proportion of its gross domestic product. Whereas most industrial developed countries spend about 5 per cent of GDP and developing countries about 4 per cent, China spends nearer 3 per cent. To be specific, government figures say that in 2002 and 2003 China spent 3.28 per cent of GDP on education, 0.04 percentage points down from 2001. This is despite the fact that in 1993, the State Council had promised to raise the ratio to 4 per cent by 2000. According to the United Nations Development Programme (UNDP), India spent 4.1 per cent of its GDP on education in 2000–2 (UNDP 2005: 255–6). Beijing does not deny that its expenditure on education is 'well below the world's average of 4.1 per cent for developing countries and merely half that of the developed ones' (Xinhua 2005). Moreover, what it does spend is extremely unevenly spread over the education system and over the various parts of the country. In 2002 only 23 per cent of the finance spent on education was earmarked for the rural areas. In some places the universities get some 90 per cent of the local state funds (Li 2005: 6).

Table 8.1 Numbers of students in the Chinese education system at various levels (millions)

Year	Primary	Secondary (regular)	Tertiary
1950	28.92	1.31	0.14
1965	116.21	9.34	0.67
1978	146.24	65.48	0.86
1980	146.27	55.08	1.14
1981	143.33	48.60	1.28
1982	139.72	45.29	1.15
1983	135.78	43.98	1.21
1984	135.57	45.54	1.40
1985	133.70	47.06	1.70
1986	131.83	48.90	1.88
1987	128.36	49.48	1.96
1988	125.36	47.62	2.07
1989	123.73	45.54	2.08
1990	122.41	45.86	2.06
1991	121.64	46.84	2.04
1992	122.01	47.71	2.18
1993	124.00	47.39	2.54
1994	130.00	49.82	2.80
1995	131.95	53.71	2.90
1996	136.15	57.38	3.02
1997	139.95	60.18	3.17
1998	139.54	63.01	3.41
1999	135.48	67.71	4.13
2000	130.13	73.69	5.56
2001	125.44	78.36	7.19
2002	121.57	82.88	9.03

Sources: NBS various years, especially 2004: 779

The size of China's education system

Due to the size of the Chinese population, China's education system is obviously the largest in the world. Table 8.1 gives details of the number of students in the system at various levels.

The numbers in primary schools rose dramatically before the Cultural Revolution, those in the secondary schools during the Cultural Revolution – one of the few good things the Cultural Revolution did for education – as well as since the mid-1990s, and those at tertiary level especially since the late 1990s. Students at primary level actually fell in number during the reform period. This is partly because the cohort has got smaller due to the one-child policy, but privatisation is no doubt another reason. I should also point out that during the Cultural Revolution primary schools mostly fell from six to five years, so many who would formerly have been at the top primary level became bottom-level secondary. This may explain some of the gains in the numbers at secondary level. However, even allowing for this, it does seem that the reform period has seen far more students progressing into secondary school and even higher education than has ever been the case before. There has been a big jump in tertiary-level students since the turn of the century. Clearly, more and more people believe it is in their interests from a career point of view to obtain a higher education degree. Moreover, as China has seen increasing numbers of people with money to spend, more and more of them want to invest in their children's education, believing this to be crucial to their career. If there is one point on which Confucianism, Republican and Communist ideology might agree on, it is that education is a critical issue for China's future.

The structure and curriculum of China's education system

The three main education levels in China are, as elsewhere, primary, secondary and tertiary. Below that, many children attend nurseries and kindergartens. The length of primary and secondary education is usually six years, though during the Cultural Revolution a concerted attempt was made to reduce the time children spent at primary school to five years. The Chinese subdivide secondary or high school into junior (three years) and senior (three years). Because education is compulsory for only nine years, the break between junior and senior secondary school is an important one for Chinese students. Apart from the regular secondary schools, there are many vocational ones as well, such as for teacher training, agriculture, engineering, foreign languages, the arts and so on. Universities are likewise comprehensive, teaching and researching all, or almost all, the main branches of knowledge, or vocational, just as at the secondary level.

At primary level, the curriculum includes Chinese language, arithmetic and numeracy, history, geography, physical culture, music, art and a foreign language, usually English. Most time is given to Chinese language and arithmetic. Another important subject is 'moral education' *(deyu)* which covers things such as discipline, good manners, hygiene and truthfulness. In a national list of ten regulations for primary school pupils, the first item is to 'have a warm love for the motherland and the people, study well, and make progress every day' (quoted in Cleverley 1985: 233–4).

Table 8.2   Illiteracy and semi-literacy in China

Census	Percentage illiterate and semi-literate
1964	38.10
1982	22.81
1990	15.88
2000	6.72

Sources: NBS various years

The secondary school curriculum includes Chinese language, mathematics, physics, chemistry and other sciences, a foreign language, history, geography, politics, physiology, music, fine arts and physical education. In junior secondary school, nearly 40 per cent of the students' time goes to Chinese and mathematics and 16 per cent to foreign languages, while in senior secondary school the natural sciences and mathematics take up about half the time, and Chinese and a foreign language about 30 per cent. In the 1980s, population education was introduced into some senior secondary schools because of the fundamental importance of the one-child-per-couple policy. The secondary-level school year is nine months.

The 1980s saw a major expansion of technical and vocational secondary schools in China in fields ranging from commerce and legal work to the arts and forestry. In the countryside, agricultural secondary schools allow students to acquire some knowledge of agricultural science and technology. There is also a system of adult education which runs courses ranging from basic literacy and numeracy to university-level programmes.

Teachers

Traditionally, teachers were highly respected members of the community. However, the Cultural Revolution (as noted earlier) saw them subjected to various forms of humiliation, especially since Mao encouraged students to condemn their teachers as reactionaries. When I visited China in January 1977, I found that one of the first things to change in education after the Gang of Four fell was that students no longer regarded it as politically expedient to criticise their teachers, who were reclaiming their position of social respect. Unfortunately, during the reform era, in a context of limited state funding for education, teachers are not particularly well paid. Consequently, many gifted students shun the teaching profession, opting instead for 'choicer' professions, such as business, law or medicine, which are more likely to earn them higher salaries. This has the effect of pushing down the teaching profession's social status. Teachers at tertiary level frequently moonlight to supplement their not very high salaries and good ones can earn a considerable amount of money that way. Pressures on teachers and their status vary according to level, being greatest at primary level.

The number of teachers has continued to rise at most levels, especially at the higher end of the education system. For instance, the number of teachers in ordinary secondary schools rose from 3.033 million in 1990 to 4.537 million in 2003. However, at lower levels it is in decline in the early twenty-first century. Primary school teacher numbers were 5.86 million in 2000 but only 5.703 million in 2003 and falls at kindergarten level are even sharper (NBS 2004: 777).

An interesting phenomenon is the process of feminisation of the teaching profession, which mirrors similar trends in the West. The proportion of female teachers has risen significantly at all levels. In primary schools, where numbers of students and teachers are greatest, proportions of female teachers rose from 39.6 per cent in 1985, to 46.6 per cent in 1995 and 52.9 per cent in 2002 (NBS 2003: 726).

Literacy

The censuses have figures on illiteracy and semi-literacy, and hence on literacy. These are shown in Table 8.2. I should point out that the figures below from the 1964 census assumed illiteracy and semi-literacy meant those people aged 12 or over knowing few or no characters, whereas the definition underlying the later three censuses was that illiteracy and semi-literacy covered those aged 15 or over knowing few or no characters. In other words, the cohort aged 12 to 14 is included in the 1964 figures, but not in those for 1982, 1990 and 2000.

If the census figures are to be believed, the drop in illiteracy and semi-literacy has been remarkable in China. Even if the absolute figures given are lower than reality, the relativities showing the progression over time are very impressive. The United Nations Development Programme's *Human Development Report* for 2005 gave literacy for China's people aged 15 and above at 78.3 per cent in 1990, rising to 90.9 per cent in 2003 (UNDP 2005: 259). The UNDP's figures are less positive than those in Chinese government's censuses, but agree in showing a sharply rising literacy rate.

There are several reasons for this rise in literacy. One is that the 1986 nine-year compulsory education law has brought about a renewed emphasis on basic education and hence literacy, even if authorities have not been able to implement it to nearly the extent they might have wished for. Another is that the gradual shift in the direction of modern attitudes and a modern society has made education and literacy more necessary to get good jobs that help modernise the country, which means that people are more prepared to make sacrifices for their children to acquire literacy. A third reason is that non-government programmes, like Project Hope, have enabled even very poor people to obtain basic education and hence advance literacy. One of these programmes concerns the education of girls, which is so crucial a part of education as a whole.

The education of girls

Educating girls is critical for a modernising or modernised society. And one benefit for a country like China is that educated women tend to want fewer children than illiterate and ignorant ones. On the whole, the PRC has succeeded in ensuring that the great majority of girls do in fact get some education. However, there are unfortunately exceptions. In rural China some parents are still reluctant to pay for their daughters' education. Some believe their daughters need the feminine arts they can get from their mother more than schooling; others do not consider education for girls a sensible investment. This is why there are still girls who do not go to school and also some who go for a brief period, perhaps a year or two, and then withdraw. One of the measures taken to improve this situation is Project Spring Bud (*Chunlei jihua*).

Female adult literacy, adult meaning aged 15 and over, was lower than male at the beginning of the century. According to the 2005 *Human Development Report*, female literacy in 2003 was 86.5 per cent, against 90.8 per cent of literacy rate in the whole country (UNDP 2005: 308). Still, this is a significant rise compared with the '2000 view', given in the 2002 *Human Development Report*, of only 76.3 per cent adult female literacy (UNDP 2002: 223). The 2003 figures for India are 47.8 per cent literacy for females, only 65 per cent of male literacy, so China is considerably less unequal in gender literacy than India (UNDP 2005: 309).

Challenges ahead

Several challenges face the Chinese education system in the twenty-first century. Firstly, the government has to find ways of allocating more money to education. The government also needs to find ways of expanding education to the poorer classes more effectively. The user-pays policies that have affected education as much as every other facet of society have made the education system more unequal. This has meant that some people have fallen through the social safety net. It is of crucial importance that all people enjoy educational opportunities; otherwise literacy, numeracy and other major indices will fall, to the detriment of the country's overall development. It is reasonable to educate people in patriotism and to serve their country. However, the government needs to find better ways of creatively integrating this into the curriculum. There needs to be even more priority given to girls' and women's education. Finally, the government should allocate more to teacher training to ensure that there are more and better teachers. Education is certainly something that really matters to society, and needs the highest possible priority.

The health system

Chinese people have developed health care systems from very ancient times, including well-known techniques such as acupuncture. When we consider traditional Chinese health care, we also think of breathing exercises, gymnastics and massage. Confucian ideology discouraged the rise of a medical profession, instead encouraging as many people as possible to have enough medical knowledge to assist those nearest to them.

The nineteenth and first half of the twentieth century saw the introduction of modern Western medicine, which competed strongly with traditional medicine for patients and government support. Due to poverty, war and lack of proper hygiene, health standards in China tended to be low. However, there were definitely improvements under Chiang Kai-shek's government: despite the war against Japan and the subsequent Civil War, life expectancy at birth increased from about 24 in the period 1929–31 (Banister 1988: 62) to about 32 in 1950.

The health system under Mao

The First National Health Conference of August 1950 laid down the following policies, which became hallmarks of the Maoist era: to give everybody access to health care; prevention before cure; and to integrate traditional and modern medicine. The CCP put great emphasis on eradicating epidemics and improving immunisation, as well as on setting up maternal and child health centres. It also took steps to train medical personnel and increase the number of professional doctors. Although the attempts to set up a health care network included the countryside, the cities were very much better served. From 1965, Mao launched a campaign to shift the balance of health care towards the countryside, and during the Cultural Revolution started a programme known as the 'barefoot doctors'. Mostly young, these were ideologically inspired paramedics. They received very little training, but were supposed to learn on the job and cater for the most common and simple peasant ailments, as well as give guidance on birth control. By 1973 there were about two of these barefoot doctors for every production brigade, a subdivision of a commune.

At about the same time, the CCP introduced a very basic system of medical insurance into the countryside. What happened in essence was that each commune or production brigade member paid a standard fee into a collective pool. These monies paid for the various health needs of the community, such as medicines, immunisation and a portion of hospital costs. By 1973 about 70 per cent of production brigades had a cooperative medical system. Another very important feature of the Cultural Revolution was a return to traditional medicine. In the 1970s, acupuncture was adopted as a local anaesthetic, even for complex operations.

Many people were sceptical of the effectiveness of 'mass participation in medicine', of the attacks on the medical profession, and of novel practices such as using acupuncture as anaesthetic. The rural health system still lagged behind its urban counterpart and hygiene standards remained low. Yet the fact is that ordinary peasants had greater access to health care than before. One scholar praises China's achievements in basic health care under Mao for going 'way beyond those achieved by countries with a similar per capita income' (Pearson 1995: 108).

Reform and the health system

The reform period has witnessed important changes in China's health system. We can sum them up as follows:

213

- The user-pays system has become much more prevalent. The collapse of the commune system meant that medical insurance in rural areas has disappeared with the 'barefoot doctors'.
- The emphasis has changed from a system that allowed weakly trained medical practitioners to serve many people at low cost to better trained doctors providing better but less affordable medical services.
- The government no longer struggles to bridge the gap in health standards between the rural and urban areas, with the result that the gap in health delivery and standards of health between the cities and the countryside has widened further.
- The system has become much more commercialised. Many health professionals sell medicines with the aim of making a profit rather than curing their patients.
- There is much more emphasis on high-grade technology than there used to be, increasing amounts of foreign imported equipment and the cost of health provision.
- More attention is devoted to curative medicine, especially in the cities, and less to preventive.
- There is much more focus on medicine relevant to disabilities than there used to be. One specialist attributes this to the fact that Deng Xiaoping's son, Deng Pufang, who is himself disabled and confined to a wheelchair, used his influence to put disabilities medicine on the national agenda (Pearson 1995: 101).

Some data on the health system in the reform period

In 1995, according to the World Health Organization (WHO), China spent 3.9 per cent of its GDP on health, rising to a respectable 5.3 per cent in 2000 (WHO 2002: 202). The problem, however, is that the proportion of the cost paid for privately has been rising, being 53.3 per cent in 1995 and 63.4 per cent in 2000 (ibid., 202). Hospitals are extremely expensive in China, measured against average incomes. The average stay in a Ministry of Health-run hospital in Beijing costs almost 11,500 yuan, equivalent to about US$1,400, which is half a year's salary for the typical city resident in China (Murphy 2003: 25). The implication is clear: getting the excellent health delivery available from good hospitals with foreign equipment is really more for the rich than the average person nowadays. To be fair, the government has become increasingly aware of the severity of the problems, and the Hu Jintao government has assigned health system reform a high priority in order to make it more equitable. By 2005, for example, 156 million farmers had become part of a pilot cooperative medical system in rural areas, which provided them with basic medical insurance. Funds came from central and local budgets and voluntary contributions by the farmers themselves (UNDP, China 2005: 90).

Table 8.3 shows official figures for some major health indicators in China during the reform period. It indicates the number of health institutions (including hospitals and clinics), technical personnel (including doctors and nurses) and the number of hospital beds. Finally, it shows the number of doctors per 100,000 of the population.

Table 8.3 Health service indicators

Type of health service	1978	1990	1995	2000	2003
Health institutions	169 732	208 734	190 057	324 771	291 323
Hospitals (clinics)	64 309 (94 395)	62 126 (129 332)	67 460 (104 406)	65 944 (240 934)	62 968 (204 468)
Hospital beds (millions)	1.847	2.592	2.806	2.908	2.955
Total technical personnel (millions)	2.464	3.898	4.257	4.491	4.306
Doctors (millions)	1.033	1.763	1.918	2.076	1.868
Nurses (millions)	0.407	0.975	1.126	1.267	1.266
Doctors per thousand people	107	154	158	168	148

Source: NBS 2004: 860–1

National Bureau of Statistics of China (NBS 2004: 861) notes a stricter demand for doctors to be certified since 2002, which may explain the decline in numbers of doctors. It may be worth adding that the WHO (c. 1999) has made estimates for the rate of physicians and other medical personnel per 100,000 people. For China in 1998, the rate is 161.7, which is very similar to the figures given in the table and obviously based on official sources. These figures show China in a reasonably positive light for its level of development. For instance, Brazil had 127.2 physicians for every 100,000 people in 1996, India only 48 in 1992, Vietnam only 48 in 1998 and Indonesia only 16 in 1996.

One major recognised test of a national health system is life expectancy at birth. Here China's achievement is quite impressive, relative to its level of economic development and considering the vast and still fairly impoverished peasantry. By the mid-1970s, life expectancy at birth in China was about 63, and rose to around 66 by 1981. During the 1990s it was steady at about 69, but rising to 70 in the late 1990s (see Mackerras 2001: 222). The WHO (2002: 178) puts life expectancy at birth in 2001 at 71.2. This compares with 68.7 for Brazil, 60.8 for India, and 65.9 for Indonesia (ibid.). The major industrial countries are, not surprisingly, somewhat ahead, with Japan at 81.4 (ibid.: 180). What these figures show overall is that the health of the Chinese is improving. But although the life expectancy figures are quite impressive, they have not risen as rapidly in the period of reform as might have been expected had the improving health delivery system been more equitable than has in fact been the case.

Disease crises and health care management

The first years of the twenty-first century struck China with two disease crises, which forced Beijing to rethink the management of China's health care system. In 2001, the human immunodeficiency virus/acquired immune deficiency syndrome

(HIV/AIDS) was exposed as being far more serious than the government had so far maintained. Less than two years later, early in 2003, came the revelation of the severe acute respiratory syndrome (SARS). Both are contagious viruses, and both are relatively new to human beings. HIV/AIDS was first conclusively identified in 1981, while SARS developed late in 2002 in Guangdong Province. What transmits AIDS is the contamination of the bloodstream with body fluids that contain the virus, such as blood and semen, through such means as sexual intercourse, shared HIV-contaminated needles, and transfusion of contaminated blood. SARS is a pneumonia-like disease spread by close contact with infected people, such as inhalation of droplets caused by coughing.

Several HIV/AIDS-risk factors in China have intensified since the late years of the twentieth century. The most important is certainly injected drug use, with about 68 per cent of those with HIV being identified as intravenous drug users, mainly in China's south and west (Li 2004: 3). Official figures issued in March 2004 claimed that drug abuse had grown from about 70,000 registered abusers in 1990 to just over 1 million drug abusers in 2003, with nearly 5 million not registered (Thompson 2005). Another is the growth of prostitution: heterosexual sex mostly between sex workers and their clients accounts for some 10 per cent of HIV cases (Li 2004: 3). Official figures say there were over 3 million sex workers in China in 2001. Based on data from HIV sentinel surveillance sites, the WHO (2001: 44) reported that only about 10 per cent of these sex workers always used condoms with clients and 'close to half reported never using condoms'. The number of men who have sex with men has also grown, and since they also tend not to use condoms, a major Chinese government/United Nations survey released in December 2004 ranked them as representing 'a high potential for an HIV epidemic' (State Council and UN 2004: 6).

In 1996 the gynaecologist and AIDS worker Dr Gao Yaojie exposed a scandal in Henan province, which had allowed corrupt officials and entrepreneurs to make money from AIDS-infected blood plasma collection centres, the result being the spread of AIDS in the province. According to the 2004 joint survey (State Council and UN 2004: 1), 'infection through commercial blood and plasma donors primarily occurred before 1996, so the number of AIDS patients and AIDS-related deaths may have reached its peak already in this group'.

In November 2001, Beijing held the first Chinese conference on HIV/AIDS and issued its first five-year plan against the virus, involving big increases in sentinel sites of HIV surveillance. In February 2004, the government set up its State Council AIDS Working Committee to supervise the prevention and control of HIV/AIDS, which in March issued a comprehensive strategy of HIV/AIDS prevention, including increases in funding, education and measures designed to increase condom use among affected people. In April 2005, the government announced a crack-down on drug use, including much bigger budgets for police training and equipment and the establishment of detoxification units (Thompson 2005).

Estimates of HIV/AIDS vary wildly. Early in 2002, UNAIDS, a joint venture of UN organisations designed to coordinate responses to HIV/AIDS, put out a figure of about 1.25 million AIDS sufferers in China, also warning that, unless very prompt and decisive action was taken, China would have about 10 million sufferers by 2010. A more conservative figure came from the joint Chinese government/United Nations survey of late December 2004, which claimed there were somewhere between 650,000 and 1.02 million at the end of 2003 (State Council and UN 2004: 1). However, AIDS activist Wan Yanhai gives the far higher estimate of 5 to 10 million in 2004, likely to rise to 20 million by 2020 (Watts 2004).

In the first half of 2003, China was struck with a different virus. The WHO became aware of the outbreak in Guangdong, Hong Kong and Vietnam in February but became alarmed the following month, adopting the new name SARS. At first, China remained very defensive about it, and at a press conference on 3 April Health Minister Zhang Wenkang refused to concede the severity of the problem. Meanwhile, SARS spread to Beijing and other places in China. During April, China's new leadership reconsidered the situation and swung into action. It immediately dismissed Zhang Wenkang and a senior Beijing CCP official over the issue. Soon after, the post of health minister was given to Wu Yi, well known for her determination and ability to get things done. Authorities allocated significant sums of money to fighting the virus, and the military built a special 1,000-bed hospital within a week. The government declared a 'people's war', taking strong measures to quarantine the disease, such as closing campuses and cancelling the May Day week-long holiday for that year to prevent people travelling and spreading the disease. The big fear was that if the disease spread to the countryside it would be more or less impossible to control. These measures seem to have been effective.

On 24 June the WHO lifted its travel ban on Beijing, thus declaring that China had beaten the SARS virus. Towards the end of July 2003, the Chinese government announced that its last SARS patients had been discharged. Thankfully, the 2003 SARS outbreak was not nearly as serious as it could have been. By the time the WHO lifted its travel ban on Beijing, the total number who had caught the disease worldwide was about 8,400, including about 800 deaths (Kahn 2003), the great bulk being in China, including Hong Kong. The numbers are minuscule compared to a whole host of diseases worldwide in a comparable period. We saw earlier that with HIV/AIDS ball-park figures are in millions, not hundreds.

The political implications are clear from the dismissal of senior officials, who were asked to take the blame for what had been in effect a cover-up of a serious situation. But what is particularly interesting is that the SARS crisis burst at exactly the same time as the National People's Congress was appointing Hu Jintao as China's new president and Wen Jiabao as the new premier. Admittedly, Hu Jintao had become CCP general secretary in November 2002, and already had shown more interest in the poorest levels of society than Jiang Zemin. Yet the crisis seemed to be the new leadership's first real test. What the SARS outbreak did was to reveal the rural health system's inadequacies and inequities. An infectious-disease expert working with WHO in Beijing quoted Wu Yi as saying that it was SARS that really galvanised the government into allocating meaningful funding and taking other actions to rebuild the rural health system (Murphy 2003: 24). At the time China claimed its hospitals had discharged their last SARS patients, the signs were that China might use the strategy it had developed to defeat SARS against HIV/AIDS, including providing necessary funds and facilities and training more people around the country in prevention methods (Chang 2003).

However, despite the progress, the Chinese government is still not nearly open enough in dealing with major health scares and epidemics. Other outbreaks occurred in 2004 and 2005, the most important being avian influenza, popularly known simply as 'bird flu'. Journalist Jonathan Watts (2005) quoted an international health expert as saying: 'SARS and bird flu led to improvements and promises of more openness, but there are big questions about the reporting system. China is still far from transparent. There are too many disincentives for officials and farmers to report problems.'

A bird flu outbreak was first reported in China in February 2004. By the end of 2005, authorities in China, Vietnam, Thailand and elsewhere had ordered millions of poultry slaughtered to prevent the virus from spreading. Migratory birds are of course all but impossible to control, the disease spreading across the great Eurasian continent. A few people living close to infected poultry had caught the disease, including in China. The major fear, which had not occurred by the end of 2005, is that the virus will jump species by mutating from one affecting birds to one that affects humans. In that case a world-wide pandemic could kill millions of people throughout the world. Preventive measures and preparation in case such a disaster should occur become essential.

It is clear that China faces big challenges in the field of health delivery. That it is a critical issue in contemporary China is beyond doubt. Failure to continue overall rises in the health of the people, to stem the HIV/AIDS epidemic or to prevent major outbreaks of diseases such as bird flu would be disastrous for Chinese development.

Economic inequality in Chinese society

The discussion so far has focused on several social issues affecting contemporary Chinese society. While noting positive developments, such as an expanding educational system, raised literacy levels, modernised health care and greater equality for women, it is hard not to conclude that alongside these achievements, Chinese society is also becoming increasingly unequal. The problem of economic inequality affecting Chinese ethnic minorities has been examined in the preceding chapter, while regional economic equality was analysed in Chapter 3. This section will focus on the question of economic inequality in Chinese society, its sources and scope.

Land reform, collectivisation, and the elimination of private enterprise

When the CCP came to power in 1949, it made concerted attempts to eradicate social and economic inequalities. It carried out a radical land reform from 1949 to 1952. This was a catastrophic movement and resulted in the death of approximately 800,000 landlords. However, it did succeed in eradicating landlordism, and in equalising land holdings. According to Stockman (2000: 186), by the mid-1950s, about 2 to 3 per cent of peasants were classified as rich, about 60 per cent as 'middle peasants' and about 30 as poor. The rich hired labour, whereas the poor did not have enough land but had to hire out their own labour. On the whole, rural China in the early 1950s became 'a realm of smallholders'. Using the Gini ratio measure of inequality, one study compares rural income inequality in the 1930s with that in 1952, and finds that the degree of inequality in the structure of rural incomes went down from 0.33 to 0.22, the fall being due to agrarian reform (Roll 1980: 139). (The Gini ratio is a simple figure from 0 to 1, where 0 means that all household income is equally shared among the whole population, and 1 means that a single person has everything, while nobody else has anything. So obviously the lower the Gini ratio is, the less the inequality.) This fall by one-third is a very significant drop.

Mao followed his initial land reform with the collectivisation of rural areas, and the introduction of rural people's communes in 1958. Although Mao's commune movement was disastrous in many ways, for example being at least partly responsible for the massive famine that occurred from 1959 to 1961 (discussed in Chapter 6), it did promote further social equalisation. Private ownership of land and other resources, though not housing, was abolished.

In the cities, the CCP eliminated the capitalist class of property owners. In 1956, it substantially curtailed private enterprise, thus severely limiting the ability of small capitalists to earn profits. Mao was very keen to reduce the gap between the city and countryside, and the rural people's communes aimed at increasing rural wealth on a cooperative basis. Mao's government also consciously developed industrial bases in previously under-developed rural areas.

So did all this actually make Chinese society more equal? One authority makes the following observation:

> Prior to 1966, China had already achieved a significant degree of equality while continuing to maintain popular support and growth. Income gaps were significantly reduced while material goods were rather equally dis-tributed relative to income. Within this narrow range, if the retrospective judgments of émigrés can be trusted, material rewards were effectively linked to performance. And there was a judicious admixture of moral and idealistic commitment ... to the goal of national growth for the sake of a strong people and nation ... (Parish 1984: 119)

There were other respects in which China became a more equal society. We have already discussed the status of women and education in the preceding sections. Classes were overturned so that many previously 'on top' were pushed down, while those at the bottom were raised up. Within the urban economy, private enterprise was totally abolished, not just restricted. Piece rates, bonuses and prizes were eliminated. Some managers and higher officials were demoted for a time, a process known as 'downward transfer' (*xiafang*). According to Parish (1984: 87–9), China became much more equal than other developing societies, at least in terms of income: the poorest 40 per cent of China's urban households got 25 per cent of total income distributed in cities, while in 23 developing market states, the poorest 40 per cent got only 15 per cent of urban incomes, a difference with China that I would argue puts it in a very favourable light. The Gini ratio of per capita household income fell in the cities from about 0.2 around 1964 to about 0.16 in 1980, showing falling income inequalities in the cities before and after the Cultural Revolution (Parish 1984: 90; Khan *et al.* 1993: 60; Stockman 2000: 187). The year 1980 was probably about the same as the end of 1978 when the reform policies were introduced.

Nobody would claim that Chinese society was characterised by equality at the time Mao died in 1976, either in the distribution of resources and wealth or in social terms. Power was very closely held in the hands of the CCP: 'Senior cadres received generous but unrecorded perquisites, and their income often was further increased by "back door" activities and other forms of corruption' (Griffin and Zhao 1993: 2). Moreover, there were big costs in terms of the suffering, persecution and deaths of large numbers of individuals. However, it is probably fair to say that Chinese society was less unequal in economic terms by the end of Mao's rule than at virtually any other time in its long history.

Economic inequalities during the reform period

When Deng Xiaoping introduced his reform policies in 1978, the emphasis shifted 'from equity to efficiency' (Wang and Hu 1999: 4). With the launch of the household responsibility system, rural incomes began diverging as some peasants proved to be more entrepreneurial than others. At the same time, the incomes between peasants and employees in rural TVEs also diverged. In the urban centres, industry returned to rewarding efficiency and expertise with higher salaries. The entry of foreign-funded enterprises or Sino-foreign joint ventures, where salaries were generally higher than in the state sector, further diversified incomes among the industrial workers. Finally, the rise of unemployment in the rural and urban areas, to some extent conditioned by the privatisation process and corporatisation of state-owned enterprises (also discussed in Chapter 3), created a new lower class in China, unknown during the Mao period.

As a result from the above processes, within both urban and rural China, income disparities have intensified during the reform period. An intensively researched study, based on surveys taken in 1988 and 1995, found that inequalities in China grew significantly over those years, both in the cities and countryside, with Gini ratios rising from 0.23 to 0.33 in the urban areas and 0.34 to 0.42 in the countryside (Khan and Riskin 2001: 144–5). The authors of the study also comment that by 1995 China had become 'one of the more unequal of the Asian developing countries', with inequality in income distribution greater than in countries like India, Pakistan or Indonesia (Khan and Riskin 2001: 49).

China's official statistics do not fully concur with the above conclusion. In the countryside the per capita annual net income of rural households, measured in Chinese yuan, was 133.6 in 1978, the year the reforms began, 686.3 in 1990, and

Table 8.4 International income inequalities measured by the Gini ratio

	2003	2004
Brazil	0.607	0.591
Chile	0.575	0.571
China	0.403	0.447
Egypt	0.344	0.344
France	0.327	0.327
Hong Kong	0.434	0.434
India	0.378	0.325
Indonesia	0.303	0.343
Japan	0.249	0.249
Malaysia	0.492	0.492
Philippines	0.461	0.461
Poland	0.316	0.316
Singapore	0.425	0.425
South Africa	0.593	0.593
South Korea	0.316	0.316
Taiwan	0.345	n/a
Thailand	0.432	0.432
United States	0.408	0.408
Vietnam	0.361	0.361
Zimbabwe	0.568	0.568

Source: UNDP 2003: 281–5; UNDP 2004: 188–91

2622.2 in 2002 (all figures are after taxation is deducted). The comparable figures for urban households (again after taxation) were 343.4, 1510.2 and 8472.2 (NBS 2004: 357). Between 1978 and 1990, per capita net incomes of rural households multiplied 5.1 times, while over the same period the comparable urban incomes multiplied 4.4 times, and though in absolute terms the gap had grown, in relative terms, the countryside did better. Between 1990 and 2003, the rural incomes multiplied by 3.8 times, while those in the cities multiplied by 5.6 times, meaning that in both relative and absolute terms, the gap accelerated during the 1990s. Another approach produces a different way of viewing the figures. If all incomes are counted on the basis of stable 1978 prices, then the year 2003 shows rural household income as having risen by 550.7 per cent, while urban rose by 514.6 per cent (NBS 2004: 357), a rise that is only slightly less, but on a much larger basis.

Gini ratios for all China, both urban and rural combined, rose markedly in the late twentieth century. The World Bank estimate for China's overall Gini ratio in 1979/80 was 0.33 (Griffin and Zhao 1993: 8), while Khan and Riskin (2001: 43) put it at 0.452 in 1995, although I think we should add the acknowledgement that the World Bank for the same year calculated it as somewhat less: 0.415. However, both agree that it was very high and was rising at the time. The World Bank indicators for 2003 put China's Gini coefficient at 0.403, based on a 1998 survey (UNDP 2003: 284), which is a bit less than the World Bank's figure for 1995, and much less than Khan and Riskin's figure, though admittedly quite a bit more than the World Bank's 1979/80 figure. However, the indicators from the same source for 2004 show a significant rise to 0.447 based on a survey taken in 2001 (UNDP 2004: 189). The UNDP, China, claimed (2005: 30–1) that China's Gini coefficient for 2002 was 0.45, this number having risen 50 per cent since 1978 (0.3) to pass the 'alarm boundary' figure of 0.4. It also said that the disparity between incomes in urban and rural regions had grown some 600 per cent between 1990 and 2003 (UNDP, China 2005: 24–5). Looking at the big picture of disparities from the beginning of the reform period to the early twenty-first century, what emerges is that, overall, urban and rural disparities have worsened.

It may be useful to put China into an international perspective. UNDP, China (2005: 13) states that, from the latest data, China ranked number 90 out of the 131 countries for which material was available in terms of income inequality, a very serious situation indeed. Table 8.4 shows the World Bank figures for various countries and territories for 2003 and 2004.

Some of the figures are the same in both lists, with no new surveys being taken. But China is the country that shows the biggest rise, from 0.403 to 0.447. In the 2004 figures, though not the 2003, it is significantly worse than all other Asian countries except the Philippines and Malaysia. It is also not only worse than India, but India shows slight improvement between the two years, whereas China is getting more unequal.

The elimination of absolute poverty

One area where China has done quite well in international terms is the elimination of absolute poverty. Several trends are apparent. In the early reform period, approximately until the mid-1980s, poverty came down greatly by comparison with the late 1970s. From the mid-1980s, there was a fall in the rate at which rural poverty declined and an *increase* in the urban poverty rate (Khan and Riskin 2001: 147). In 1994, due to increasing concern over poverty, the authorities formalised a plan to eliminate absolute poverty by the year 2000. This had some success *in its own terms*, with the number of rural poor halving in 1998 compared to 1990. Although absolute poverty persists in the early twenty-first century, it is drastically lower than it was at the beginning of the reform period in the late 1970s, let alone in 1949. I emphasised the phrase 'in its own terms' because

Chinese figures show much lower absolute figures than World Bank estimates. According to figures issued at an international conference in Chengdu in September 2001, the World Bank estimates show 280 million rural poor in 1990, and 106 million in 1998, while Chinese official figures claim 85 million in 1990 and 42 million in 1998. One of the main reasons for the wildly different figures is that the official Chinese figures put the boundary for absolute rural poverty at US$0.66 per day, while the World Bank puts it at US$1 per day. However, what is perhaps most striking about the two sets of figures is that they agree that the number of absolute poor went down greatly between 1990 and 1998. Indeed, the World Bank reductions are even bigger than the official Chinese ones, both in absolute and relative terms.

Conclusion

The critical issues of family, gender, education, health, and social equality/inequality discussed in this chapter suggest that the Chinese people and their government face gigantic problems in modernising the country and in meeting the vast needs of society. There are links among these matters. For example, family systems and societies that limit females' access to education or allow them to lag too far in terms of health will inevitably suffer disadvantages against those that are more inclusive, especially in the long term.

The privatisation of key social services, such as health delivery and education, has a way of widening inequalities in any society. Certainly it has done that in China and many other parts of the world in the last decade or two. China therefore has to be cautious about letting inequalities get too wide and allowing its social services to run down too much. In other words there is a need for balance between the models of socialism and capitalism. It is generally expected that governments that call themselves socialist will intervene in the economy and society somewhat more than those emphasising private entrepreneurship. So it is ironic to find the avowedly Marxist-Leninist CCP adopting the user-pays principle in the social services with such enthusiasm. There is irony also in the fact that for a long time it did relatively little to address the growing social inequality in recent years.

However, it does seem that new leaders Hu Jintao and Wen Jiabao are more concerned about inequality than was Jiang Zemin. In March 2004, they introduced economic policies that focused more on sustainability and on narrowing income gaps than on outright development. As we have seen above, the December 2005 *China Human Development Report*, the compilation of which was supported and partly led by the Chinese government, pulled no punches about the seriousness of the problems of inequality in China. It also enunciated a coordinated policy to alleviate them, the most important already taken being to abolish agricultural taxes across the country as a way of reducing urban–rural disparities (UNDP, China 2005: 90). A range of policy recommendations included allocating much more money to social services, and introducing a progressive tax system, so that high-income groups pay much more than those on lower incomes (UNDP, China 2005: 100, 115).

Will this emphasis on sustainability solve the problems? In the short term it will not, because inequalities tend to gather a momentum of their own, which is very difficult to halt. As for the longer term, we shall have to wait and see. However, the new leadership is almost certainly genuinely concerned about these problems for the very simple reason, which they have repeatedly enunciated themselves, that social inequalities cause instability. Social disturbances are already frequent and have the potential to accelerate, even to the extent of tearing the country apart.

And there is an even more serious issue for the leadership. Social instability has the potential to bring about the overthrow of the CCP. The CCP currently shows no sign of being willing to resign power, and is large and strong enough to get its way. But that does not constitute a guarantee of indefinite power. The logic is simple: if the CCP wants to retain power indefinitely, it must do something about the problems of inequality and instability.

References

Baker, H. D. R. (1979) *Chinese Family and Kinship*, New York: Columbia University Press.

Banister, J. (1988) 'The Aging of China's Population', *Problems of Communism* 37/6 (November–December): 62–77.

Bastid, M. (1984) 'Chinese Educational Policies in the 1980s and Economic Development', *China Quarterly* 98 (June): 189–219.

Bossen, L. (2003) 'Women and Development', in R. E. Gamer, *Understanding Contemporary China*, Boulder, CO, and London: Lynne Rienner Publishers.

Chang, L. (2003) 'China May Apply Lessons from SARS to Fight AIDS', *Wall Street Journal* (4 August), online.

Cheng, K. M. (1995) 'Education – Decentralization and the Market', in L. Wong and S. Macpherson (eds), *Social Change and Social Policy in Contemporary China*, Aldershot: Avebury, pp. 70–87.

Cleverley, J. (1985) *The Schooling of China: Tradition and Modernity in Chinese Education*, Sydney, London, Boston: George Allen & Unwin.

Croll, E. (1983) *Chinese Women Since Mao*, London: Zed Books, New York: M. E. Sharpe.

—— (1995) *Changing Identities of Chinese Women*, London and Hong Kong: Zed Books and Hong Kong University Press.

Deng Xiaoping (1984) *Selected Works of Deng Xiaoping (1975–1982)*, Beijing: Foreign Languages Press.

DP, NBS (Department of Population, Social Science and Technology Statistics, National Bureau of Statistics, China) (comp.) (2002) *Zhongguo renkou tongji nianjian (China Population Statistics Yearbook)*, Beijing: China Statistics Press.

French, H. W. (2005) 'Protesters Say Police in China Killed Up to 20', *New York Times* (10 December), online.

Griffin, K. and Zhao, R. (1993) 'Introduction', in K. Griffin and R. Zhao (eds), *The Distribution of Income in China*, Houndmills, Basingstoke: Macmillan, New York: St. Martin's Press, pp. 1–22.

Hook, B. (ed.) (1991) *The Cambridge Encyclopedia of China*, 2nd edn, Cambridge: Cambridge University Press.

Huang, W. (2005) 'Working for Harmony, Creating a Harmonious Society Will Take the Effort of Every Government Employee and Every Citizen, Says Premier Wen Jiabao', *Beijing Review* 48/11 (17 March): 23–5.

IPS (Institute of Population Studies, Chinese Academy of Social Sciences) (1994) *Dangdai Zhongguo funü diwei chouyang diaocha ziliao* (*Sampling Survey Data of Women's Status in Contemporary China*), Beijing: International Academic Publishers.

Johnson, K. A. (1983) *Women, the Family and Peasant Revolution in China*, Chicago and London: University of Chicago Press.

Judd, E. (1994) *Gender and Power in Rural North China*, Stanford, CA: Stanford University Press.

Kahn, J (2003) 'Beijing Effectively Beats SARS, W.H.O. Declares', *New York Times* (24 June), online.

Khan, A. R., Griffin, K., Riskin, C. and Zhao, R. (1993) 'Household Income and its Distribution in China', in K. Griffin and R. Zhao (eds), *The Distribution of Income in China*, Houndmills, Basingstoke: Macmillan, New York: St Martin's Press, pp. 25–73.

Khan, A. R. and Riskin, C. (2001) *Inequality and Poverty in China in the Age of Globalization*, Oxford, New York: Oxford University Press.

Kwei, C. (ed.) (1968) *The Chinese Year Book*, 7 vols, premier issue 1935–6, final issue 1944–5, Shanghai: Nendeln, Liechtenstein: Kraus Reprint.

Li, S. (2005) 'Fairer Distribution of Funds Key to a Better Education', *China Daily* (23 February): 6.

Li, W. Z. (2004) *Customizing HIV/AIDS Prevention Programs in China: Emerging Issues for Women*, New York: Department for General Assembly and Conference Management, United Nations Headquarters.

Mackerras, C. (1985) 'Education in the Guomindang Period, 1928–1949', in D. Pong and E. S. K. Fung (eds), *Ideal and Reality, Social and Political Change in Modern China, 1860–1949*, Lanham, MD: University Press of America, pp. 153–83.

—— (2001) *The New Cambridge Handbook of Contemporary China*, Cambridge: Cambridge University Press.

Mackerras, C., McMillen, D. H. and Watson, A. (eds) (1998) *Dictionary of the Politics of the People's Republic of China*, London and New York: Routledge.

Murphy, D. (2003) 'A Shot in the Arm', *Far Eastern Economic Review* 166/22 (5 June): 24–5.

NBS (National Bureau of Statistics of China) (comp.) (2003) *Zhongguo tongji nianjian 2003* (*China Statistical Yearbook 2002*), Beijing: China Statistics Press.

—— (2004) *Zhongguo tongji nianjian 2004* (*China Statistical Yearbook 2004*) Beijing: China Statistics Press.

Parish, W. L. (1984) 'Destratification in China', in J. L. Watson (ed.), *Class and Social Stratification in Post-Revolution China*, Cambridge: Cambridge University Press, pp. 84–120.

Pearson, V. (1995) 'Health and Responsibility; But Whose?', in L. Wong and S. Macpherson (eds), *Social Change and Social Policy in Contemporary China*, Aldershot: Avebury, pp. 88–112.

Rawski, E. S. (1979) *Education and Popular Literacy in Ch'ing China*, Ann Arbor: University of Michigan Press.

Roll, C. R., Jr (1980) *The Distribution of Rural Incomes in China, A Comparison of the 1930s and the 1950s*, New York and London: Garland Publishing.

Seybolt, P. J. (1973) *Revolutionary Education in China, Documents and Commentary*, White Plains, NY: International Arts and Sciences Press.

State Council AIDS Working Committee Office and UN Theme Group on HIV/AIDS in China (2004) *HIV/AIDS Prevention, Treatment and Care in China (2004)*, Beijing: State Council AIDS Working Committee Office, National Center for AIDS/STD Prevention and Control, China CDC, UNAIDS China Office.

Stockman, N. (2000) *Understanding Chinese Society*, Cambridge: Polity Press.

Thompson, D. (2005) 'The "People's War" Against Drugs and HIV/AIDS', *China Brief* 5/14 (21 June), accessed 23 August 2005 from www.jamestown.org.

UNDP (United Nations Development Programme) (2002) *Human Development Report 2002, Deepening Democracy in a Fragmented World*, New York, Oxford: Oxford University Press.

—— (2005) *Human Development Report 2002, International Cooperation at a Crossroads, Aid, Trade and Security in an Unequal World*, New York: United Nations Development Programme.

UNDP, China (2005) *China Human Development Report 2005*, Beijing: United Nations Development Programme, China Country Office, online at www.undp.org.cn.

Wang, S. and Hu, A. (1999) *The Political Economy of Uneven Development, The Case of China*, Armonk, NY, and London: M. E. Sharpe.

Watts, J. (2004) 'Chinese Walls Come Down', *Guardian* (11 September), online.

—— (2005) 'China in Denial Over Foot and Mouth Cull, Attempt to Hide Slaughter Echoes Response to Bird Flu and Sars', *Guardian* (24 May), online.

WHO (World Health Organization) (2001) *HIV/AIDS in Asia and the Pacific Region*, Geneva: World Health Organization.

—— (2002) *The World Health Report 2002, Reducing Risks, Promoting Healthy Life*, Geneva: World Health Organization.

—— (1999) 'WHO Estimates of Health Personnel, Physicians, Nurses, Midwives, Dentists and Pharmacists' (1998), accessed 27 June 2003, at www3.who.int/whosis/health_personnel/health_personnel.cfm.

Woodside, A. and Elman, B. A. (1994) 'Afterword: The Expansion of Education in Ch'ing China', in B. A. Elman and A. Woodside (eds), *Education and Society in Late Imperial China, 1600–1900*, Berkeley: University of California Press, pp. 525–60.

Xinhua (2005) 'Education Can Break Vicious Poverty Cycle'. Accessed 23 September 2005 at www.chinaview.cn.

Yang, Y., Zhang, T. and Xiong, Y. (1988) *Zhongguo shaoshu minzu renkou yanjiu (Research on the Populations of China's Minority Nationalities)*, Beijing: Nationalities Press.

Yao, X. (2000) *An Introduction to Confucianism*, Cambridge: Cambridge University Press.

9

Cross-Strait relations and China's reunification prospects

C_ZESLAW_ T_UBILEWICZ_*

Introduction

Contrary to claims by the Chinese Communist Party (CCP), who trace Taiwan's unity with the mainland to ancient times (*The Taiwan Question and Reunification of China* 1993), the island's formal relationship with China began in the late seventeenth century, and ended two centuries later. The island returned to the Republic of China's (ROC) sovereignty in 1945, and four years later became the focal point of conflict between the Chinese communists and the governing Nationalist Party (Kuomintang, KMT). Having been defeated in the civil war in 1949, the KMT moved the ROC's government and capital to Taiwan. Since then, the island has acted as an alternative China that is capitalist and more democratic than its arch rival, the People's Republic of China (PRC).

Located 100 miles off China's coastline, Taiwan remains the last major territory over which Beijing claims sovereignty that is yet to be reunited with the PRC. Relations between mainland China and the rebel island are of critical importance for contemporary China for at least three reasons. First, the existence of Taiwan, de facto independent of Beijing, is a reminder of the unfinished civil war and is symbolic of the failure of the Chinese state to extend its power to all regions over which it claims sovereignty. Second, the United States' (US) involvement in cross-Strait relations exposes a Chinese vulnerability to foreign pressure that is reminiscent of the 'unequal treaties' era. Above all, however, the

Notes * Islands controlled by Taipei
        △   Islands recovered by the PRC in 1955

Figure 9.1   Map of the Taiwan Strait

future of China hinges upon a solution to the Taiwan question. If China finds a unification formula agreeable to the Taiwanese people, it could close the chapter of civil war and shed the legacy of foreign powers' interference in its domestic affairs. By doing so, a united China could become an undisputed political and economic power in East Asia and beyond. If, however, driven by an impatient nationalistic agenda, it carries out the reunification through coercion (whether military or economic), the resulting conflict with Taiwan (and over Taiwan, if foreign powers get involved) could not only devastate the island's prosperity, but also destroy the peaceful international environment that is necessary for China's continued economic development. Such a conflict would also undermine Chinese economic growth, upset social stability, test the durability of the PRC regime, and antagonise Western powers. At the same time, however, Taiwan's success at sustaining de facto sovereignty over a prolonged period might set a 'wrong' example to other parts of China, where the CCP has failed to suppress secessionist sentiments. Thus, a successful solution to the Taiwan problem in the relatively foreseeable future is critical to the CCP's ambitions of safeguarding China's national interest and territorial integrity, and transforming China into an economic and military power that is internationally confident and respected.

China and Taiwan before 1949

Contacts between Taiwan and the mainland might date back to at least the sixth century CE, but when the Portuguese spotted the island in 1590, Taiwan was neither a part of China, nor populated by the Chinese. The majority of inhabitants were the aborigines of Malayo-Polynesian origin who dominated the indigenous population of Taiwan until the mid-seventeenth century (Lai *et al.* 1991: 13; Roy 2003: 12). Because China expressed neither territorial claim to Taiwan nor any interest in colonising Taiwan, the island easily fell to the Dutch colonisers, who governed it from 1624 to 1662 (Ho 1978: 7–8; Winckler 1988: 49). In 1663, the Dutch were defeated by the Ming loyalist, Zheng Chenggong, who transformed the island into a haven for anti-Qing militants. For this reason, the Qing Emperor Kang-xi's forces invaded Taiwan and incorporated it into the empire as a Fujianese prefecture in 1683 (Spence 1999: 57). The Qing, however, showed no interest in either developing it economically or strengthening its military defences. Only in response to the military threats posed to Taiwan by the Western imperialists (Ho 1978: 13; Lai 1991: 14; Finkelstein 1993: 47) did they upgrade the island to the status of a province in 1885 and make efforts to modernise its economy.

Taiwan as a Japanese colony

In 1895, China signed the Treaty of Shimonoseki with Japan, which ceded Taiwan to Japan (Spence 1999: 222). The Japanese developed Taiwan's economy and reoriented it economically towards Japan. Politically, they instituted a military dictatorship and agreed to modest self-government reforms only in the mid-1930s. Socially, they attempted to transform the Taiwanese into loyal imperial subjects who were fluent in Japanese and practised Japanese customs and religion (Lai *et al*. 1991: 26; Chu and Lin 2001: 110; Roy 2003: 43). The achievements of this 'Japanisation' were reflected in the absence of any significant anti-Japanese underground resistance during the Sino-Japanese war from 1937 to 1945 (although some Taiwanese established anti-Japanese organisations on the Chinese mainland; Jacobs 1990: 88). About 80,000 Taiwanese served in the Japanese army as soldiers, while 126,000 supported the army in non-combat positions (Roy 2003: 53). Yet the islanders welcomed Taiwan's return to China in 1945. Despite all efforts by Japanese, ethnically and culturally the Taiwanese continued to define their identity as Chinese.

The 28 February Uprising

Enthusiastic as they were about return to the motherland, the Taiwanese expected the positive aspects of the Japanese rule to continue. These included an efficient and uncorrupted administration; law and order; employment opportunities in the government bureaucracy; and continuing economic prosperity. But they also hoped that China would grant the island political autonomy and elevate it to the rank of province. The mainland Chinese, however, having suffered under the Japanese occupation for eight years, felt apprehensive about the Japanese-speaking Chinese, many of whom had served as spies or conscripts in the Japanese occupation forces on the mainland. Rather than making Taiwan a province, the ROC government placed it under a military government, a status associated with a conquered enemy territory (Roy 2003: 60).

Fifty years of separation from China might not seem a lengthy period in 3,000 years of China's recorded history, but these fifty years were formative for modern China's political, social and cultural identity. As a Japanese colony, Taiwan did not experience the Boxers' Uprising, the fall of the Manchu dynasty, the establishment of the Republic of China, the May 4th Movement, the Northern Expedition, the rule of the KMT, and the wartime atrocities committed by the Japanese army. When the KMT-appointed first governor-general, Chen Yi, arrived in Taiwan in October 1945, his task was, therefore, not only to bring the island's economy back to the pre-war levels, but also to integrate it politically and culturally with the mainland.

Taiwan's dependence on Japanese imports made its swift economic recovery difficult. Economic hardships, compounded by rising unemployment among the locals, led to increased crime and disorder. The Taiwanese were further frustrated by corruption among the mainland officials, reduced employment opportunities in the administration, and the channelling of the island's resources to the mainland economy. The mainland troops' low discipline also undermined the initial goodwill of the Taiwanese people towards China (Lai *et al*. 1991: 65–75; Finkelstein 1993: 57–8). The political reforms in mid-1946, which included the establishment of the Taiwan Provincial Council (the first in Taiwan's history), as well as the opening of district, city and township councils to free elections, proved insufficient to counterbalance the rising anti-China resentments on the island. Tensions exploded following a minor incident on 27 February 1947 when agents of the Taipei City Monopoly Bureau attempted to confiscate smuggled cigarettes from a Taiwanese widow, Lin Chiang-mai. The incident resulted in the death of a bystander, and hundreds of Taiwanese demanded the punishment of the agents responsible for the shooting. On 28 February, large crowds mounted attacks on the Monopoly Bureau headquarters, vandalised mainland Chinese businesses, took over the radio station, and physically assaulted mainlanders. Within a few days, the whole island was engulfed in violent anti-Chinese rioting during which an estimated 1,300 mainland Chinese lost their lives. Mainland troop reinforcements arrived on 8 March and suppressed the uprising by 13 March, killing an estimated 8,000 Taiwanese in the process (Lai *et al*. 1991: 8).

Following the uprising, the KMT made Taiwan a province, appointed a civilian governor and called for new elections. These conciliatory gestures, however, were invalidated with the proclamation of martial law in mid-May 1949, which suspended the protection of civil rights. In addition, many provisions of the 1947 constitution were replaced or superseded by 'Temporary Provisions Effective during the Period of Communist Rebellion' (Chu and Lin 2001: 114). Meanwhile, many Chinese fled the mainland as the communist forces progressively defeated the KMT. By December 1949, when the KMT government officially retreated to Taiwan, an estimated 2 million Chinese had settled on the island.

Taiwan during the Civil and Korean wars

Prior to the Cairo Conference in November 1943 (which returned Taiwan to China) neither the KMT nor the CCP considered the island as a part of Chinese territory, and both parties supported Taiwan's independence (Hsiao and Sullivan 1979). In the KMT's draft constitutions of 1925, 1934 and 1936, the island was not included as part of Chinese territory. Recovery of Taiwan became Chiang Kai-shek's objective only after the Allies made the recovery of Axis-occupied areas one of the major principles of the Atlantic Charter in 1941 (Lee, B. 1999: 15–16). Similarly, the CCP changed its position on Taiwan only after the Cairo Conference. Prior to the early 1940s, the Chinese communists considered the Taiwanese as a distinct nationality and indicated their support for their liberation movement (Mao 1934; Hsiao and Sullivan 1979: 447–9).

Following the Cairo Conference and Taiwan's formal return to China, the KMT and CCP no longer viewed Taiwanese sovereignty as an option, subject to Taiwanese preference. When the civil war broke out in 1946, the communists intended to capture Taiwan. In July 1949, Mao Zedong ordered the Third Field Army to prepare for landing operations on the island. The communists' failure to occupy the offshore islands of Jinmen, in October, and Dengbu, in November, however, reminded Mao of the necessity of Soviet military assistance if the invasion was to succeed. The Soviets responded positively to Mao's request (Goncharov *et al*. 1994: 99–100). In April 1950, when the People's Liberation Army (PLA) successfully recovered Hainan Island, Taiwan's fate seemed sealed. Still, two months later, Beijing postponed the invasion of Taiwan until the spring and summer of 1951

(Chen 1994: 101). The Korean War, however, invalidated this plan, as it diverted military resources from the invasion of Taiwan to Korea (Gong 2001: 143–4). More importantly, it reminded the Americans of the strategic importance of Taiwan.

Prior to the outbreak of the Korean War, the Truman administration had been disillusioned with the corrupt and incompetent KMT regime, and considered the support of the Nationalists too costly and contrary to its objective of containing the Soviets in Europe (Finkelstein 1993: 197–8; Chen 1994: 115–16; Garver 1997: 12–14). Hence, in January 1950, President Truman made an announcement disassociating the US from defending Taiwan. However, the outbreak of the Korean War reminded Washington that the communist occupation of Taiwan could create an enemy territory in the centre of the US's western strategic parameter (Garver 1997: 28). President Truman ordered the Seventh Fleet to the Taiwan Strait in June 1950, thereby transforming the Taiwan issue from a Chinese domestic affair into a Sino-American conflict. As the presence of the Seventh Fleet denied Taiwan to the PRC (and neutralised the KMT's plans to invade the mainland), Washington became the chief obstacle to the objective of national reunification on both sides of the Taiwan Strait.

Taiwan Strait Crises

The first crisis: 1954–5

In the 1950s, neither the KMT nor the CCP gave up on a military solution to the unfinished civil war. By mid-1950, Taipei held some thirty small, offshore islands which later proved useful for staging raids against the PRC and its maritime commerce and, in the longer term, were to become the launching pad for an attempted recovery of the mainland. Faced with nagging attacks in 1952, Beijing initiated a campaign to retake these offshore islands. The bombardment of two major offshore islands, Jinmen and Mazu (see Figure 9.1) in September 1954 precipitated the outbreak of the first Taiwan Strait Crisis. Some commentators have suggested that Beijing's attack was driven by its intention to prevent the United States from including Taiwan in its multilateral defence arrangements in Southeast Asia. And as such, it was meant to warn the US against signing a defence pact with Taiwan (Chang and He 1993: 1507; Christensen 1996: 195). If these were indeed the Chinese communists' political objectives, they failed. The crisis prompted Washington to sign the Mutual Defence Treaty in December 1954, which obliged Washington to come to Taiwan's defence if the island was attacked by the Communist forces, and, in March 1955, led to President Eisenhower's public announcement of Washington's intention to use nuclear weapons in the cross-Strait conflict. Militarily, the first Strait Crisis was China's success as Beijing recovered Yijiangshan and Dachen islands off the Zhejiang coast (see Figure 9.1): occupying Jinmen and Mazu was not reportedly its objective at the time (Chang and He 1993: 1507). Whether fearing the outbreak of nuclear war or being content with the accomplishment of its military goals, Beijing ceased shelling the offshore islands in May 1955.

The second crisis: 1958

In contrast to the first Taiwan Strait Crisis, the second crisis, which began in August 1958 with the renewed shelling of Jinmen and Mazu, had vague objectives. It could have resulted from the Eisenhower administration's announcement in May 1957 that it would install nuclear-capable missiles on Taiwan, undermining the status quo in the Strait (Pinsker 2003: 362), or, as Christensen argues (1996: 204–5, 229), the crisis may have been intended to build a sense of national threat among the Chinese people in order to mobilise their support for the Great Leap Forward. According to Khrushchev, Beijing ended the crisis in mid-September 1958 without invading the offshore islands in order to keep Chiang Kai-shek's military within the reach of the PLA's artillery (Khrushchev 1993: 80–1). Whiting (2001) concurs, suggesting that for Mao the KMT forces on Jinmen symbolically and geographically linked the ROC to the mainland and allowed Beijing to strain ROC–US relations any time by increasing tension over the offshore islands. (Similarly, for Chiang Kai-shek, the offshore islands played a symbolic role of linking Taiwan with the mainland.) Since late October 1958, China has shelled Jinmen on odd-numbered days, mostly with propaganda leaflets, and has not resorted to a military offensive against any territory controlled by Taipei.

The 'one China' question

For Chiang Kai-shek, Taiwan was a part of China that temporarily housed the ROC government. Chiang did not recognise the legality of the PRC regime and maintained that there was only one China, the ROC. The PRC regime also claimed that there was only one China, namely, the PRC. The PRC reasoned that Taiwan was a part of the PRC, although temporarily under a rebel administration. Both governments' claims to represent 'one China' prevented the international community from recognising both Chinas as two separate entities. Given US support for the ROC and Soviet support for the PRC, the majority of pro-US states maintained diplomatic ties with Taipei, while all communist states established relations with Beijing. The ROC represented China at the United Nations (UN), but the communist and developing states demanded that China's UN representation be switched to the PRC. These demands were satisfied in October 1971 when the PRC replaced the ROC as China's representative. Rather than lobby the UN member-states on the issue of dual representation, which would have legitimised the PRC regime, the ROC opted to withdraw from the UN (Garver 1997: 259–60). To a large extent, Taipei's defeat at the UN resulted from the emerging Sino-American rapprochement, prompted by Washington's hopes to enlist Beijing's partnership in its global containment of Soviet communism (Harding 1992: 4). Taking a cue from Washington's communication with Beijing, US allies supported the PRC's membership in the UN and began switching allegiances to China. By January 1979, Taiwan's pool of diplomatic partners had shrunk from 42 in 1972 to 22, while the PRC's allies had increased to from 85 to 120.

Capitalising on Taiwan's importance in the United State's geopolitical strategy, Beijing worked relentlessly to undermine the US's partnership with Taiwan. The Shanghai Communiqué, which President Nixon signed during his visit to China in February 1972, 'affirmed' Washington's ultimate objective to withdraw its forces from the island, and, before that happened, to 'progressively' reduce its military presence on Taiwan. It also 'acknowledged' the United States' 'one China' policy and 'affirmed' its interest in a peaceful settlement of the Taiwan question by the Chinese themselves (*Shanghai Communiqué* 1972). Despite the exchange of liaison offices by Beijing and Washington in 1973, and President Ford's visit to China in 1975, America was too preoccupied with its domestic crises to formally shift its China policy. Only in January 1979 did the Carter administration establish official ties with Beijing, cut diplomatic relations with Taipei, abrogate the Mutual Defence Treaty (which formally ended in 1980) and withdraw its military from the island. Yet, in a joint communiqué, Washington merely 'acknowledge[d] the Chinese position that there is but one China and Taiwan is part of China' (*Joint Communique* 1979).

The January 1979 de-recognition not only undermined the ROC's international standing but also its very ability to survive. However, the US Congress's enactment of the Taiwan Relations Act (TRA) in March 1979 saved the island from China's possible takeover. Although the TRA was ambiguous in terms of the US's commitment to Taiwan's defence, it did provide Washington with an option to defend the island, even in the event of Taiwan being confronted with boycotts or embargoes. It also assured Taipei of the continued provision of defensive arms 'in such quantity as may be necessary to enable Taiwan to maintain a sufficient self-defence capability' (*Taiwan Relations Act* 1979). As a follow-up to the establishment of Sino-American relations, the Taiwan Relations Act was an articulation of America's continued commitment to the status quo in the Taiwan Strait and a reminder of the centrality of US involvement in the solution to the Taiwan question.

Sino-Taiwanese dialogue

The US recognition of the PRC rendered Taiwan more vulnerable to the mainland's pressure and infused Beijing with confidence that reunification with Taiwan, on its terms, was within its reach. More relaxed about the future, Beijing abandoned its liberation rhetoric and began stressing the peaceful road to reunification. Yet, it never renounced the possibility of using military force against Taiwan (Chiu 1990: 10).

Beijing's peace overtures

In January 1979, the National People's Congress (NPC) issued a 'Message to Compatriots on Taiwan', which called for the establishment of 'three links' (mail, transport and trade) and 'four exchanges' (economic, cultural, technical and sporting)

(Lee, B. 1999: 20). At the same time, in a symbolic gesture, Beijing ceased shelling Jinmen and Mazu. In September 1981, the Chairman of the NPC's Standing Committee, Marshall Ye Jiangying, articulated the 'Guidelines on Making Taiwan Return to the Motherland in a Peaceful Unification' ('nine-point proposal'). Ye called for negotiations between the ruling parties, the CCP and the KMT (rather than between the two governments), and in doing so emphasised China's non-recognition of the ROC's statehood. Ye promised that after eventual reunification, Taiwan – as a special administrative region (SAR) – would enjoy 'a high degree of autonomy' and could retain its armed forces, while Beijing would not interfere in its internal affairs. Ye also pledged the mainland's non-interference in Taiwan's socioeconomic system. Article 31 of China's new constitution, enacted in December 1982, allowed for the possibility of establishing SARs. Two years later, after Sino-British negotiations over Hong Kong's future, Beijing spoke of reunification with Taiwan in the context of 'one country, two systems', under which the Taiwan SAR would be granted political and economic autonomy. A 'high level of autonomy', however, did not amount to full autonomy; a fact which Deng Xiaoping was quick to remind visiting Chinese-American scholar Winston Yang Li-yu in 1983. Furthermore, not ruling out a military solution to the Taiwan issue, Deng identified factors which could prompt China's military invasion. These included Taipei's rapprochement with the Soviet Union; proclamation of Taiwan's independence; development of nuclear weapons on Taiwan; political chaos in Taiwan; and Taipei's continued rejection of reunification talks over 'a long period of time' (Huan 1985: 1068).

The vagueness and limitations of Beijing's peace offer did not escape Taipei's attention. Chiang Kai-shek's successor, Chiang Ching-kuo, decided to sustain the long-established hostility towards the PRC, which he repackaged in 1981 as 'three nos': no negotiation, no contact and no compromise with communism (Lee, B. 1999: 21). International isolation, however, forced Taiwan to become more flexible on issues pertaining to its participation in international affairs. In 1981, for example, Taipei agreed to participate in the Olympic Games under the name 'Chinese Taipei'. Two years later, it allowed academics to participate in scholarly meetings alongside mainland representatives in third countries (Chiu 1990: 31). In the economic realm, unable to stop trade with China, Taiwan lifted the ban on indirect trade with the mainland in 1985 but continued to regulate imports from China (Lee, B 1999: 24). Popular demands to relax travel restrictions and the May 1986 incident (in which a China Airlines captain hijacked a cargo jet to Guangzhou in order to see his ageing father) forced the Taiwanese authorities to allow ROC citizens (indirect) travel to China in 1987 (Harding 1992: 157–8). In 1987, Taipei also lifted restrictions on the export of capital to China.

Dialogue formalised

President Chiang Ching-kuo's successor, Lee Teng-hui, faced with the Taiwanese business community's increasing interaction with the mainland, engaged in a dialogue with China on issues ranging from functional cooperation to a 'one China' principle. In his May 1990 inaugural address, he spelt out the conditions under which negotiations over reunification should take place, namely, the PRC's adoption of democracy and market economy; Beijing's renunciation of the use of force against Taiwan; and China's non-interference in Taiwan's foreign relations. Lee emphasised the principle of equality if any future negotiations were to be held. Further guidelines on reunification came in February 1991, when the National Unification Council – established by Lee in 1990 – projected a three-state process leading to eventual unification with China. During the first stage, the two sides would acknowledge each others' political existence, end bilateral hostilities and allow each others' international identity, while China would establish democratic rule on the mainland. In the second stage, the two sides would cooperate with each other internationally and expand economic relations. In the final stage, the two sides would agree on a constitutional system for a unified China (Clough 2001: 207–8; Ijiri 1997: 42). The ROC's termination of the 'Temporary Provisions' in May 1991 formally ended the ROC's state of war with the CCP and renounced Taipei's long-standing claim to be the legitimate government of all China.

In March 1991, Taipei established the Straits Exchange Foundation (SEF), authorised by the governmental Mainland Affairs Council to negotiate with the mainland on practical matters. Beijing responded in December with the Association for Relations Across the Taiwan Strait (ARATS). The organisations provided both sides with a nominally non-official channel to engage in dialogue without compromising their respective stands on the 'one China' question. Both were led by prominent personalities: Koo Chen-fu (a leading businessman, member of the KMT's Standing Committee, and President Lee's advisor) headed SEF and Wang Daohan (a former mayor of Shanghai, and closely associated with PRC President Jiang Zemin) chaired ARATS. With the intensified economic, social and cultural contacts between the mainland and Taiwan, Koo and Wang's agenda was full of pending solutions to functional problems that inconvenienced the evolution of unofficial relations. During their first meeting in Singapore in April 1993 – preceded by an oral agreement acknowledging an existence of 'one China' (the '1992 consensus') – Koo and Wang settled matters such as the authentication of documents, the handling of registered mail, and a schedule for meetings between officials of both organisations. In the following two years, SEF and ARATS reached further agreements on handling fishing disputes and the hijacking of planes, among other things. The second Koo–Wang meeting was scheduled for July 1995 (Clough 2001: 215–6).

Alongside these explorations of solutions to practical problems, both Beijing and Taipei elaborated their respective positions on the question of unification and 'one China'. China's first White Paper on Taiwan, *The Taiwan Question and Reunification of China* (1993), reiterated Beijing's position that Taiwan was an inalienable part of China and should be reunified under the 'one country, two systems' formula. Under this formula Taiwan would retain its own armed forces, but would be prevented from buying new weapons or engaging in diplomatic activities. Taipei's response in July 1994 agreed to the existence of 'one China', but stressed that 'one China' had been split into two political entities, one of which was the ROC, a de facto sovereign state with the right to engage in international activities and to enter international organisations (Clough 2001: 208–9; Lee, B. 1999: 41). President Jiang Zemin's 'Eight-Point Proposal' of January 1995 revealed emerging flexibility among the Chinese leadership on the Taiwan issue. Jiang suggested that Beijing was prepared to talk with the Taiwan authorities about 'any matter' on an equal footing, as long as they accepted the premise of 'one China'. He proposed that negotiations should be held on ending the state of hostility between the two sides and accomplishing peaceful reunification. Jiang did not renounce China's right to use force against Taiwan, but he made a significant qualification, saying, 'If used, force will not be directed against our compatriots in Taiwan, but against the foreign forces who intervene in China's reunification and go in for "the independence of Taiwan"'. He also invited Taiwanese leaders to visit the mainland 'in their proper status'. Most interestingly, the term 'PRC' did not appear in the statement, which implied that Beijing no longer insisted on 'one China' to refer to the People's Republic (Chu 2000: 207). Officially, Taipei dismissed Jiang's proposals as containing nothing new. In his six-point rebuttal in April 1995, Lee certainly did not propose anything new either when he called on China to renounce the use of force against Taiwan and stressed the existence of two distinct political entities.

Renewed tensions

By the late 1980s, Taipei was engaging in a dual strategy vis-à-vis the mainland: it appeared committed to a functional cooperation with Beijing and cautiously explored the possibilities of eventual reunification; but it also pursued a strategy that stressed Taiwan's independence and sovereignty and negated the 'one China' principle, the very foundation of the dialogue with Beijing.

Flexible diplomacy

Between 1979 and 1987, the ROC lost official ties with six states. Although it managed to gain new allies, ending up with a total of twenty-two a year later, its new diplomatic partners tended to be small, relatively poor and of little significance in world geopolitics (see Table 9.1). More dramatic action was needed if Taipei wished to increase its pool of diplomatic partners and strengthen unofficial relations with those states that recognised the PRC. The fundamental shift in Taiwan's foreign policy came during Lee Teng-hui's presidency. In mid-1988, President Lee called for 'flexible diplomacy', which aimed at the consolidation of existing diplomatic ties or gaining new diplomatic allies, development of semi-official ties with the states that maintained diplomatic relations with China, and participation in inter-governmental organisations (Wu 1995: 31; Hsieh 1996: 76). The end of the Cold War also facilitated the execution of 'flexible diplomacy', because the disappearance of the Soviet empire effectively devalued the so-called 'China card', reducing the PRC's leverage in world affairs (Hsieh 1996: 71). Moreover, Taiwan's booming free market economy contrasted with the economic downturn

Beijing experienced in the aftermath of the June 4th tragedy. Furthermore, given the international isolation of China after the Tiananmen event, Beijing's foreign policy focused on regaining respectability in the international community. China appeared willing to make a number of compromises to mend international fences and appeared less concerned with various states' unofficial ties with Taiwan.

By the mid-1990s, 'flexible diplomacy' had expanded Taipei's international profile. Taiwan had maintained diplomatic relations with 30 states and unofficial relations with 150 states. It had also established 90 offices in 60 states that did not recognise Taiwan (Han 1995: 175). Its achievements at expanding non-official relations with the PRC's allies were particularly impressive. These included President Lee's unofficial visits to Southeast Asian countries in 1993–4 (Chen 2002: 38), as well as the establishment of unofficial ties with most post-communist states in East Central Europe, including Russia (Tubilewicz 2002). With regards to the West, Taipei used its Six-Year National Development Plan (1991–6), valued at US$300 billion, to consolidate relations with the Western powers, who resumed cabinet-level dialogue with Taipei in order to win contracts for large infrastructure projects (Wu 1995: 32–3; Hsieh 1996: 89; Joei 1994: 319). Taiwan's relations with Western Europe also included arms deals, of which the French sale of Mirage 2000-5 jet fighters (worth US$4 billion) in 1992 stole the world's headlines. In 1993, Taipei launched a campaign to re-enter the UN. A year earlier, with US support, it managed to secure membership – as Chinese Taipei – in the Asia-Pacific Economic Cooperation.

Mainland commentators concluded that Taiwan's diplomatic achievements resulted from a 'financial-aid offensive' which took advantage of the mainland's 'temporary difficulties' and utilised foreign exchange reserves to buy off countries in need. The *Beijing Review* warned that the mainland's difficulties 'will soon be overcome' (Li 1990: 29). In the aftermath of Deng Xiaoping's trip to the south in early 1992, the Chinese economy regained its momentum. By the mid-1990s, China had emerged as an undisputed economic powerhouse, amassing the world's second largest foreign currency reserves, becoming a magnet for foreign investments, and dramatically expanding trading relations. Accordingly, an increasing number of states seeking economic advantages in the Chinese market chose to toe Beijing's line on the Taiwan issue (Wu 1996: 56).

Domestically, the Taiwanese did not rally behind the strategy to dispense with hard-earned wealth in exchange for diplomatic favours. The missile crisis of 1995–6 (discussed below) in particular demonstrated the irrelevance of 'flexible diplomacy', as it failed to protect Taiwan from China's military threat.

The missile crisis

Following the US Congressional legislation of the TRA in 1979, Beijing intensified efforts to limit, and ultimately eliminate, US arms sales to Taiwan. Convinced of the significance of a 'strategic relationship' with China against the Soviet Union, the Reagan administration bowed to Chinese pressure (Chiu 1990: 24). In August 1982, Washington signed a joint communiqué with Beijing which spelt out limits to

Table 9.1 The gains and losses of Taipei's 'flexible diplomacy'

Year	Gains of 'flexible diplomacy'	Gains of PRC diplomacy	Number of ROC allies
1989	Bahamas Grenada Liberia Belize		26
1990	Lesotho Nicaragua Guinea-Bissau	Saudi Arabia	28
1991	Central African Republic		29
1992	Niger	South Korea	29
1994	Burkina Faso	Lesotho	29
1995	Gambia		30
1996	Senegal	Niger	30
1997	Sao Tome and Principe Chad	Bahamas St Lucia South Africa	29
1998	Marshall Islands	Central African Republic Guinea-Bissau Tonga	27
1999	Macedonia Papua New Guinea Palau	Papua New Guinea	29
2001		Macedonia	28
2002		Nauru	27
2003	Kiribati	Liberia	27
2004	Vanuatu	Dominica Vanuatu	26
2005	Nauru	Grenada Senegal	25

arms sales to the island. Washington pledged not to exceed, either in qualitative or quantitative terms, the level of arms supplied to Taiwan before 1979, and to gradually reduce arms sales to Taiwan over an unspecified period of time until a 'final solution' was found for Taiwan. However, President Reagan's 'six assurances' also sought to reassure Taipei that Washington would not set a date for ending arms sales to the ROC, would not mediate in the intra-Chinese conflict, would not change its position regarding China's sovereignty over Taiwan, and would not exert pressure on Taiwan to enter into negotiations with China (Dean 2001: 77; Goldstein and Schriver 2001: 154). Furthermore, Reagan's interpretation of the 1982 communiqué specified that if the PRC changed the balance of military power in the Taiwan Strait in its favour, then the US would help Taiwan match these improvements. Yet US arms sales to Taiwan did gradually temper off in the 1980s. However, they jumped again to US$6 billion in 1993, when the Bush administration approved the sale of 150 F-16 jet fighters to Taiwan (Mann 1999: 127; Lilley 2001: 162, 165).

Although the Clinton administration was vocal on the question of China's human rights record, it trod carefully on the Taiwan issue (Dean 2001: 92). Having conducted a comprehensive review of policy towards Taiwan in 1994, the administration opted for minor changes to the pattern of existing non-official relations, and rejected the possibility of granting visas to top-ranking ROC leaders. In June 1995, however, bowing to Congressional pressure, President Clinton allowed President Lee to attend a reunion at Cornell University (where Lee obtained his Ph.D. in 1968). While unofficial, this was the first ever visit by the ROC president to the United States, and a crowning achievement for 'flexible diplomacy'. Beijing was furious, considering Lee's US visit a challenge to the 'one China' principle, as well as evidence of the failure of the conciliatory policy on Taiwan. It cancelled a scheduled meeting between the ARATS and SEF, postponed a series of high-level meetings with the US, and recalled its ambassador from Washington.

In July–August 1995, Beijing replaced peace initiatives with military intimidation, when the PLA conducted military exercises in the Taiwan Strait. In December 1995, China launched amphibious manoeuvres in the Taiwan Strait which coincided with the parliamentarian elections in Taiwan. Beijing ignored the appearance of a US aircraft carrier in the Strait (the first since 1979 and allegedly prompted by weather conditions), and launched a second series of military exercises off Taiwan in March 1996, shortly before Taiwan's first presidential elections.

Having exhausted diplomatic solutions to escalating tensions, Washington, determined to remain a key player in East Asia and fulfil its security obligations to Asian allies, and concerned about Taiwan's economic well-being, sent two aircraft carriers near Taiwan in the largest deployment of US naval forces in East Asia since the Vietnam War (Mann 1999: 330–7; Ross 2000: 91–112). China ended its war games soon after the presidential elections in late March 1996. The missile crisis demonstrated US commitment to Taiwan's security, and undermined the credibility of China's peaceful strategy towards Taiwan. It also constituted Beijing's first direct attempt at influencing Taiwanese democratic processes.

Taiwan's democratisation

Given the minority status of the mainlanders on Taiwan, any democratisation of the political process on the island needed to involve a shift of power to the native Taiwanese and the public debate of the 'one China' issue and the political status of Taiwan. For these reasons, Chiang Kai-shek maintained martial law on Taiwan, outlawing the formation of political parties and suspending free elections to the national legislative bodies. Elections to a nominally 'national' legislature held on Taiwan would have contradicted Chiang's claim that Taiwan was only a part of China, a claim that justified the KMT's dominance of political power in Taiwan. Elections to provincial, municipal and township assemblies, however, were allowed, as they did not undermine the 'one China' principle and served the purpose of strengthening the KMT's local power base through a patron–client network (Tien 1996: 8, 19; Rigger 1999: 81–3). Towards this goal, Chiang also promoted enlargement of the KMT's membership and a 'Taiwanisation' of the KMT. The KMT grew from about 34,000 in 1949 (representing 0.8 per cent of the population) to 1 million by the late 1960s. By the early 1950s, 60 per cent of the KMT's members were native Taiwanese (Huang 1996: 114; Roy 2003: 81), but mainlanders continued to occupy key leadership positions in the government and the KMT's Standing Commitee.

The lifting of martial law

Chiang Ching-kuo accelerated the process of the 'Taiwanisation' of the KMT by recruiting native Taiwanese into the central governmental and party decision-making bodies (Huang 1996: 116). More importantly, however, he initiated a gradual opening of the electoral process. In response to Taiwan's ousting from the UN and its de-recognition by the United States (which exposed the fiction of 'one China' ruled by the KMT and questioned the legitimacy of the state), the KMT leadership felt compelled to enhance its legitimacy and gain public support through democratisation (Tian and Chu 1994: 3; Chu and Lin 2001: 118). Coinciding with this limited political opening, a loosely coordinated opposition movement, Tangwai (literally meaning 'outside the party/KMT'), emerged and made considerable gains in local elections. As the KMT's attempts at repressing the opposition movement proved unsuccessful, Chiang Ching-kuo lifted martial law in 1987 in order to prevent Taiwan from becoming embroiled in chronic political turmoil. Yet the lifting of martial law heralded neither democracy nor a sanctioning of the advocacy of Taiwanese independence, as it was followed with legislation that prohibited political activities supporting separatism. It was the Legislative Yuan's legalisation of political parties in 1988 that officially opened the political scene for competition with the KMT. However, Taiwan's major opposition party, the Democratic Progressive Party (DPP), formed in September 1986 on the basis of the 'Tangwai' movement, could only compete with the KMT in local elections, as elections to the National Assembly (a legislative body empowered to elect a president and amend the constitution) and the Legislative Yuan (the chief law-making body) were restricted to supplementary elections, when seats were vacated by lifelong legislators elected on the mainland in 1947.

Evolution of Taiwanese democracy

Major political reforms in Taiwan arrived with the presidency of Lee Teng-hui, whose reform agenda included a progressive democratisation of the Taiwanese political system. Due to his efforts, in 1991, the 'Temporary Provisions' were lifted; lifelong legislators were forced into retirement, and free elections were held for the National Assembly. In 1992, Article 100 of the Criminal Code, which criminalised the advocacy of sedition, was revised making it legal to advocate independence. At this time, the first election for the entire Legislative Yuan was held. The process of establishing democratic institutions and procedures was completed in March 1996 when the ROC president and vice-president were elected by popular ballot for the first time in Taiwanese (and China's) history (Rigger 1999: 148–77).

Domestically, Taiwanese democratisation drew criticism from the so-called 'non-mainstream' faction within the KMT (composed mostly of the mainlanders). This faction opposed direct elections on the ground that they would favour Taiwanese nationalism (Bellochi 2001: 132). In 1992, the 'non-mainstream' faction left the KMT and formed the New Party. Moves towards direct elections were also opposed by those fearing negative reaction from Beijing. Indeed, the Chinese leadership was concerned about the impact of Taiwanese democratisation on cross-Strait relations. It was not until the presidential elections in 1996, however, that Beijing concluded that the most serious challenge to the reunification agenda came not from the US involvement in the cross-Strait conflict but from the democratic pro-independence forces on Taiwan

At first, the DPP electioneered on the platform of Taiwanese independence. The DPP considered this strategy a viable alternative to the KMT's socioeconomic development programme because the sub-ethnic division between the mainlanders and the native Taiwanese transcended socioeconomic problems (Chu and Lin 1996: 83). At the party convention in October 1991 the DPP's radical faction pushed through an amendment to the party charter which made the attainment of Taiwan's independence the DPP's long-term goal. In 1992, the DPP proposed a new draft constitution for the 'Republic of Taiwan'. The DPP's poor results for the National Assembly election (held shortly after the party embraced the independence platform), however, forced it to include socioeconomic issues in its political programme (Chu and Lin 1996: 86). In the December 1992 elections to the Legislative Yuan, the DPP moderated its calls for independence and gained 32 per cent of the vote, positioning itself as the second largest political party on the island and a viable alternative to the KMT (Chiou 1994: 33).

The DPP's decision to broaden its electoral appeal was also necessitated by the KMT's successful transformation into a Taiwanese party. Under Lee, the KMT's party machinery fell almost entirely into the hands of Taiwan-born party bureaucrats and politicians. Furthermore, the KMT stole the DPP's pro-Taiwan agenda on issues related to Taiwan's international standing. A post-1992 Legislative Yuan election survey revealed that the KMT enjoyed a substantial advantage over the DPP on issues related to national identity, with more than 60 per cent of respondents identifying themselves with the KMT's stance (Chu and Lin 1996: 93).

Until the mid-1990s, Beijing's involvement in Taiwanese democratic politics was indirect, relying primarily on reminding the Taiwanese voters of the dangers of supporting pro-independence forces and mobilising political support in Taiwan (e.g. the New Party). Following President Lee's visit to the United States, China decided to influence the presidential elections of March 1996 directly by staging military exercises. Ironically, Beijing's action, intended to intimidate the Taiwanese electorate into voting against Lee, boosted his popularity. Lee Teng-hui won elections with 54 per cent of the popular vote. The missile crisis is also believed to have helped the DPP, which won a landslide victory in county magistrate and city mayor elections in November 1997, gaining control of areas containing more than 71 per cent of Taiwan's population (Zhao 2003: 41; Peterson 2004: 29).

The rise of Taiwanese identity

Chiang Kai-shek's efforts to strengthen the islanders' Chinese identity – through making Mandarin the official language of the state bureaucracy, media and education, through renaming streets to remind people of the Confucian values and the mainland, through teaching China's history and geography (while portraying Taiwan as historically part of China), and through withholding support for Taiwanese indigenous culture – did not entirely succeed (Chiou 1994: 29; Dreyer 2003: 5). Other factors worked against Chiang's efforts such as the collective memory of the 28 February Uprising and the bottom-up movement of literary nativisation, which started in the 1960s, and returned the Taiwanese to their cultural roots. Taiwan's gradual democratisation allowed the discourse on national identity to move beyond a cultural realm. The DPP's rising fortunes in local and national elections confirmed Chiang Kai-shek's fears that democracy would impact on Taiwan's identity and its relationship with the mainland. Before the DPP came to power, however, it was the KMT's Lee Teng-hui – himself a Taiwanese native – who promoted 'Taiwan first' values. During Lee's presidency, history books emphasised the Taiwanese past, rather than that of the mainland; mainland-born politicians campaigned in local dialects, rather than in Mandarin; and the memory of the 28 February Uprising became public through the setting up of a museum dedicated to the event.

Surveys conducted by the Election Center at National Chengchi University monitored the steady rise in Taiwanese identity among Taiwanese citizens and a corresponding decline in Chinese (mainland) identity (although these quantitative studies do not reveal the meanings that respondents attached to the notion of 'identity'). While the incidence of 'double identity' (people identifying themselves as both Chinese and Taiwanese) was at its highest in the mid-1990s, by the late 1990s Taiwanese identity had surpassed the double identity ratio, and reached 50 per cent by the year 2000. Among the three ethnic groups in Taiwan, the

Fujianese (Hoklo), Hakka and the mainlanders, the mainlanders identified them-selves most strongly with China. However, half of the mainlander respondents chose double identity in 2000, while six years earlier 50 per cent of them had iden-tified with Chinese only. The majority of DPP supporters have been staunch in their Taiwanese identity throughout the years. In 2000, the proportion of KMT supporters who identified as Taiwanese surpassed, for the first time, those who reported double identity (Ho and Liu 2002).

Consistent with the rise in the number of people identifying as Taiwanese are statistics detailing the rise in support for Taiwan's independence. In 1992, public opinion surveys revealed that 12.4 per cent of respondents supported Taiwanese independence, while 56.9 per cent supported unification. Ten years later, almost 50 per cent of respondents supported the status quo, 27.7 per cent hoped for unification, and 24 per cent for independence (Hsieh 2004: 484). When asked whether Taiwan should seek independence if peace could be guaranteed in the Taiwan Strait, 37.7 per cent of respondents agreed in 1993, while seven years later, the percentage jumped to 60.89 per cent (Hamrin and Zheng 2004: 341). The marked rise in Taiwanese identity and support for either the status quo in the Taiwan Strait or outright independence not only boosted the electoral chances of the DPP but also forced the KMT to further embrace the 'Taiwanese' and distance itself from the mainland.

The DPP era in cross-Strait relations

In his May 1996 inaugural address, President Lee proposed a 'journey of peace' in which he offered to meet the mainland leaders and no longer demanded China's renunciation of force as the precondition for cross-Strait negotiations However, despite this offer, Lee remained wary of Taiwan's closer interaction with China. In 1996 he called on Taiwanese businessmen to 'avoid haste, be patient' when doing business with the mainland, and limited investments in a single project in China to US$50 million (Clough 2001: 206). In a mid-1999 state-ment to the *Deutsche Welle*, Lee described cross-Strait ties as special state-to-state relations ('two-state theory'), and cemented his 'troublemaker' status in China, who viewed these statements as confirming his intention to divide China's territory and undermine its sovereignty (Lee, Teng-hui 1999: 12; *Renmin Ribao* 1999, 14 July). In protest against Lee's 'theory', Beijing suspended the Wang–Koo dialogue, which had restarted in 1998. By late 1999, China's top priority, however, was to prevent the DPP's candidate, Chen Shui-bian, from winning the presiden-tial election, scheduled for March 2000.

Chen Shui-bian's first term

In late 1999–early 2000, Beijing had to prepare itself, for the first time, for the eventuality that Taiwan's leader would come from the party that put independence in its charter. Once again, Beijing decided to apply military pressure to prevent

Taiwanese voters from voting for the 'pro-independence' candidate. China staged five large-scale military exercises, from October 1999 to February 2000, and issued a second White Paper on Taiwan, which spelt out the conditions under which the mainland would use force against Taiwan. These were:

1   any major event leading to the separation of Taiwan from China in any name;
2   any invasion of Taiwan by foreign countries;
3   the Taiwanese authorities' rejection of cross-Strait reunification through peaceful negotiations (*The One China Principle and the Taiwan Issue* 2000).

Military intimidation, however, did not produce its desired results. Chen won the elections, although his success owed more to the split within the KMT camp which fielded two candidates (officially, Lien Chan, and James Soong, who ran as an independent) than to China's heavy-handed involvement.

Contrary to the Chinese leaders' statements suggesting some dramatic action after Chen's election, Beijing reacted to his success with a wait-and-see policy. President Chen, in a conciliatory move, announced the 'one if and five nos' during his inaugural speech in May 2000, distancing him from the DPP's tradition of promoting Taiwan's independence. In essence, Chen promised that if the PRC gave up any plans to use military force against Taiwan, then Taipei would maintain the status quo by promising 'five nos': no declaration of independence, no change in national title of the Republic of China, no change of constitution, no referendum on independence, and no abolition of the Guidelines for National Unification. A year later, Chen proposed 'the new five nos', namely, no provocation against the mainland, no misjudgment of the situation, no acting as a US pawn, no zero-sum game with the mainland, and no halt in Taipei's efforts to improve cross-Strait ties (Zhao 2003: 44). However, Beijing waited for Chen's deeds, rather than his words.

The Chen administration sent a series of conciliatory signals to Beijing: the ban on travel and trade between the mainland and the Taiwan-held offshore islands (the 'three small links') was lifted; the 'no haste, be patient' policy was ended; Taiwanese investment in high technology was legalised; and links between Taiwanese and Chinese banks were permitted. The DPP government also relaxed the terms of entry for mainland visitors, allowed mainland journalists to stay and cover Taiwanese news, and in early 2003, agreed to a series of chartered, indirect flights between the mainland and the island (Mainland Affairs Council 2005). At the same time, however, Chen continued his predecessor's 'flexible diplomacy' (albeit with lesser success, see Table 9.1) and sought both high-level transits through the US and advanced arms sales from the US. He also continued to apply for membership in intergovernmental organisations, and pushed the 'Taiwan iden-tification' campaign to new heights, symbolised by the addition of the phrase 'issued in Taiwan' on the cover page of ROC passports.

Beijing refused to resume cross-Strait talks, as in its view, President Chen's policies confirmed his determination to advance Taiwan's independence. Instead, Beijing appealed directly to the Taiwanese people by extending the olive branch to Chen's political rivals, the KMT and People's First Party (PFP), known as the pan-Blue camp. The PFP was established by Soong after his unsuccessful presidential bid in 2000 and like the post-Lee Teng-hui KMT it favoured eventual reunification with China. Beijing's united front tactics also involved Taiwanese businesspeople who were mobilised to apply pressure on Chen's leadership. Beijing did not give up on the military intimidation of Taiwan either, modernising its military in order to make it ready for an invasion of the island. Internationally, it continued to isolate Taiwan and worked hard to convince Washington that the breakdown of the status quo in the Taiwan Strait would not serve US strategic interests.

President Chen's sliding popularity in Taiwan, in no small measure caused by the poor economy, forced him to play the China card by returning to the strategy of promoting the island's independence. Chen dusted off his predecessor's 'two-state theory' when, in August 2002, he declared that 'with Taiwan and China on each side of the Taiwan Strait, each side is a country' (President Chen, 'One Country on Each Side' 2002: 1). At the same time, however, in order to appeal to those favouring the status quo or reunification with China, Chen continued to paint a rosy picture of the cross-Strait reconciliation process. In mid-August 2003 he drew up a three-stage blueprint for Taiwan's interaction with the mainland. In the first stage, Taiwanese government officials would complete all necessary preparations for direct transport and trade links with China by the end of 2003. In the second stage, the ROC government would resume cross-Strait talks after the March 2004 presidential elections. By the end of 2004, the two sides would reach the final stage: direct air and sea links (*South China Morning Post*, 14 August 2003). Given the timing of Chen's remarks on reconciliation with the mainland, Chen's comments were designed to win over neutral voters ahead of the presidential elections in March 2004.

2004 presidential elections

During the presidential election campaign, the 'one China' issue emerged as a key issue. At first, Chen's opponents, Lien Chan of the KMT and James Soong of the PFP (electioneering on a united ticket), said little about the prospects of cross-Strait relations, except that they would handle the issue with a greater pragmatism. Instead, their campaign attempted to highlight Chen's mismanagement of the Taiwanese economy. In response, Chen constructed his re-election campaign around the issue of strengthening Taiwan's national identity and exposing China's military threat. As a part of this strategy he proposed the Referendum Law, which was passed in November 2003. Beijing (as well as the United States) feared that Chen would hold a formal independence referendum concurrently with presidential elections in March 2004. Responding to domestic and international pressure, President Chen revised his plans. His 'peace referendum' merely asked the Taiwanese whether they would support a peaceful solution to the Taiwan Strait conflict and whether Taipei should engage in talks with Beijing on peace and stability in the Taiwan Strait. The 'Peace referendum' failed to obtain support from over 50 per cent of registered voters, as required by the Referendum Law.

Chen's rise in the polls in 2003 (to some extent caused by his successful transit via the United States in October–November 2003) forced the opposition to change its tactics. To counter Chen's platform for a new constitution by 2008, Lien and Soong made it explicit that they did not support the imminent reunification with the mainland. Shortly before the elections, the opinion polls indicated that the Lien–Soong ticket was more likely to win by a narrow margin. The certainty of their victory, however, was undermined a day before elections by an assassination attempt on President Chen and Vice President Annette Lu. On 20 March 2004, President Chen was re-elected by a margin of 0.228 per cent (or 30,000 votes) over the combined pan-Blue opposition ticket. While the shooting incident to some extent could explain Chen Shui-bian's electoral victory, it does not explain the sharp rise in the number of his supporters, from 39.3 per cent of the electorate in the 2000 elections to 50.11 per cent in 2004, a rise of 1.5 million votes. For China, the election results manifested the pro-independence forces' rise to dominance in Taiwanese politics and the likely continuity of their rule on the island (Yaun 2004: 9).

In contrast with its stance in the two previous presidential elections, Beijing was reserved in voicing its political preferences, possibly fearing that any backlash against Chen would only strengthen his appeal to the Taiwanese voters. The PRC broke its silence in mid-November 2003, amid deliberations on the Referendum Law, and issued several threats that it would not stand by if Taiwan declared independence. Following the elections, the Taiwan Affairs Office blamed Chen Shui-bian for tension across the Taiwan Strait and undermining stability in the Asia-Pacific. It stressed that China's desire for the 2008 Olympic Games to be successful would not stop it from acting against the island (*South China Morning Post*, 15 April 2004).

China's push and pull

In an inaugural address in May 2004, President Chen vowed to stabilise cross-Strait relations and establish a 'peace and stability framework' for cross-Strait cultural, economic and trade exchanges. Two months earlier, however, in an interview with the *Washington Post* (24 March 2004), he had rejected the 'one China' principle and instead proposed 'one principle, four issues'. The one principle referred to the principle of peace, while the four issues were:

- establishment of a mechanism for negotiation;
- negotiations based on equality and reciprocity;
- establishment of political relations;
- prevention of military conflict.

To Beijing, Chen's refusal to acknowledge the existence of 'one China' confirmed once more his pro-independence stance and the hypocrisy of his 'peace overtures' to the mainland. The Chinese media chose to focus on the protests against Chen's re-election mounted by the KMT and PFP supporters, rather than on Chen's new proposal for cross-Strait dialogue (*Christian Science Monitor*, 24 March 2004; *People's Daily Online*, 21 May 2004).

Thompson and Zhu (2004) argue that Chen's re-election signified the failure of China's 'two-handed strategy', whereby the 'soft hand' tempted the island to return to China via opening its market to Taiwanese businesspeople, while the 'hard hand' sought to deter Taiwan's *de jure* independence by deploying missiles across the Taiwan Strait and declaring its readiness to use military force when necessary. They further suggest that a 'push–pull approach' in which Beijing emphasises military deterrents to prevent the island from permanent separation from the mainland has replaced the 'two-handed strategy'. It could be argued that the reason for Beijing's tougher stand on Taiwan's 'separatists' was their victory in presidential elections. Yet the failure of the DDP and its ally, the Taiwan Solidarity Union (a fiercely pro-independence party, formed by former President Lee in August 2001), to capture a majority in the December 2004 elections to the Legislative Yuan undermined the theory of rising pro-independence sentiments on the island. It also ensured that, lacking a legislative majority, President Chen would be unable to push through his controversial proposal for revising the constitution, which he planned to carry out by 2008. Still, Beijing resorted to a 'hard push' when legislating the Anti-Secession Law in March 2005, which formalised China's well-known position on the use of 'non-peaceful means' against Taiwan in the event of Taipei's declaration of independence. The timing of the Anti-Secession Law was curious in light of the results to the Legislative Yuan in 2004 and the relaxation in cross-Strait tensions, as evidenced by the first direct – albeit charter – flights between Taiwan and the mainland during the Chinese New Year in 2005 and President Chen's declaration to reopen cross-Strait talks and initiate a cross-Strait cargo transportation plan. The Anti-Secession Law reflected Beijing's pessimism about long-term trends in cross-Strait relations, as well as the domestic political risks involved in reversing the earlier decision to consider such a law (Christensen 2005). As it provided a legal basis for China's eventual invasion of Taiwan, the DPP fiercely opposed it. Internationally, the Anti-Secession Law was not welcomed by the United States, while the European Union used its passage as an excuse to postpone the lifting of an arms embargo on China, imposed after the June 4th tragedy.

Alongside the 'hard push', which reminded Taiwanese leadership of China's long-standing policy on national reunification, Beijing pursued a 'pull approach'. It hosted Lien Chan and James Soong in April–May 2005. Lien left China with three gifts: two pandas (China's national icon); the removal of import duties on eighteen categories of farm goods (projected to increase Taiwan's agricultural exports to China by US$318 million annually); and the lifting of the ban on mainland citizens visiting the island. (It is believed that lifting this ban will create 70,000 jobs in Taiwan's tourist and retail industries; *China Post*, 13 May and 16 June 2005.) In July 2005 Beijing revised residency requirements for Taiwanese businesspeople, making it easier for them to apply for long-term residency. A month later, Beijing more than halved tuition fees paid by Taiwanese students enrolled at mainland universities, and introduced a scholarship programme for one-fifth of them (*Shanghai Daily*, 26 July 2005; *China Post*, 31 August 2005). Lien's tour resulted in an outburst of pro-China euphoria on the island. Opinion surveys indicated support for his visit by over 50 per cent of those polled, raising concerns among DPP supporters of its impact on forthcoming elections to the National Assembly, held in mid-May 2005. However, the DPP achieved a 42.5 per cent share of the vote, against 38.9 per cent for the KMT, making the DPP the largest party in the Assembly. These results showed the failure of 'panda diplomacy' to translate sympathy for cuddly bears into political gains. The National Assembly subsequently voted on a reform package which dissolved the Assembly and stipulated that future constitutional amendments, including national name or territorial changes, would need to gain approval from three-quarters of the Legislative Yuan members and more than half of total eligible voters in a national referendum. In light of these constitutional changes, President Chen's plan to replace the 1947 constitution with a new version relevant to contemporary Taiwan by 2008 will be difficult to implement.

Cross-Strait economic relations

The Chinese leadership hopes that progressive economic integration between the mainland and Taiwan will counter the anti-unification tendencies ensuing from the rise of Taiwanese identity through democratic politics. Sino-Taiwanese economic interaction began in the late 1980s, when the rising costs of labour and land, combined with an appreciation of the Taiwanese dollar, undermined the competitiveness of Taiwan's labour-intensive industries. The mainland's cheap labour, geographic proximity and cultural affinities convinced Taiwanese businesspeople to shift operations to China. In 1992, Taiwan became China's second largest investor (after Hong Kong), jumping from fourth position in 1991. China also emerged as Taiwan's leading trading partner. Sino-Taiwanese trade tripled between 1989 and 1992, and doubled in the following three years (see Table 9.2).

President Lee, weary of the political consequences of an over-reliance on the China market, encouraged Taiwanese businesspeople to explore markets in Southeast Asia, Central America and East Central Europe. However, economic experts suggest that Lee's restrictive policy was ineffective as investors invested in China through third countries (Ho and Leung 2004: 738), and even Taiwanese official statistics reveal that the flow of investments to the mainland accelerated, rather than slowed down after 1996 (see Table 9.3). By September 2001, when President Chen replaced the 'no haste, be patient' policy with 'active opening, effective regulation', the Taiwanese annually invested twice as much in the mainland as they used to in the mid-1990s. According to Taiwanese official data, ROC investments in China stood at US$47.26 billion by the end of 2005, while the mainland official data indicated US$90.29 billion in contracted investments. Other estimates put the value of Taiwanese total investments in China at over US$100 billion (Ho and Leung 2004: 738). Investments stimulated trade, as key capital goods were sourced from the island. Between 1995 and 2004, Taiwan's trade with the mainland more than tripled (see the ROC estimates in Table 9.2). In 2002, China became Taiwan's largest export market (followed by the US) and, a year later, Taiwan's largest trading partner (surpassing the US).

With growing trade came an influx of Taiwanese businesspeople (and tourists) to the mainland. While roughly one million Taiwanese travelled to China

Table 9.2 Taiwan's trade with China (in millions of US dollars)

Period	PRC Customs Statistics			Estimates made by Mainland Affairs Council, ROC		
	Exports	Imports	Total	Exports	Imports	Total
1989	—	—	—	3,331.9	586.9	3,918.8
1990	2 255.0	319.7	2 574.6	4 394.6	765.4	5 160.0
1991	3 639.0	594.8	4 233.9	7 493.5	1 125.9	8 619.4
1992	5 881.0	698.0	6 579.0	10 547.6	1 119.0	11 666.6
1993	12 933.1	1 461.8	14 394.9	13 993.1	1 103.6	15 096.7
1994	14 084.8	2 242.2	16 327.0	16 022.5	1 858.7	17 881.2
1995	14 783.9	3 098.1	17 882.0	19 433.8	3 091.4	22 525.2
1996	16 182.2	2 802.7	18 984.9	20 727.3	3 059.8	23 787.1
1997	16 441.7	3 396.5	19 838.2	22 455.2	3 915.4	26 370.6
1998	16 629.6	3 869.6	20 499.2	19 840.9	4 110.5	23 951.4
1999	19 537.5	3 951.7	23 489.2	21 312.5	4 522.2	25 834.7
2000	25 497.1	4 994.9	30 492.1	25 009.9	6 223.3	31 233.1
2001	27 339.4	5 000.2	32 350.0	21 945.7	5 902.2	27 847.9
2002	38 063.1	6 585.9	44 649.0	29 465.0	7 947.7	37 412.5
2003	49 362.3	9 004.7	58 367.0	35 357.7	10 962.0	46 319.7
2004	64 778.6	13 545.2	78 323.8	44 960.4	16 678.7	61 639.1
2005	74 684.4	16 549.6	91 234.0	56 275.9	20 093.7	76 369.6

Source: Adapted from Mainland Affairs Council, ROC (2006) *Cross-Strait Economic Statistics Monthly* 158. http://www.mac.gov.tw/big5/statistic/em/158/5.pdf.

between 1987 and 1989, since 1990 (when 890,500 travelled to China) the numbers have increased annually, and in 2005 the annual number of Taiwanese visitors to China quadrupled. Cumulatively, from 1987 until 2005, 38 million Taiwanese went to China. It is estimated that over 300,000 Taiwanese have settled in Shanghai alone, and between 500,000 and 1 million Taiwanese live in China at any time (out of Taiwan's total population of 23 million) (Chao 2004: 697). As developing good relationships with the authorities is often the key to a venture's profitability, Taiwanese companies have toed Beijing's line and steered clear of supporting the DPP (Zhao 2003: 51–2). During the 2004 presidential elec-

Table 9.3 Taiwan's investment in China (in millions of US dollars)

Period	ROC data Amount approved	PRC data Contracted Amount	Realized Amount	Realization Ratio
1991	174.16	3 310.30 (including pre-1991 data)	861.64	26.03
1992	246.99	5 543.35	1 050.50	18.95
1993	1 140.37 (2 028.05)	9 964.87	3 138.59	31.50
1994	962.21	5 394.88	3 391.04	62.86
1995	1 092.71	5 849.07	3 161.55	54.05
1996	1 229.24	5 141.00	3 474.84	67.59
1997	1 614.54 (2 719.77)	2 814.49	3 289.39	116.87
1998	1 519.2 (515.41)	2 981.68	2 915.21	97.77
1999	1 252.78	3 374.44	2 598.70	77.01
2000	2 607.14	4 041.89	2 296.28	56.81
2001	2 784.15	6 914.19	2 979.94	43.10
2002	3 858.76 (2 864.30)	6 740.84	3 970.64	58.90
2003	4 594.99 (3 103.80)	8 557.87	3 377.24	39.46
2004	6 940.66	9 305.94	3 117.49	33.50
2005	6 006.95	10 358.25	2 151.71	20.77
Accumulated to 2005	47 256.18	90 293.06	41 774.76	46.27

Source: Adapted from Mainland Affairs Council, ROC (2006) *Cross-Strait Economic Statistics Monthly* 158. http://www.mac.gov.tw/big5/statistic/em/158/5.pdf.

Note: Figures in parenthesis represent the amount of previously unregistered investments, according to the revision of the 'Statutes Governing Relations between the People of Taiwan Area and Mainland Area' on 14 May 1997

tions, Taiwanese businesspeople in China openly endorsed the KMT's candidate (*Asia Times Online*, 4 February 2004).

Pro-independence forces on Taiwan fear that the island's dependence on China will eventually lead to its loss of economic independence. Without the trade surplus with China, which in 2005 equalled either US$36.18 billion (228.7 per cent of Taiwan's total foreign trade surplus) or US$58.13 billion (367.5 per cent of Taiwan's total foreign trade surplus) depending on the source of statistical data, Taiwanese total foreign trade would have registered negative growth since the mid-1990s. In the early 2000s, more than 50 per cent of Taiwan's outbound investment went to China (compared with only 9.5 per cent in 1991). In 2003, investment in China took 4 per cent of Taiwan's gross domestic product (GDP), while the US and Japan's investment in China accounted for only 0.05 per cent and 0.06 per cent of their GDP respectively (*Taipei Times*, 4 June.2004). There is also a brain drain taking place, with rising numbers of Taiwanese professionals moving to the mainland in search of jobs and/or business opportunities.

Yet, it could be also argued that economic interdependence – where China offers labour, land and business-friendly regulations and Taiwan supplies financing, technology and managerial skills – benefits both sides, and China has as much to lose from ending this economic partnership as Taiwan. An estimated 50,000 Taiwanese companies employ millions of Chinese workers. In Guangdong's Dongguan county alone, 3 million workers have found jobs in Taiwanese-owned factories. Across the mainland, Taiwanese companies account for around 40 per cent of China's total exports (conservative estimates suggest 14–18 per cent) and 65 per cent of China's information technology exports (Cheng 2001; Meer and Keliher 2003; *South China Morning Post*, 3 September 2003; Tung 2003: 4). Some analysts even argue that China has no economic leverage over Taiwan whatsoever (Meer and Keliher 2003). Beijing's reluctance to use economic threats against Taiwan during the 1995–6 and 1999–2000 crises implies its concerns over the consequences of such a threat for the Chinese economy, and for its exports, social stability and image among international investors (Tung 2003). Ironically, economic interdependence – rather than rendering Taiwan vulnerable to Chinese pressures – might have strengthened Taiwan's hand in its dealings with China.

The US factor

Beijing understands that economic integration, if it ever leads to eventual political unification, will take a long time to bear results. In the meantime, China is determined through military intimidation to prevent Taipei from moving towards formal independence, and it attempts to weaken Taiwan's relationship with the United States. In June 1998, Beijing scored a significant victory when President Bill Clinton during his China visit explicitly declared a 'three nos' policy on Taiwan: no support for Taiwan's independence; no to two Chinas or one Taiwan-one China, and no to Taiwan's membership in international organisations for which statehood was a requirement (Dean 2001: 104). Clinton did not change his policy on Taiwan following President Chen's election in 2000. When Chen made his first transit via the US in August 2000, Washington made sure that his transit was unquestionably low-profile. In contrast, President George W. Bush – considering China a 'strategic competitor' that challenged US geostrategic superiority in the Asia-Pacific – vowed to strengthen ties with Taiwan. Following the spy plane incident in April 2001 (where a US surveillance plane collided with a Chinese fighter mid-air), President Bush declared he would 'do whatever it takes to help Taiwan defend itself' (Shih 2004: 4). His declaration was soon followed with deeds: a robust arms package (which included submarines); relaxed rules concerning the Taiwanese leaders' transits via the US; no commitment to the 'three nos' policy; and stronger interaction with the Taiwanese military.

The September 11 terrorist attacks on the United States in 2001, however, altered the geostrategic context of Washington's relations with Beijing and Taipei. The need for China's support for the US global war on terror, and more specifically, for the US invasion of Afghanistan and Iraq, as well as Beijing's perceived leverage over North Korea's nuclear ambitions, triggered Washington's shift from a hard-line stand on China to a policy resembling the 'strategic engagement' of the Clinton era. Seeking a dialogue with China on diplomatic and economic issues, the Bush administration re-emphasised the 'one China' policy, publicly 'opposed' Taiwan's independence (a marked shift from 'no support'), and replaced pro-Taiwan rhetoric with irritation over Taipei's attempts to upset the status quo in the Taiwan Strait. Interestingly, the 2003 referendum controversy revealed the limits of US influence on Taiwan and demonstrated China's new perception of the US's role in cross-Strait relations. In December 2003, President Bush, in the company of visiting PRC Prime Minister Wen Jiabao, opposed any actions from President Chen that might unilaterally change the status quo in the Taiwan Strait (Fang 2004: 552). Bush did so partly in response to Beijing's request to prevent Taiwan from holding a referendum. Wen's request legitimised the US role in the intra-China conflict, but – disappointingly for China – Washington's pressure did not prove any more effective in convincing Taiwan's pro-independence camp to drop controversial policies, than Beijing's own efforts. As Chen Shui-bian electioneered on the anti-China platform, he could hardly back down on the issue of a referendum and risk alienating his supporters.

Future scenarios

Given the dynamic nature of the Sino-Taiwanese relationship, it is impossible to predict the model both sides of the Taiwan Strait might eventually agree upon as a solution to their long-standing conflict. Below are listed a few possible scenarios of the future evolution of cross-Strait relations.

The status quo

The most likely scenario is a continuity of the status quo. Given its commitment to domestic economic development, the goal of creating a well-off society and its ambition to host exemplary Olympic Games in 2008, Beijing is likely to pursue its existing policies of isolating Taiwan internationally and building a united front with the Taiwanese business community and the pan-Blue camp. It will also try to contain any moves within the pro-independence camp that might lead to Taiwan's formal independence. The Chen administration, for its part, will probably avoid upsetting the status quo, because of US objections, its desire to secure the island's continuing economic well-being, and the majority of Taiwanese citizens' preference for maintaining the status quo.

War

War is an unlikely scenario, reserved for the occasion of Taipei's declaration of independence. However, China prepares for it earnestly through its military modernisation programme, purchases of advanced weapons from Russia, and the stockpiling of short-range ballistic missiles opposite Taiwan, of which an estimated 500 currently target the island and 50–75 are added annually to the inventory (*South China Morning Post*, 1 August 2003; Blank 2004). In contrast to China's rising military budgets (which have been increasing by double digits over most of the past fifteen years and are equivalent to 4–5 per cent of China's GDP), Taiwan's total defence budget peaked in 1994 and thereafter declined, currently making up about 2.5 per cent of Taiwan's GDP (Fang 2004: 558; *Taipei Times*, 5 March and 9 July 2005). Analysts predict that, because of the disparities in armaments procurement, the conventional force balance across the Taiwan Strait is likely to tip in China's favour in five to ten years (Shambaugh 2000: 119; *Taipei Times*, 9 July 2005). The issue of Taiwan's defences is further compounded by domestic politics. Attempting to demonstrate the Chen administration's ineffectiveness and their pro-China position, the pan-Blue legislative majority vetoed the government's bill to procure advanced US weapons, offered by the US in 2001.

The most important implication of China achieving military parity with Taiwan is its implied ability to stage a successful invasion of the island. Military experts, however, are divided over China's capacity to conquer Taiwan. Some argue that at least until 2010 China will not be able to do so (O'Hanlon 2000), while others caution that Beijing could stage a successful invasion if it allocated enough resources to its execution (Wood and Ferguson 2001). Washington's involvement in the intra-Chinese conflict is another unknown. Its non-involvement in a potential Sino-Taiwanese military conflict would send a worrying signal to US allies in Asia (and beyond), as well as symbolise its readiness to defer to China in regional matters, thereby resetting the pecking order of powers in East Asia. It would also show disregard for Taiwan's democratic achievements, thus questioning Washington's commitment to furthering democracy worldwide. Given all these ramifications, it is rather unlikely that the United States would ignore China's invasion of Taiwan (Rahman 2001: 70–2).

One country, two systems

The United States has showed no interest in 'one country, two systems' as a model for Taiwan's reunification with the mainland (Mann 1999: 153–4). Neither did President Lee, who dismissed it as 'wishful thinking' (Lee, B. 1999: 54). The political and economic difficulties that Hong Kong encountered after the handover in July 1997 did not help China make a convincing case for 'one country, two systems' either. The Taiwanese public also saw the Hong Kong people's fear of Article 23 (an anti-subversion law) as an example of the gradual erosion of freedom enjoyed by Hong Kong people. Following the National People's Congress's interpretation of the Basic Law (Hong Kong's mini-constitution) in April 2004, Taipei declared that China had assumed full control of the political process in Hong Kong and the 'one country, two systems' formula was a fraud. In an interview with the *Washington Post* (29 March 2004), President Chen further emphasised that 'what has happened in Hong Kong has shown that ['one country, two systems'] is a total failure'. The majority of Taiwanese people share President Chen's sentiments: 70–80 per cent of them reject it as a solution to the problems of cross-Strait relations (Mainland Affairs Council, www.mac.gov.tw/english/index1-e.htm).

Federacy

The 'one country, two systems' model is essentially a form of federacy. In this kind of political arrangement, an otherwise unitary state develops a federal relationship with a territorially, ethnically or culturally distinct community, while all the other parts of the state remain under unitary rule (Stepan 1999: 20). Currently, federacy functions in Denmark's relationship with Greenland and Finland's with the Aaland Islands. However, the Danish and Finnish models do not offer a solution to the cross-Strait conflict. Firstly, Taiwan would find it difficult to accept the federacy model as its implementation would require the demilitarisation of Taiwan. Furthermore, China would be unlikely to agree to any international agreement on Taiwan's autonomy that is guaranteed by an international organisation because it would undermine its sovereign claims to the island (Taiwan Strait IV 2004: 8). Moreover, Greenland's current ambitions to become sovereign, despite its budgetary dependence on Denmark (*Gazeta Wyborcza*, 16 November 2005), suggest the limitations of the federacy solution to maintaining a federal relationship between two distinct communities over an indefinite period.

Confederation

In mid-2001, KMT Chairman Lien Chan floated the idea of confederation as a solution to the unification problem. He suggested that confederation, or union of two equals, could be formed upon the '1992 consensus' as a transition phase in China's unification process. The Lien-proposed confederation was to conform to the principles of parity, separate jurisdiction, peace and gradual progress, was not intended as an alternative form of Taiwanese independence, and was neither a commonwealth nor a federation (*A Brief on the 'Confederation'* 2001). Lien's ideas were not included in the KMT party programme out of uncertainty over their implications in the forthcoming legislative elections. The pro-independence camp dismissed them as a 'proposal to save the KMT's sinking ship' (*Taipei Times*, 9 July 2001). Vice Premier Qian Qichen's 'anything can be discussed' response to the *Washington Post*'s question regarding China's acceptance of a loose confederation with Taiwan (5 January 2001) suggested that Beijing did not rule out the confederation idea outright. Yet the confederation model would force Beijing to accept the equal status of Taiwan and its de facto sovereignty for an indefinite period. And for these reasons, China is unlikely to embrace the confederation model as its first choice.

Conclusion

After Hong Kong's and Macau's return to China in 1997 and 1999 respectively, reunification with Taiwan topped the PRC regime's agenda, alongside social stability and economic development. Faced with waning appeal for Marxism-Leninism and Mao Zedong Thought, the nominally communist leadership has increasingly resorted to the banner of nationalism to strengthen its domestic legitimacy and has transformed the reunification project from a relic of the civil war to China's 'sacred right [...] to safeguard national unity and territorial integrity' (*The Taiwan Question and Reunification of China* 1993). Party-state official pronouncements portray the Taiwan issue as the last reminder of China's past national humiliations, and the main obstacle to China assuming its rightful dominant position in East Asia and beyond. Accordingly, Taiwan's separation from China has become a highly emotional subject, and one for which China is ready to sacrifice all it has achieved since 1949. 'No one should underestimate China's resolve to achieve unification', for which Beijing was ready to 'pay any price', the PRC Taiwan Affairs Office spokesperson reminded the world after President Chen's re-election in 2004 (*South China Morning Post*, 15 April 2004). Of the three possible situations which are said to trigger China's 'non-peaceful' response, Taiwan's formal declaration of independence is the most likely to be followed by Beijing's military action.

With Taipei refraining from any such formal declaration, Beijing's resolve to 'pay any price' for national unification has yet to be tested. Domestically, the CCP leadership faces a myriad of challenges, including restructuring of the state-owned sector, regional economic disparities, rising unemployment, public finance reform, restless ethnic minorities and dormant demands for political reforms. To address these challenges effectively, China needs a stable and peaceful international environment. The nationalist agenda to reunify with Taiwan does not invalidate the objective of economic development as long as Beijing and Taipei find a reunification formula agreeable to both sides. But any attempt to forcefully reunify Taiwan could backfire economically and politically, with possibly dire consequences for the Chinese economy, social stability and the CCP's survival.

Occasional military threats notwithstanding, the Chinese leadership seemingly understands the dangers involved in pushing the reunification agenda against the wishes of the Taiwanese public. Since the late 1970s when it floated its first peaceful proposal, Beijing has shown increasing flexibility in accommodating the sensitivities of the Taiwanese leaders and people. It no longer defines 'one China' as the PRC, no longer rejects dialogue on an equal footing, and no longer insists on 'one country, two systems' as the only method of reunification. Above all, however, it hopes that Taiwan's growing economic dependence on the mainland will render the island susceptible to China's pressures, and eventually lead to a reunification.

So far, neither military intimidation nor economic cooperation has convinced the Taiwanese people to embrace reunification with China. Given the European Union's experience, economic integration does not automatically result in political integration. Ultimately, the Taiwanese identity, and Taiwan's distinctive democratic political culture, institutions and procedures are more likely to determine the Taiwanese people's future attitudes to reunification.

The US's self-accorded right to defend Taiwan against China's invasion, enshrined in the TRA, introduces a foreign element to the intra-Chinese conflict and, thus far, it has prevented that conflict from escalating into a military stand-off. Although suspicious of Washington's geostrategic objectives, Beijing has not only resigned itself to tolerating US involvement in the cross-Strait dialogue but recently has even attempted to enlist its support in limiting the pro-independence agenda on the island. Ironically, the often vilified Americans may ensure that the Taiwan issue, critical as it is to the Chinese nationalist agenda, will not escalate to the point where the economic prosperity of the Greater China and the stability of East Asia are sacrificed on the altar of Chinese national honour.

Note

*   The author wishes to thank Professor J. Bruce Jacobs and Dr Cheung Wai Kwok for their insightful comments on the first draft of this chapter.

References

A Brief on the 'Confederation' Concept in the Draft Platform of the Kuomintang Party (2001) Accessed 6 November 2005, at www.gio.gov.tw/taiwan-website/5-gp/election/major/major02b.htm.

Bellochi, N. H. (2001) 'Taiwan's Domestic Political Developments and Their Impact on US–Taiwan Relations', in Hungdah Chiu, Hsing-wei Lee and Chih-Yu Wu (eds), *Implementation of Taiwan Relations Act: An Examination after Twenty Years. Maryland Series in Contemporary Asian Studies* 2, pp. 127–46

Blank, S. (2004) 'China–Taiwan Arms Race Quickens', *Asia Times Online*. 24 February. Accessed 5 November 2005, at www.atimes.com.

Chang, G. and He, Di (1993) 'The Absence of War in the US–China Confrontation over Quemoy and Matsu in 1954–55: Contingency, Luck, Deterrence?', *American Historical Review* 98/5: 1500–24.

Chao Chien-min (2004) 'National Security vs. Economic Interests: Reassessing Taiwan's Mainland Policy under Chen Shui-bian', *Journal of Contemporary China* 13/41: 687–704.

Chen Jian (1994) *China's Road to the Korean War: The Making of Sino-American Confrontation*, New York: Columbia University Press.

Chen Jie (2002) *Foreign Policy of the New Taiwan: Pragmatic Diplomacy in Southeast Asia*, Cheltenham: Edward Elgar.

Chen Shui-bian (2002) 'One Country on Each Side', *Taiwan Communiqué* 102.

Cheng, A. T. (2001) 'The United States of China', *Asiaweek.com*, 6 July. Accessed 3 November 2005, at www.asiaweek.com.

Chiou, C. L. (1994) 'Emerging Taiwanese Identity in the 1990s: Crisis and Transformation', in G. Klintworth (ed.), *Taiwan in the Asia-Pacific in the 1990s*, Sydney: Allen & Unwin, pp. 21–43.

Chiu Hungdah (1990) 'The Taiwan Relations Act and Sino-American Relations', *Occasional Papers/Reprints Series in Contemporary Asian Studies* 5, Maryland: School of Law, University of Maryland.

Christensen, T. (1996). *Useful Adversaries: Grand Strategy, Domestic Mobilization, and Sino-American Conflict, 1947–1958*, Princeton: Princeton University Press.

—— (2005) 'Have Old Problems Trumped New Thinking? China's Relations with Taiwan, Japan, and North Korea', *China Leadership Monitor* 14 (Spring). Accessed on 3 November 2005, at www.chinaleadershipmonitor.org.

Chu Yun-han (2000) 'Making Sense of Beijing's Policy toward Taiwan: The Prospect of Cross-Strait Relations during the Jiang Zemin Era', in Hung-mao Tien and Yun-han Chu (eds), *China Under Jiang Zemin*, Boulder, CO, and London: Lynne Rienner Publishers, pp. 193–212.

Chu Yun-han and Tse-min Lin (1996) 'The Process of Democratic Consolidation in Taiwan: Social Cleavage, Electoral Competition, and the Emerging Party System', in Tien Hung Mao (ed.), *Taiwan's Electoral Politics and Democratic Transition*, Armonk and London: M. E. Sharpe, pp. 79–104.

Chu Yun-han and Jih-wen Lin (2001) 'Political Development in 20th Century Taiwan: State-Building, Regime Transformation and the Construction of National Identity', *China Quarterly* 165: 102–29.

Clough, R. (2001) 'Taiwan–Mainland Relations', in Huangdah Chiu, Hsin-wei Lee and Chih-yu Wu (eds), *Implementation of Taiwan Relations Act: An Examination after Twenty Years. Maryland Series in Contemporary Asian Studies* 2, pp. 201–19.

Dean, D. (2001) 'US Relations with Taiwan', in Huangdah Chiu, Hsing-wei Lee and Chi-Yu Wu (eds), *Implementation of Taiwan Relations Act: An Examination after Twenty Years. Maryland Series in Contemporary Asian Studies* 2, pp. 69–108.

Dreyer, J. T. (2003) 'Taiwan's Evolving Identity', *Woodrow Wilson Center's Asia Programme Special Report* 114: 4–10.

Fang Hsu-hsiung (2004) 'The Transformation of US–Taiwan Military Relations', *Orbis* 48/3: 551–61.

Finkelstein, D. M. (1993) *Washington's Taiwan Dilemma, 1949–1950*, Fairfax: George Mason University Press.

Garver, J. W. (1997) *The Sino-American Alliance: Nationalist China and American Cold War Strategy in Asia*, Armonk, NY: M. E. Sharpe.

Goldstein, S. M. and Schriver, R. (2001) 'An Uncertain Relationship: The United States, Taiwan and the Taiwan Relations Act', *China Quarterly* 165: 147–72.

Goncharov, S. N., Lewis, J. W. and Xue Litai (1993). *Uncertain Partners: Stalin, Mao, and the Korean War*, Stanford: Stanford University Press.

Gong Li (2001) 'Tension across the Taiwan Strait in the 1950s: Chinese Strategy and Tactics', in R. S. Ross and Jiang Changbin (eds), *Re-examining the Cold War: US–China Diplomacy, 1954–1973*, Cambridge, MA, and London: Harvard University Press, pp. 141–72.

Hamrin, C. L. and Zheng Wang (2004) 'The Floating Island: Change of Paradigm on the Taiwan Question', *Journal of Contemporary China* 13/39: 339–49.

Han, S. H. (1995) 'Time to Welcome Taiwan Back into the United Nations', *Asian Affairs: An American Review* 22/3 (Fall): 172–80.

Harding, H. (1992) *A Fragile Relationship: The United States and China Since 1972*, Washington: The Brookings Institution.

Hsiao, F. S. T. and Sullivan, L. R. (1979) 'The Chinese Communist Party and the Status of Taiwan, 1928–1943', *Pacific Affairs* 52/3: 446–67.

Hsieh Chiao Chiao (1996) 'Pragmatic Diplomacy: Foreign Policy and External Relations', in P. Ferdinand (ed.), *Take-off for Taiwan*, London: The Royal Institute of International Affairs. 66–106.

Hsieh J. Fuh-sheng (2004) 'National Identity and Taiwan's Mainland Policy', *Journal of Contemporary China* 13/40: 479–90.

Ho, S. P. S. (1978) *Economic Development of Taiwan 1860–1970*, New Haven and London: Yale University Press.

Ho Szu-yin and I-chou Liu (2002) 'The Taiwanese/Chinese Identity of the Taiwan People in the 1990s', *American Asian Review* 20/2: 29–74.

Ho Szu-yin and Tse-kang Leung (2004) 'Accounting for Taiwan's Economic Policy toward China', *Journal of Contemporary China* 13/41: 733–46.

Huan Guo-cang (1985) 'Taiwan: A View from Beijing', *Foreign Affairs* 63/5: 1065–80.

Huang Teh-fu (1996) 'Elections and the Evolution of the Kuomintang', in Tien Hung Mao (ed.), *Taiwan's Electoral Politics and Democratic Transition*, Armonk and London: M. E. Sharpe, pp. 105–36.

Ijiri, H. (1997) 'Taiwan's "Pragmatic Diplomacy" and Its Implications for the Chinese Mainland, Japan and the World', in M. H. Yang (ed.), *Taiwan's Expanding Role in the International Arena*, Armonk, NY: M. E. Sharpe, pp. 37–49.

Jacobs, J. B. (1990) 'Taiwanese and the Chinese Nationalists, 1937–1945: The Origins of Taiwan's "Half-Mountain People" (Banshan ren)', *Modern China* 16/1: 84–118.

Joei, B. T. K. (1994) 'Pragmatic Diplomacy in the Republic of China: History and Prospects', in J. C. Hu (ed.), *Quiet Revolutions on Taiwan, Republic of China*, Taipei: Kwang Hwa Publishing Company, pp. 297–330.

Joint Communiqué on the Establishment of Diplomatic Relations between the United States of America and the People's Republic of China (1 January 1979). Accessed 19 October 2005, at www.china.org.cn/english/taiwan/7832.htm.

Khrushchev, N. (1993) 'Memuary Nikity Sergeevicha Khrushcheva', *Voprosy Istorii* 2: 77–91.

Lai Tse-han, Myers, R. H. and Wei Wou (1991) *A Tragic Beginning: The Taiwan Uprising of February 28, 1947*, Stanford: Stanford University Press.

Lee, B. (1999) 'The Security Implications of the New Taiwan', *Adelphi Paper* 331: 11–86.

Lee, Teng-hui (1999) 'Understanding Taiwan: Bridging the Perception Gap', *Foreign Policy* 78/6: 9–14.

Li Jiaquan (1990) 'Essential Elements', *Beijing Review*: 27–31.

Lilley, J. R. (2001) 'US–Taiwan Relations and the People's Republic of China (PRC): A Personal Retrospective', in Huangdah Chiu, Hsing-wei Lee and Chi-Yu Wu (eds), *Implementation of Taiwan Relations Act: An Examination after Twenty Years. Maryland Series in Contemporary Asian Studies* 2, pp. 147–73.

Mainland Affairs Council (2005) *Taipei's Olive Branches*. Accessed 20 September 2005, at www.mac.gov.tw.

Mann, J. (1999) *About Face: A History of America's Curious Relationship with China From Nixon to Clinton*, New York: Alfred A. Knopf.

Mao Zedong (1934) *Report to the Second National Congress of the Workers' and Peasants' Representatives*. Accessed 15 October 2005, at www.marxists.org/reference/archive/mao/selected-works/volume–6/mswv6_18.htm.

Meer, C. and Keliher, M. (2003) 'Taiwan's Economic Leverage Over China', *Asian Wall Street Journal*, 12 August.

O'Hanlon, M. (2000) 'Why China Cannot Conquer Taiwan', *International Security* 25/2: 51–86.

Peterson, A. (2004) 'Dangerous Games Across the Taiwan Strait', *Washington Quarterly* 27/2: 23–41.

Pinsker, R. (2003) 'Drawing a Line in the Taiwan Strait: "Strategic Ambiguity" and its Discontents', *Australian Journal of International Affairs* 57/2: 353–68.

Rahman, C. (2001) 'Defending Taiwan, and Why It Matters', *Naval War College Review* 54/4: 69–93.

Rigger, S. (1999) *Politics in Taiwan: Voting for Democracy*, London and New York: Routledge.

Ross, R. S. (2000) 'The 1995–96 Taiwan Strait Confrontation: Coercion, Credibility, and the Use of Force', *International Security* 25/2: 87–123.

Roy, D. (2003) *Taiwan: A Political History*, Ithaca and London: Cornell University Press.

Shambaugh, D. (2000) 'A Matter of Time: Taiwan's Eroding Military Advantage', *Washington Quarterly* 23/2: 119–33.

Shanghai Communiqué (1972) Accessed 18 October 2005, at www.china.org.cn/english/china-us/26012.htm.

Shih, E. (2004) 'The Conduct of US–Taiwan Relations, 2000–2004', *Centre for Northeastern Asian Policy Studies Working Paper*.

Spence, J. (1999) *The Search for Modern China*, New York and London: Norton.

Stepan, A. (1999) 'Federalism and Democracy: Beyond the US Model', *Journal of Democracy* 10/4: 19–34.

Taiwan Relations Act (1979) Accessed 18 October 2005, at www.taiwandocuments.org/tra01.htm.

'Taiwan Strait IV: How an Ultimate Political Settlement Might Look' (2004) *International Crisis Group Asia Report* 75.

The One China Principle and the Taiwan Issue (2000) Accessed 2 November 2005, at www.gwytb.gov.cn:8088/detail.asp?table=WhitePaper&title=White%20Papers%20On%20Taiwan%20Issue&m_id=4.

The Taiwan Question and Reunification of China (1993) Accessed 9 November 2005, www.gwytb.gov.cn:8088/detail.asp?table=WhitePaper&title=White%20Papers%20On%20Taiwan%20Issue&m_id=3.

Thompson, A. and Zhu Feng (2004) 'When All Else Fails: Beijing Conservative Stance on Taiwan', *China Brief* 4/14. Accessed on 3 November 2005, at www.jamestown.org.

Tien Hung-mao (1996) 'Elections and Taiwan's Democratic Development', in Tien Hung Mao (ed.), *Taiwan's Electoral Politics and Democratic Transition*, Armonk and London: M. E. Sharpe, pp. 3–26.

Tien Hung-mao and Yun-han Chu (1994) 'Taiwan's Domestic Political Reforms, Institutional Change and Power Realignment', in G Klintworth (ed.), *Taiwan in the Asia-Pacific in the 1990s*, Sydney: Allen & Unwin, pp. 1–20.

Tubilewicz, C. (2002) 'The Little Dragon and the Bear: Russian-Taiwanese Relations in the Post-Cold War Period', *Russian Review* 61/2: 276–97.

Tung Chen-yuan (2003), 'China's Economic Leverage and Taiwan's Security Concerns with Respect to Cross-Strait Economic Relations', *The Taiwan Workshop*, Fairbank Center. Harvard University. Accessed 11 November 2005, at www.fas.harvard.edu/~fairbank/tsw/text/Tung.htm.

Whiting, A. S. (2001) 'China's Use of Force, 1950–96, and Taiwan', *International Security* 26/2: 103–31.

Winckler, E. A. (1988) 'Mass Political Incorporation 1500–2000', in E. A. Winckler and S. Greenhalgh (eds), *Contending Approaches to the Political Economy of Taiwan*, Armonk and London: M. E. Sharpe, pp. 41–66.

Wood, P. M. and Ferguson, C. D. (2001) 'How China Might Invade Taiwan', *Naval War College Review* 54/4: 55–68.

Wu Linjun (1995) 'Does Money Talk?: The ROC Economic Diplomacy', *Issues and Studies* 31/12: 22–35.

—— (1996) 'The ROC's Economic Diplomacy after the March Crisis: Can Money Talk Again?', *Issues and Studies* 32/12: 51–66.

Yuan Peng (2004) 'The Taiwan Issue in the Context of New Sino–US Strategic Cooperation', *Centre for Northeast Asian Policy Studies Working Paper*, Washington: The Brookings Institution. Accessed 30 August 2005, www.brookings.edu/dybdocroot/fp/cnaps/papers/yuan2004.pdf.

Zhao Suisheng (2003) 'Beijing's Wait-and-See Policy Toward Taiwan: An Uncertain Future', *East Asia* 20/3: 39–60.

Index